Music of
the Counterculture Era

James E. Perone

American History through Music
David J. Brinkman, Series Editor

GREENWOOD PRESS
Westport, Connecticut • London

Library of Congress Cataloging-in-Publication Data

Perone, James E.
    Music of the counterculture era / James E. Perone.
      p. cm.—(American history through music)
    Includes bibliographical references and indexes.
    ISBN 0–313–32689–4 (alk. paper)
    1. Popular music—United States—1961–1970—Social aspects. 2. Popular music—
United States—1971–1980—Social aspects. 3. Counterculture—United States—History—
20th century. 4. Nineteen sixties. 5. Nineteen seventies. 6. Popular culture—United
States—History—20th century. I. Title. II. Series.
ML3918.P67P47   2004
781.64'0973'09046—dc22   2004040432

British Library Cataloguing in Publication Data is available.

Copyright © 2004 by James E. Perone

Library of Congress Catalog Card Number: 2004040432
ISBN: 0–313–32689–4

First published in 2004

Greenwood Press, 88 Post Road West, Westport, CT 06881
An imprint of Greenwood Publishing Group, Inc.
www.greenwood.com

Printed in the United States of America

The paper used in this book complies with the
Permanent Paper Standard issued by the National
Information Standards Organization (Z39.48–1984).

10 9 8 7 6 5 4 3 2 1

Contents

Series Foreword

The elements of music are well known. They include melody, rhythm, harmony, form, and texture. Music, though, has infinite variety. Exploring this variety in the music of specific time periods, such as the Colonial and Revolutionary Period, the Roaring Twenties, and the Counterculture Era, is the purpose of the "American History through Music" series. The authors of each volume describe the music in terms of its basic elements, but more importantly, focus on how the social, economic, political, technological, and religious influences shaped the music of that particular time. Each volume in the series not only describes the music of a particular era but the ways in which the music reflected societal concerns. For these purposes, music is defined inclusively; this series considers such diverse musical genres as classical, folk, jazz, rock, religious, and theater music, as each of these genres serve as both reflections of society and as illustrations of how music influences society.

Perhaps the most important conclusion that readers will draw from this series is that music does not exist independently of society. Listeners have enjoyed music throughout time for its aesthetic qualities, but music has also been used to convey emotions and ideas. It has been used to enhance patriotic rituals, and to maintain order in social and religious ceremonies. The "American History through Music" series attempts to put these and other uses of music in an historical context. For instance, how did music serve as entertainment during the Great Depression? How did the music of the Civil War contribute to the stability of the Union—and to the Confederacy? Answers to these and other questions show that music is not just a part of society; music *is* society.

The authors of "American History through Music" present essays based in sound scholarship, written for the lay reader. In addition to discussing important genres and approaches to music, each volume profiles the composers and performers whose music defines their era, describes the musical instruments and technological innovations that influenced the musical world, and provides a glossary of important terms and a bibliography of recommended readings. This information will help students and other interested readers understand the colorful and complex mosaics of musical history.

David J. Brinkman
University of Wyoming

Preface

Much has been written and much has been said about the American counterculture era, the period 1960–1975. This era was defined by the sit-in by four Black students at a Greensboro lunch counter at one end (1960) and the end of the Vietnam Conflict at the other end (1975). Without doubt, this was one of, if not the, most turbulent periods in the history of the United States, short of a civil war. The growing restlessness of baby boomers with respect to parental authority, the increasing availability of mind-altering drugs, the establishment of rock music, the struggles of the Civil Rights movement, and especially the controversy surrounding the Vietnam Conflict all came together to create the political and social struggles of the era. To an extent greater than in earlier periods of political and social upheaval in the United States, music was part of the struggle. Music related to the various aspects of the counterculture was not only there for the "insiders," it was on radio airwaves and on television, many times in forms seemingly geared toward a more general audience.

This book presents background information, musical and lyrical descriptions, analysis, and criticism of the songs that refer to, were affected by, and responded to the events of one of the most controversial eras in the history of the United States of America. Although I have not detailed every counterculture song of the period, I have attempted to discuss representative songs: songs that were used actively as part of the movement on the streets and songs that were issued commercially on vinyl albums and 45-rpm singles. I will also deal with songs that perhaps became best known through their exposure on television.

We will begin our study with an overview of the counterculture era, including discussion of the various aspects of what commonly has been called "the movement." We will then take a look at various parts of the counterculture that were reflected in music, beginning with the protests against the Vietnam Conflict and then continuing to the struggles of various oppressed groups for empowerment, radical political movements, and various lifestyle choices, including the hippie lifestyle and recreational drug use. I have also included an A–Z of music and the counterculture that provides brief overviews of the work of various musicians and counterculture political figures and definitions of various counterculture phenomena such as "Deadheads" and "Woodstock."

Throughout the discussion of the specific songs of the era, I have consciously avoided providing direct musical and textual quotations for two reasons: (1) obtaining permissions would be a nearly insurmountable obstacle and, much more importantly, (2) I strongly believe that it is essential to hear, to experience the music of this or any other era in order to more fully grasp its significance; to *very* roughly paraphrase a quotation that I have seen variously attributed to Laurie Anderson, John Lennon, Martin Mull, Thelonious Monk, and Elvis Costello (among others), reading about music (without experiencing it) is like dancing about architecture. (Incidentally, it was Elvis Costello who said in a 1983 interview, "Writing about music is like dancing about architecture—it's a really stupid thing to want to do" [White 1983, 52]). Most of the commercially successful (and even many of the obscure) songs of the era are available on compact disc reissues; therefore, the reader should be able to obtain a representative collection of this musical material. Because the world of reissues, file downloading, and the like is so dynamic, so ever-changing, I have not provided a discography or a guide indicating exactly how to get recordings. World Wide Web–based sources like cdnow.com, allmusic.com, and amazon.com are great resources both for information and for purchasing new or used copies of compact discs. Due to the many legal wranglings taking place related to file sharing and downloading, and (as mentioned earlier) due to the dynamic nature of today's digital age, I hesitate to recommend specific websites for that sort of thing.

The reader is advised that I have used quotation marks for song titles and for titles of individual jazz compositions. Longer "classical" instrumental works, multimovement song cycles, musical shows, and titles of other major works are italicized. These standard title formats are important to keep in mind, especially when separating discussion of, say, the musical *Jesus Christ Superstar* from the song of the same name.

My aim in this project has been to create a guide to the songs of the counterculture era, one that can be understood and appreciated by scholars ranging from high school and college students to the general public. Although I have included discussion of the musical materials of many songs, I have tried to use as little musical jargon as possible. It is my hope that the reader finds this book to be a way into the music of one of the most sociologically interesting eras in American musical history, suggesting some of the reasons for the music; the relationships between war, drugs, particular lifestyle choices, and struggles of various minority groups and particular songs; and some of the relationships between the songs themselves.

Acknowledgments

This book could not have been written without the valuable assistance of a number of people. I wish first to thank Karen Perone for offering moral support throughout this and all of my book projects for Greenwood Press, and for offering much-needed input at every stage of every project.

Over the course of writing several books, the entire staff at Greenwood Press has been most helpful and cooperative. I wish to extend special thanks to Senior Editor Rob Kirkpatrick, and to Martha Mesiti and John Donohue, copy and production editors, respectively, for helping me in the fine-tuning of this book.

I also wish to thank my friend and colleague, Dr. Kelly F. Lowe. Dr. Lowe's insights into music as rhetoric and his uncanny ability to quote obscure passages from the writings of Hunter S. Thompson never cease to amaze me.

Finally, I wish to thank the outstanding, though under-appreciated, British songwriter Nick Lowe, for asking the musical question, shortly after the time period discussed in this book, "What's so funny 'bout peace, love, and understanding?" And, thanks to Elvis Costello for asking the question so well in his recording of the song. That rhetorical question represents the heart of the movement. . . .

1

Background

HISTORICAL PERSPECTIVE OF THE COUNTERCULTURE

Just what did it mean to be part of "the movement," or "the counterculture" in the 1960s and the first half of the 1970s? Historian Terry H. Anderson (*not* the journalist of hostage fame) asserts that the counterculture movement could be defined in terms of organizations, leaders, ideologies, or specific social causes, but he concludes that a truer definition would have to lump all of these together. Although not all activists worked toward the same ends on all of the same causes—one person, for example, might focus entirely on the anti-war aspects of the movement—there was considerable overlap between the various social causes. In the preface of his book *The Movement and the Sixties*, Anderson writes,

> *movement* in this book connotes all activists who demonstrated for social change. Anyone could participate: There were no membership cards. Activists usually appeared at the protest because they held similar positions on an issue. Sara Evans, a civil rights volunteer, later wrote, "Above all the term 'movement' was self-descriptive. There was no way to join; you simply announced or felt yourself to be part of the movement—usually through some act like joining a protest march. Almost a mystical term, 'the move-

ment' implied an experience, a sense of community and common
purpose." (Anderson 1995, xv–xvi)

Despite Anderson's broad approach, it would be useful at least to consider
briefly some of the individual movements and lifestyle choices that made up
this counterculture, particularly those that influenced or were influenced or
reflected by the music of one of the most turbulent decade-and-a-half-long
periods in the history of the United States. Later, when considering specifics
of the music of the counterculture era, I will also break the counterculture
up into several parts. The reason for this approach is that the music itself
tended to address one or maybe two separate aspects of the counterculture.
Rarely did a pop song, for example, reflect the hippie lifestyle, glorify psychedelic drugs, protest the United States involvement in Southeast Asia, and
support Black Power while taking a feminist/Back to the Land stance. The
reader must remember, however, that although the example I just posed
might seem a bit ludicrous, there will be some overlap between the various
"parts" of the counterculture.

A survey of the existing literature on the counterculture era reveals some
disagreement about just how to define the limits of this time period: some
writers focus almost entirely on the 1960s, while others deal primarily with
the 1965–1974 period (the period during which U.S. ground troops were in
Vietnam). The previously mentioned Terry H. Anderson defines his study
by means of two great bookends, Greensboro on one end and Wounded
Knee and the end of the Vietnam Conflict on the other. One-time member
of the Students for a Democratic Society, anti-war and progressive activist
Tom Hayden supports Greensboro as the starting point of the counterculture
movement, explaining that, "On February 1, 1960, the historic events of the
decade unexpectedly began. Four unknown black students staged a sit-in at
a segregated lunch counter in Greensboro, North Carolina, and started what
was soon called 'the movement' " (Hayden 1988, 31).

The counterculture continued to broaden after its start at Greensboro, with
the Civil Rights movement spawning the first great student revolt of the
1960s, when on September 2, 1964, eight University of California at Berkeley students were suspended for distributing leaflets and soliciting funds for
civil rights organizations on campus property. This event marked the beginning of the Berkeley Free Speech movement. Counterculture activities on
college and university campuses in the form of demonstrations for civil
rights and against the Vietnam Conflict would continue into the 1970s, although the May 4, 1970 shooting of four students by members of the Ohio

National Guard at Kent State University, and the similar killings in Mississippi at Jackson State University just days later, drastically changed the nature of campus demonstrations.

The seeds of the women's liberation (as it later came to be known) were
also sown during the first several years of the 1960s, with author Jerome L.
Rodnitzky suggesting that a politically based women's movement was in part
influenced by the presidency of John F. Kennedy (1961–1963). Betty Friedan's publication of *The Feminine Mystique* in 1963 was another early step
in the establishment of the women's movement. Friedan would continue to
be central to the movement through her formation of the National Organization for Women (NOW) in 1966. By 1968, the movement would be known
as women's liberation, connoting a revolutionary breaking of a slavery-like
bondage. Perhaps symbolic of the most extreme, radical arm of the movement was radical feminist Valerie Solanas's 1968 shooting of pop artist Andy
Warhol. As author Rodnitzky suggests, "Warhol recovered from his wounds,
but perhaps women's liberation never did" (Rodnitzky 1999, 27). Although
the Solanas incident caused a serious black eye for the movement (despite
the fact that the movement distanced itself from the actions of Valerie Solanas), by the end of the 1960s and the early 1970s a less-radical movement
would sweep the nation. This was fueled in part by music written and performed by female pop stars such as Carly Simon and Carole King. By the
middle of the 1970s an entire subgenre of women's music had developed,
keeping the movement alive well after the time span with which this book
will deal.

Although not to gain national prominence for several years, the use of
psychedelic drugs and the hippie lifestyle also began around 1963. Author
Ken Kesey used the royalties from his book *One Flew over the Cuckoo's Nest*
to fund what were called "acid tests," in which members of his circle, known
as the Merry Pranksters, took LSD (the drug was legal until 1966) in a party-
like atmosphere beginning in 1963. According to author and music critic
Barney Hoskyns, who documented San Francisco's Haight-Ashbury district
during the second half of the 1960s in his book *Beneath the Diamond Sky*
(1997), this early hippie lifestyle of the Merry Pranksters was fueled by the
music of the Grateful Dead, the Jefferson Airplane, and other rock groups.
Hoskyns writes that members of the San Francisco Beat scene in the North
Beach area referred to the Merry Pranksters and other LSD-taking, long-
haired, young people as "hippies," a pejorative term originally used by
African-American jazz musicians to describe the "white beatnik hangers-on
in the jazz scene" (Hoskyns 2001, 109). Originating in the North Beach area,

the hippie scene found a more hospitable home in the Haight-Ashbury district of San Francisco. Despite the apparent tension between the established beatniks and the hippies, Bruce Cook, author of *The Beat Generation*, quotes an early commentator on the start of the hippie "movement" as saying that the hippies were "no more than Beats plus drugs" (Cook 1971, 196). According to writer Christopher Mele, by the mid-1960s "the hippies had constructed a subculture based around widespread social change" (Mele 2000, 159). Music critic Edward Macan writes that this "counterculture consisted largely of young, middle-class white people who had consciously rejected the lifestyle of their parents in favor of more experimental paths" (Macan 1996, 15–16). Macan continues by describing the hippies as sharing a concern with spirituality and politically transforming American society through such things as "uncovering new realms of perception and consciousness" through the exploration of Eastern religions and the use of hallucinogenic drugs, communal and sometimes nomadic living, opposition to the war in Vietnam, and opposition to law enforcement agencies as agents of oppression (Macan 1996, 16).

The relationship between the hippies and the beatniks can also be seen in the way in which the famous Beat writer and subject of Jack Kerouac books, Neal Cassady, was able to play a central role in both groups. Although Kerouac himself did not relate well with the Merry Pranksters (he was quite ill at the time Kesey's followers finally met the great Beat author), Cassady traveled with the Pranksters, sometimes driving their "magic" bus. He is featured prominently in many of the surviving photographic documents of the group's activities.

Both Paul Perry (1996), in his book *On the Bus*, and Hunter S. Thompson (1967), in his book *Hell's Angels*, document the somewhat surprising synergy that developed in 1965 and 1966 between Kesey's Pranksters and the Hell's Angels motorcycle gang. Despite their many differences, the two groups shared a spirit of rebellion against the prevailing power structure and against the social norms of "conventional" America. They shared a keen desire for freedom on their own terms. Rock critic Joe S. Harrington (2002) points to drugs as the link between the motorcycle gang and Kesey's Pranksters. The Hell's Angels and other such groups formed an easily identifiable "biker" subculture as part of the overall counterculture. I will discuss music relating to this biker subculture in the "Hippie Lifestyle" part of Chapter 5.

Marijuana and LSD continued to be mind-altering drugs of choice throughout the counterculture era, although by the late 1960s, LSD seemed to be fading from the scene somewhat. The increasing violence of the Vietnam Conflict and the demonstrations against it, along with the violent debacle in Chicago at the 1968 Democratic National Convention and the subsequent election of Richard Nixon in the 1968 presidential election, coincided with an increased use of harder, addictive drugs like heroin. Jill Jonnes, in her book *Hep-Cats, Narcs, and Pipe Dreams: A History of America's Romance with Illegal Drugs* (1996), details this change. In addition, other painkillers and barbiturates, or downers, became increasingly popular as the U.S. and world situation became increasingly ugly at the end of the 1960s and the early 1970s. In fact, 1969 and 1970 found the world witnessing the drug-related deaths of such prominent counterculture musicians as Jimi Hendrix, Janis Joplin, and Jim Morrison, to name the three best-known casualties.

Interestingly, the Merry Pranksters were to become important early members of the Back to the Land movement in the late 1960s. The communal nature of the Pranksters and the Grateful Dead, a band linked with Ken Kesey's acid tests, certainly resembled the lifestyle in the rural communes of the Back to the Land movement. As we shall see, this movement helped to support a return to the musical style (but not necessarily the lyrical style) of traditional folk and country music. The Back to the Land movement was also strongly linked to the environmental movement and increasing concern over food processed by multinational corporations. Organic foods first came into prominence at this time, and the relationship between the Back to the Land movement and the later increased interest in organic foods is explored in Warren J. Belasco's book *Appetite for Change: How the Counterculture Took on the Food Industry 1966–1988* (1989). It should be noted that many of the voices heard in present-day protests over irradiated food and genetically engineered food grew out of this movement.

Around 1970, various "special interest" groups emerged. In particular, a potent, radicalized Black Power movement separated itself from the Martin Luther King, Jr.–led Civil Rights movement. Some Black militants openly carried guns, testing the limits of weapons laws, and making a point that they would respond to illegal intimidation and violence directed at them by law enforcement personnel by defending themselves. Afrocentric education was encouraged and some activists demanded nationhood for Black America.

By 1970, an active gay rights movement began in larger cities in the United States. According to Stuart A. Kallen, "by 1973 there were nearly 800 organizations fighting for gay rights both locally and nationally" (2001, 28).

From a musical standpoint, the lesbian movement would generate the most important material, at least within the historical limits of the present study. Music by and directed at openly gay men dealing specifically with gay issues and building gay pride began to be heard at the end of our timeframe as the disco era began.

The entire counterculture era seems to have peaked in 1968. The fiasco of anti-war rallies turned violent at the 1968 Democratic National Convention, the murder of audience members at the Rolling Stones' 1969 concert at Altamont, California, the 1970 Kent State University and Jackson State University shootings, and the landslide reelection of President Richard Nixon in 1972 all combined to deflate the movement.

But did counterculture music originate in 1960, peak during 1968, the so-called year of revolution, and simply stop in 1975? The short answer is: no. The pro-labor union songs of the 1930s and 1940s, sung by folk-style groups like the Weavers, the folk songs of the late nineteenth century that were adapted to support the violent labor strikes in Oakland, California, or the anti-slavery songs of the mid-nineteenth century might all be considered to be precedents for the music of the era under study in this book. And, the songs of punk rockers and rappers bring alternative lifestyles and rejection of the values of the dominant society through the 1970s to today.

Study of the earlier history of the vibrant 1960s counterculture haven of the Greenwich Village area of New York City also reveals that this was not a new phenomenon. Authors and editors such as Rick Beard and Leslie Cohen Berlowitz, in their *Greenwich Village: Culture and Counterculture* (1993), and Francis Patrick Naughton, in his dissertation, "Making the Greenwich Village Counterculture: An Analysis of the Construction of an Urban Intellectual Community" (1978), document the strong, left-leaning collection of artists, gays, feminists, and other decidedly (for the time) counterculture figures who made the district a counterculture haven as early as the 1910s. Indeed, Beard and Berlowitz trace the Greenwich Village counterculture back to the bohemians of the mid-nineteenth century, including figures such as writer Walt Whitman and writer, free-thinker, and feminist Ada Clare, among others.

And what of the impact of the 1960–1975 counterculture music today? Recently historians Peter Braunstein and Michael William Doyle lamented what they called the dehistoricizing of the 1960s and early 1970s counterculture, writing that the "casual inflation of the term 'counterculture' into a nebula of signifiers comprehending bongs, protest demonstrations, ashrams, and social nudity rears its head at seemingly any Sixties retrospective" (Braunstein and Doyle 2002a, 6). They write that "easy terms" like "counterculture" "lose their original historical mooring, become shorthand references, then shortcuts to thinking, and finally Pepsi commercial soundbites" (Braunstein and Doyle 2002a, 6). Indeed, at the time of this writing, the decidedly anti–U.S. government song "American Woman" appears frequently on a fashion-related television commercial. Similarly, although the song is outside the scope of this book, those familiar with the British punk/ new wave music of the late 1970s must be dismayed, surprised, and amused by the fact that in 2002 and 2003 the 1979 song "London Calling" by the Clash is being used in a widely televised commercial for luxury Jaguar automobiles. The point of both of these examples is that, once the counterculture sociopolitical ramifications of a work of art lose their impact through time, the work of art can become part of a much more generic popular culture.

And what of the music? Music was part of every aspect of this counterculture, playing important roles in the lives of probably every young person who was part of "the movement." Protest songs were sung at anti-war rallies, songs made overt or obfuscated references to drugs, music was used when people used recreational drugs, the development of "back-to-the-land" communes coincided with a resurgence of traditional folk and country musical styles, and so forth. This having been said, however, the reader is urged to keep in mind that we are not dealing with a huge number of musical works. One might assume, for example, that the anti-war movement, one of the largest parts of counterculture activity, and certainly one that garnered much media attention, must have generated a huge number of songs. Surely most rock musicians opposed the war and recorded anti-war material, and surely their audiences bought those recordings and helped to generate radio airplay. Historians Kenneth J. Bindas and Craig Houston studied the music of the anti-war movement and wrote,

> On the subject of the Vietnam War, one of the most important events of the sixties, rock music and its musicians were noticeably silent. Only when the American public altered its opinion toward the war did the record industry and prominent musicians redirect their music by marketing songs with antiwar themes. (Bindas and Houston 1989, 1)

In fact, the historians discovered that "antiwar rock songs comprised less that 1.5 percent of the approximately 1000 singles to make *Billboard*'s yearly top 100 chart, 1965–74" (Bindas and Houston 1989, 3).

Sometimes instead of addressing specific issues, or advocating particular counterculture lifestyles, the music of the era was more generally pro-experimentation, anti-violence, pro-youth, and anti-commercialism. Sometimes, however, music and the extra-musical world seemed to be closely linked, such as when the heavily orchestrated, psychedelic music of 1967 gave way to the harder rock of 1968, simultaneous with the growing violence of the Vietnam Conflict and the protests against it, and the increased use of harder, addictive drugs. And despite Bindas and Houston's findings concerning rock music and the Vietnam Conflict, rock music was important to the overall movement, according to those who experienced it. For example, according to one unnamed hippie quoted in Anderson 1995, "rock music is responsible more than any other single factor in spreading the good news" (Anderson 1995, 245). Anderson stresses the importance of live music and especially FM radio in spreading the counterculture's message to the so-called "freaks," due to the relatively low number of commercial interruptions, and the higher degree of freedom from a top-40-type format that FM disc jockeys had over their AM colleagues (Anderson 1995, 246). In this study, we will look at music that made the top 40, music that was heard primarily on FM radio stations, and music that was known primarily because it was performed at rallies.

Curiously, very few songs took an overall look at the movement itself. The Beach Boys' "Student Demonstration Time," Mike Love's 1971 rewrite of the Jerry Leiber and Mike Stoller song "Riot in Cell Block #9," chronicled the movement from Berkeley Free Speech through the Kent State University and Jackson State University shootings. Love's lyrics take an observer's dispassionate view of the pros and cons of using demonstrations to try to make political points. The best-known look at the conflict between the movement and mainstream American society, however, was Stephen Stills's "For What It's Worth." Recorded by the songwriter's group, Buffalo Springfield, the song made it to #7 on the *Billboard* pop singles charts in early 1967. Interestingly, the Stills song comments on the growing sense of being on the edge of intense violence. This is especially interesting because the song came out over a year before the most intense violent conflicts of the movement, which took place throughout 1968. "For What It's Worth" proved to be an eerie foretelling of the near revolution that sprang from the movement, made all the more effective by its timing and the somewhat ominous instrumental performance by Stills, Neil Young, and company. Thunderclap Newman's "Something in the Air," a fairly substantial hit in 1969, also seems to foretell a coming counterculture revolution; however, the British band's song was not nearly as timely as Stephen Stills's masterpiece.

If one were to seek out music that dealt with nearly every aspect of the 1960–1975 counterculture on one record album or compact disc, one might best turn to the musical *Hair*, which opened April 29, 1968 at the Biltmore Theatre, New York City. Although I will be dealing with specific aspects of the movement in separate chapters, I wish to deal with *Hair* in one place, so as not to have to chop up the discussion of this groundbreaking show. Since the show encompasses elements of virtually everything discussed up to this point, this seemed to be the most logical place. The show was written by James Rado, Gerome Ragni, and Galt MacDermot. Rado and Ragni, who were unemployed actors living in New York City's East Village, decided to write a show about young people with whom they had become acquainted. They then set about finding a suitable composer, settling on Galt Mac-Dermot. MacDermot, a native of Canada also living in New York, was a little older than his collaborators and was not working in a contemporary popular music style at the time. He based his score on the styles of popular music he heard on the radio. Considering the way in which the entire project developed, it could easily be argued that *Hair* is entirely artificial, especially when compared with the rock music of the era, most of which had a sort of folk-like ownership of the mass of young people. To wit, in his 1972 book *It's Too Late to Stop Now*, well-known rock critic Jon Landau wrote:

> Rock, the music of the Sixties, was a music of spontaneity. It was a folk music—it was listened to and made by the same group of people. It did not come out of a New York office building where people sit and write what they think other people want to hear. It came from the life experiences of the artists and their interaction with an audience that was roughly the same age. As that spontaneity and creativity have become more stylized and analyzed and structured, it has become easier for businessmen and behind-the-scenes manipulators to structure their approach to merchandising music. The process of creating stars has become a routine and a formula as dry as an equation. (Landau 1972, 40)

The lack of a real grassroots spontaneity did not seem to hurt *Hair*. After several preview performances in 1967 and early 1968, the show eventually succeeded in bringing the youth counterculture to Broadway. It made an immediate impact on American musical theatre and sharply divided critics. The free-form style, the loud rock music, the exploration of subject matter such as drugs ("Hashish"), alternative life styles (virtually the entire show), the hippie life style, the generation gap, interracial sexual relationships ("Black Boys," "White Boys"), free love ("Sodomy," "Black Boys," "White Boys"), the degradation of the environment ("Air"), non-Western religion and philosophy ("The Flesh Failures [Let the Sunshine In]" contains a near quote of a line from George Harrison's Hindu-inspired song "Within You, Without You"), and so forth, all came together to give many audience members and purchasers of the subsequent soundtrack album the impression that *Hair* was a true counterculture happening. Some prominent critics of the twenty-first century dismiss *Hair*, refusing to acknowledge it as a milestone rock opera. Music critic William Ruhlmann, for example, credits *Jesus Christ Superstar* (1970) as being "the first show to successfully put rock music in a theatrical context (*Hair* is really a pop/show music pastiche, not rock)" (Ruhlmann 2002). Ruhlmann's assessment aside, *Hair* does contain the rhythms and harmonic materials of 1966–1968 rock, as well as its instrumentation. The fact that at least some segment of the youth population of the late 1960s sensed an authenticity in the music of *Hair* is suggested by the fact that the Cowsills, the multigenerational group upon which the Partridge Family was modeled, took the song "Hair" to #2 on the *Billboard* pop charts in early 1969, the 5th Dimension took "Aquarius/Let the Sunshine In (The Flesh Failures)" to #1—a position the recording held for an astounding six weeks— in spring 1969, Oliver had a #3 hit single with "Good Morning Starshine" in summer 1969, and Three Dog Night's version of "Easy to Be Hard" reached #4 on the *Billboard* pop charts in autumn 1969. In addition, soul singer Carla Thomas reached #86 on the *Billboard* pop charts with "Where Do I Go." The infamous nude scene and the occasional use of real marijuana in performance also lent a certain measure of counterculture authenticity to the show (Deutsch 1988).

THE RELATIONSHIP OF MUSIC AND SOCIETY

To what extent does music reflect society and to what extent does music shape society? These questions have been debated, sometimes quite vigorously, since at least the time of the ancient Greek philosophers Plato and Aristotle. In *The Republic*, Plato wrote at some length about the need to promote some musical styles and even some of the musical modes (which are somewhat akin to scales), while banning others (Strunk 1965). Plato argued that music shapes not only society at large, but also individuals. Others (Denisoff and Levine 1971; Edwards and Singletary 1984) have argued that while music might reflect a particular time and place, music is largely ineffective as a form of rhetoric meant to convince anybody of anything. R. Serge Denisoff, one of the most prolific writers of the early 1970s on the subject of the music of protest, collected a number of essays expounding both views in the first section of *The Sounds of Social Change* (1972a). Denisoff concludes that both viewpoints are at least partially correct in the context of the various protest movements of the 1960s, with the extent to which music convinces or reflects depending upon the specific song or specific social movement in question. Three decades after Denisoff's study, the complex relationships between music and society are still subject to debate. For example, at present, debates rage about the sometimes violent lyrics found in rap and hip hop compositions. If one accepts the conclusion that music can be both reflective of society at large and influential upon society as I do, then one must attend closely to the details of particular musical works in terms of either their reactive or their promptive nature.

When dealing with music of the counterculture era in the United States, we might assume that popular music would be the focus. Such will be the case in this book, although I will deal with two major "classical" works, George Crumb's *Black Angels* and Steve Reich's *Come Out*, the former in reference to the anti-war movement and the latter in reference to the Civil Rights and Black Power movements. Some would argue that the highly experimental music of avant-garde composers like John Cage (who allowed accident and chance to play a role in the compositional process) were part of the counterculture. Since the techniques of many of these works were developed in the 1940s and 1950s, and were anticipated to some extent in the European Dada movement of several decades before that, I will deal with the avant-garde only to the extent that it either directly related to the movements and lifestyle choices under study. And what of the rest of the "classical" repertoire of the counterculture era? According to historian Ben Arnold, the Vietnam Conflict in particular led to a paradigm shift in the response of serious concert music composers to war. Arnold writes that the Vietnam conflict was a new age war, a war with a culture of protest. Composers no longer wrote compositions to support war as had Aaron Copland, Samuel Barber, Roy Harris, Gail Kubick, and dozens of others during World War II; they openly protested the war and expressed anti-government sentiments directly and to a degree unprecedented in history. (Arnold 1993, 317)

In his reference guide *Music and War: A Research and Information Guide*, Arnold presents information on approximately sixty concert compositions that either deal directly with the war or were heavily influenced by it. The author notes, however, that "while a large educated public reads novels about the Vietnam conflict, few (if any) of the art compositions dealing with Vietnam are known even in the music/academic world that produced so many of them" (Arnold 1993, 324). Indeed, perusal of concert programs of choral ensembles, symphony orchestras, concert bands, and even ensembles that predominantly perform music written in the past fifty years reveals that these works simply have not made it into the repertoire, with the possible exception of the George Crumb composition mentioned earlier.

Why the paradigm shift mentioned above? How did all the various political and social movements, not to mention the new lifestyle choices of the younger generation of the 1960–1975 period, come to be the common knowledge of nearly everyone in the United States? It has been widely suggested that the answer lies in the electronic media of the era. Media expert Marshall McLuhan (McLuhan and Fiore 1968) regarded the Vietnam Conflict as the first true media war: a war that, for the first time, was covered almost in real time on television sets across the country. Likewise, protests against the war were seen as they unfolded. In discussing the importance of television in the development of public opinion, McLuhan wrote that "a new form of 'politics' is emerging, and in ways we haven't yet noticed. The living room has become a voting booth. Participation via television in Freedom marches, in war, revolution, pollution, and other events is changing *everything*" (McLuhan and Fiore 1967, 22; italics in original). In the quarter-century since McLuhan's pronouncements, we have seen live news television, fax machines, and computer networks play crucial roles in the fall of the Soviet Union and lifting of the Iron Curtain, in the conduct of the Persian Gulf War and "Operation Iraqi Freedom," the O. J. Simpson case, and the terrorist attacks on the United States on September 11, 2001.

Back to the two burning questions: to what extent did music of the counterculture era influence hearers, and to what extent did it reflect a particular country during a particularly turbulent time? Study of the literature of the time yields diverging results, largely depending on the writer's agenda and the extent to which studies were undertaken in a scientific manner.

David A. Noebel and Jerome L. Rodnitzky are two writers of the counterculture era who disagreed in the strongest of terms politically, but who were both of the camp arguing that music shapes the individual and society. In his *Rhythm, Riots, and Revolution*, Noebel, a decidedly right-wing writer, placed the blame for the early anti-war movement—he saw the movement as something negative—and the "subversive" and "atheistic" trends in American society in general on what he called "pro-Communist" musicians like Pete Seeger, Bob Dylan, Joan Baez, Phil Ochs, and others (Noebel 1966). Rodnitzky, who has never espoused a right-wing philosophy in his writings, credited Noebel for being unusually perceptive as to the power of music as an influence. Rodnitzky wrote: "Although Noebel's specific charges lean toward the ridiculous, as a frightened professional patriot, he is one of the few individuals besides folk performers themselves who seem to grasp the persuasive power of the musical idiom" (Rodnitzky 1971b).

In apparent contrast to Noebel and Rodnitzky, Charles DeBenedetti's scholarly study with Charles Chatfield, *An American Ordeal: The Antiwar Movement of the Vietnam Era* (1990), a massive work, contains only a handful of references to music. Indeed, other studies, such as Bindas and Houston 1989, which finds that only approximately 1.5% of the records to make the pop charts between 1965 and 1974 had anything at having to do with the war, suggest that the political movements had lives of their own and did not receive a massive infusion of new bodies spurred on by musical compositions. To cite another example questioning the ability of the music of the counterculture era to exert influence, Emily Edwards and Michael Singletary, studying the relative importance of lyrics in how listeners formed their likes and dislikes of particular songs, found that only 25 percent of teens primarily liked a song because of its lyrics (Edwards and Singletary 1984, 23). Likewise, the prolific writer on the sociology of music, R. Serge Denisoff, working with Mark H. Levine, found that 41 percent of teens polled about the meaning of the notorious omni-protest song "Eve of Destruction" did not fully or correctly interpret songwriter P. F. Sloan's intended message (Denisoff and Levine 1971). This having been said, "Eve of Destruction" represents one of the more interesting songs of the counterculture era in terms of its shotgun approach to protesting virtually all of the social ills of its time, its immense popularity, and the intensity of reactions to it from the political right and from the political left. Since it is one of the few potent omni-protest songs, thus avoiding category, and since it illustrates the interconnectedness of many of the counterculture movements, let us examine it here.

"Eve of Destruction" appeared on the scene in the summer of 1965, after the Cuban Missile Crisis, and just after the introduction of U.S. ground troops in Vietnam. Also significant to its musical style was the emergence of the new folk-rock style, in which the topical lyrics of folk revival and protest music were put to rock accompaniment, earlier in the year. In fact, some of the musical clichés associated with the folk-rock styles of the Byrds and Bob Dylan (once he "went electric" and moved from an acoustic folk style to performing backed by a rock band in 1965) found their way into "Eve of Destruction." P. F. Sloan's composition, as sung by Barry McGuire in what would be a #1 hit on the *Billboard* top 100 pop charts, uses the suspended fourth which then resolves to the root position tonic chord at the end of each major section—heard in the rhythm guitar parts of such Byrds folk-rock hits as "Turn! Turn! Turn! (To Everything There Is a Season)" and "Mr. Tambourine Man"—and the electric guitars, electric bass, electric organ, drums (provided by the original members of the Grass Roots) and sneering singing style of the by-then-electric Dylan.

Songwriter P. F. Sloan, formerly a member of the Fantastic Baggys, an absolutely apolitical and totally obscure surf band, comments on the chaos in Asia, world hunger, the military-industrial complex, the nuclear standoff between the Soviet Union and the United States, racism in the United States, space exploration as a waste of money given all of the poverty in the world, and the generation gap, hence my early description of the song as a "shotgun approach" to protest. Sloan includes some obvious text painting in his musical setting. As I wrote in my *Songs of the Vietnam Conflict,*

> In a song with stanzas featuring different words but the same music and a repeated refrain phrase that includes the same words and music each time, one might expect to find text painting, the setting of particular words or phrases to music that highlights them (a rising melodic line for the word "higher," for example), in the refrain phrases. This is exactly what Sloan does in his three–fold repetition of the word "over," within a descending pitch line, suggesting the frustration felt by the singer with the character to whom the song is addressed, a character who seems quite insistent that all is basically all right with the world. (Perone 2001, 38)

Given the composer's shotgun approach, he was probably guaranteed to offend many in the political, social, and religious establishment of 1965. The conservative, fundamentalist-Christian writer David A. Noebel, for example, in his widely distributed book *Rhythm, Riots, and Revolution*, claimed that the lyrics of "Eve of Destruction" "and similar expressions are constantly being used to induce the American public to surrender to atheistic, international Communism" (Noebel 1966, 229). Although Noebel obviously felt that the song could have a widespread impact on American youth, and although Sy and Barbara Ribakove in their 1966 biography of Bob Dylan claimed that young people were deeply affected by "Eve of Destruction" (Ribakove and Ribakove 1966, 120), the previously mentioned study by Denisoff and Levine (1971) suggests that the meaning of the song was fairly widely misunderstood or incompletely understood.

Sloan's "Eve of Destruction" was banned by a number of radio stations in twenty of the fifty largest radio markets in the United States. Still, it reached #1 on both the *Billboard* and *Cash Box* pop charts. And, interestingly enough, the recording generated much negative reaction from musicians associated with the political left. Phil Ochs referred to the recording as "a bad introduction" to protest music (Cunningham and Friesen 1965). Tom Paxton said, "The fact that there has been a response by the young to these protest songs is no cause for rejoicing. Anyone who asks of these idols that they probe a bit deeper will be disappointed, because these songs never intended to tell them anything more than Mom and Dad don't understand them" (Denisoff 1990, 83). Influential blues guitarist and teacher Dave Van Ronk called "Eve of Destruction" "an awful song" (Van Ronk 1966, 21). Apparently no one liked the song, that is, except for the record-buying public.

Did the prevailing power structure and corporate America consider "Eve of Destruction" to be a dangerous song? Allow me to cite one example that suggests that it did. Three years after the initial success of and controversy surrounding "Eve of Destruction," at about the height of U.S. involvement in the war in Vietnam, the University of Buffalo Marching Band, led by Director of Bands Frank Cipolla, performed a show entitled "Give Peace a Chance" during halftime of the fall 1968 nationally televised football game between the University of Buffalo and Holy Cross University. Television network executives objected to the anti-war theme of the halftime show, with its centerpiece "Eve of Destruction," and censored the band's performance (Bewley 2000). Back in the 1960s it was commonplace for television coverage of college football to include the bands' halftime shows; this one was not seen, due to fears that the pairing of "Eve of Destruction" with the general anti-war theme of the performance was too anti-government in nature.

With such widely diverging assessments of "Eve of Destruction" in particular and of the impact of music on society in general, the rhetorical question arises: Just what is the real impact of music? Given hindsight, it appears that much of the music of the counterculture era reflects what was going on in U.S. society. It really seemed to reflect that old saw, "preaching to the choir." David A. Noebel's concerns aside, it seems unlikely that many people were swayed one way or the other by an "Eve of Destruction." That having been said, however, it is possible that the whole gestalt of "the movement," of which the music was always a part, was helped, was pushed on by the music.

The few songs of the 1960–1975 period that commented on the movement itself (aside from those anti-counterculture songs of right-wing country songwriters) in the most general terms (not dealing with specific parts of the movement) tended to chronicle or even foretell the conflicts between protesters and the official enforcers of "straight" society's rules: the police. The song that probably best captured the general sense of being on the edge of possible mass violence at each and every large demonstration was "For What It's Worth," written by Stephen Stills. The song was recorded by the composer's rock group, Buffalo Springfield, and hit #7 on the *Billboard* pop charts in early 1967. Stills eerily foretells the violence that more and more frequently was part of the demonstrations from summer 1967 through the infamous Kent State University shootings of May 4, 1970. Stills is entirely sympathetic to the protesters, and although the song does paint a them-versus-us picture of the movement, his song has a curious air of detachment. The singer clearly is part of the counterculture, but seems to be presenting a factual snapshot of what life in the movement is like during the times of impending confrontation, rather than advocating for any particular political or social cause. Incidentally, Stills and his Buffalo Springfield bandmate Neil Young were later part of Crosby, Stills, Nash & Young, the group that recorded Young's "Ohio," a biting commentary on the shootings of students at Kent State by members of the Ohio National Guard.

Another of the general movement-oriented songs came from what many readers might consider an unlikely source, the Beach Boys. Group member Michael Love took Jerry Leiber and Mike Stoller's classic rock and roll number "Riot in Cell Block #9" and added new lyrics. The resultant 1971 song, which the Beach Boys included on their album *Surf's Up*, chronicled the conflicts between the counterculture and straight society from the Berkeley Free Speech movement to the Kent State University and Jackson State University shootings. Love does not overtly take political sides, but suggests the validity of the movement; however, he warns that those who would try to affect social change through mass demonstrations that violence might very well greet them.

As we now get set to turn our attention to music associated with the various parts of the "movement" it is important for the reader to keep in mind that music of social protest was not invented in the 1960s. The history of such music, even in the United States, goes back more than 150 years. Even protest music that went against the general tide of U.S. public opinion can be found well before the 1960s. The pro-union songs of the nineteenth century and the violent labor protests of the nineteenth-century United States, although not covered very extensively in some history books, were very important events in their time. One need only read Jack London's novel *The Valley of the Moon* (1913), which was originally serialized in *Cosmopolitan Magazine*, to see the extent to which the labor strife of late-nineteenth-century Oakland, California, touched many working class residents. Although London does not detail the music of the movement of his day, those protest songs can be found in several collections. Even during a more recent period in which twenty-first-century Americans might assume that the nation had been united toward a common goal, such has not always been the case. Prior to the bombing of Pearl Harbor on December 7, 1941, for example, there was a fairly strong anti-war movement in the United States, and music was there to help further the cause. Like the pro-labor music of over one hundred years ago, the anti-war music of the 1930s and early 1940s does not receive much acknowledgment today. One of the main differences between pre-1960 protest music and music of "the movement" is that the anti-establishment music of the 1960s and early 1970s was much more prevalent than that of earlier times. It became a much greater part of the more general popular culture of its time and in doing so, has survived longer than any other earlier repertoire of anti-establishment or counterculture music.

Even before the end of the counterculture era some of the lifestyle choices, philosophies, attitudes, and even popular expressions of the 1960s were becoming near clichés. Certainly by the time of the emergence of disco music in the mid-1970s and punk rock in both the United States and Great Britain as a somewhat violent reaction both to disco and to the attitudes of the

1960s, many young people questioned the ability of 1960s-type attitudes to affect positive social and political change. We can point to musical evidence of this late 1970s questioning of the values of the counterculture, or at least the hippie lifestyle and philosophy, in the form of British pop songwriter Nick Lowe's composition "(What's So Funny 'bout) Peace, Love and Understanding." Recorded by Elvis Costello & the Attractions for their 1978 album *Armed Forces*, the song questions those who mock the 1960s values of peace, love, and understanding. A song like this could not possibly work rhetorically if those 1960s values were still held dear by the young generation in 1978.

For a final assessment of the impact of the counterculture, however, let us turn to Barry Melton, cofounder of the frequently political band Country Joe & the Fish. Melton, a full-time political activist and musician in San Francisco, had been greatly influenced by the Reverend Gary Davis, Mance Lipscomp, Doc Watson, and Bukka White, earlier folk artists who he and many other folk revival performers considered to be icons of musicality and activism. Melton and Joe McDonald formed their band in 1965 and soon thereafter toured under the sponsorship of the radical Students for a Democratic Society. He writes of the impact of the movement,

> But we did some really good things, perhaps in spite of ourselves. Most of us stopped using harmful drugs and used our brief glimpse of heaven to usher in a whole new era in psychology and religion. . . . We became conscious of our bodies, left the cities, started organic farms, and helped give the rest of the country a good idea of what constitutes a healthy diet. Or we stayed in the cities, helped to revitalize the neighborhoods, and improved the quality of life. We had the patience and tolerance to accept alternative medicine and therapies. Our questioning the basic assumptions about sex and relationships helped pave the way for both the women's and gay rights movements. We helped bring the world a whole new consciousness of the environment, and we helped tear down the Berlin wall. And, most of all, we helped teach the world that one person can make a difference. (Melton 2001, 156–57)

And now to the music of the era and the music of the movement. . . .

2

Popular Music Trends through the Counterculture Era

Before we can study the relationship between the music of the counterculture era and U.S. society, it is important to establish the general musical
trends of the time. The period 1960–1975 witnessed several styles and genres
of music come and go, and found the focus of musicians and the record
buying public shifting from individual songs to albums. In addition, listening trends in commercial radio played a role in what kinds of popular music
reached those who took part in the movement.

While the roots of youth-oriented rock music go back to rhythm and blues
(R&B) and country music of the 1940s, most historians consider the time
right around 1954 as being key in the popularization of this new, hybrid
musical genre called rock and roll. While many people have heard of such
important 1950s rock and roll pioneers as Chuck Berry, Little Richard, Elvis
Presley, Buddy Holly, Fats Domino, and Bill Haley and His Comets, and
while many people are familiar with at least some of their music, it is important for the purposes of our study to bear in mind that the end of the
1950s saw a downturn in rock and roll as the premiere youth-oriented music.
This happened for several reasons, including such diverse occurrences as
the following: (1) Little Richard turned from music to the ministry; (2) Buddy
Holly, Richie Valens, and the Big Bopper died in an airplane crash in February 1959; (3) sexual scandals temporarily forced both Jerry Lee Lewis and
Chuck Berry off the record charts; and (4) the infamous "payola" scandal (in

which disc jockeys were found to be taking bribes in exchange for giving certain records more airplay than others) called into question the integrity of the rock and roll radio industry. Record companies increasingly sought out sanitized, wholesome performers (who happened to be more acceptable to parents than some of the original rock and roll stars), turned them into stars, and had them record music often lacking the musical and lyrical edge of rock and roll. Something new had to come into the music scene to rekindle the musical interests of young people in the late 1950s and early 1960s. One of the new styles that emerged at this time was folk revival music.

That a return to more or less traditional American folk music, and newly composed music in the folk style, was gaining popularity in the late 1950s can be seen in the success of groups like the Kingston Trio. This San Francisco–based group, all of whom sang and played acoustic instruments like guitar, banjo, and bass, had ten top–10 single records between 1958 and 1963. Kingston Trio albums also sold well for their record company, Capitol Records. While some folk purists complained that the group's style was too close to that of contemporary pop music, the Kingston Trio brought old American folk songs to the public's collective ear like no other folk-styled group. And some of the folk protest musicians who emerged in the early 1960s acknowledged the importance of the Kingston Trio in bringing folk music to the forefront of American popular consciousness. For example, in a 1968 interview in *Broadside*, Phil Ochs credited the Kingston Trio and Joan Baez with being strong artists who, through their ability to win over audiences, acted as "translators" for the late 1950s and early 1960s folk song movement (Interview with Phil Ochs 1968, 13). Joan Baez herself has been widely quoted as saying that the Kingston Trio was one of her early inspirations for becoming a folk musician.

Pete Seeger, Malvina Reynolds, and Woody Guthrie were among the older, well-established folk musicians whose music continued to be important at the dawn of the 1960s. All three had come out of the leftist politics and protest song movements of the 1930s and 1940s. Guthrie's career, and indeed his life, was cut short by the ravages of the devastating illness Huntington's chorea, which kept him hospitalized during the last decade of his life. Even in his weak state, Guthrie was a tremendous influence on the new generation of left-wing folk protest singers, including Joan Baez, Phil Ochs, and most especially, Bob Dylan. Reynolds and Seeger would continue both to inspire younger musicians and themselves would be active in music of the movement during the counterculture era.

The new generation of folk revival musicians, including Joan Baez and Bob Dylan, emerged in the early 1960s. These musicians, which by 1964 would include Phil Ochs and Tom Paxton, sang older left-wing protest music and composed songs that were in the style of folk music, but that addressed the social issues of the 1960s, including racial integration, the threat of nuclear war, labor strife, and the Vietnam Conflict. While most of these musicians would continue to play an important role in the movement, primarily through their appearances at anti-war and civil rights rallies, pop music was again changing.

Folk revival music was not the only new popular form hitting the American radio airwaves and generating record sales at the beginning of the 1960s. Berry Gordy, Jr., a one-time songwriter, autoworker, and boxer, formed his Motown Records empire in Detroit, Michigan in the late 1950s. Gordy actually owned several record labels, including Gordy, Tamla, and Motown, but the popular rhythm and blues style performed by his artists has been generically labled "Motown," short for the Motor City (Detroit). Motown acts largely were solo singers and vocal groups. Generally the same set of accompanying instrumentalists would perform on many records by all of the Motown vocalists. Adding to the instantly recognizable Motown sound was a similarity of music arrangement, the use of in-house songwriters, and a common record production style. Performers like Smokey Robinson and the Miracles, the Supremes, the Temptations, the Four Tops, Stevie Wonder, Diana Ross, and the Jackson Five scored dozens of top 10 hits. Although Motown artists tended to be more successful on the *Billboard* pop charts (which weighed success among White audiences higher than among Black audiences) than they were on *Billboard* magazine's rhythm and blues charts (which more heavily leaned toward African-American audiences), Motown touched the lives of every young American of the 1960s and 1970s.

The surfing craze hit the United States like a rogue wave in 1962. Groups like the Beach Boys, Jan and Dean, and others brought the carefree southern California lifestyle to the entire nation. Stylistically, surf music combined the guitar-based rock and roll of Chuck Berry with the doo-wop harmonies of 1950s *a capella* (without instrumental accompaniment) vocal groups. The most successful of these acts, the Beach Boys, mostly recorded their own material, in the form of songs written by Brian Wilson. Wilson quickly became one of the first rock recording artists also to work as a record producer. As had been the case in the late 1950s, 45-rpm singles were foremost on the minds of record companies and recording artists. The early albums of the Beach Boys, for example, tended feature the "A" and "B" sides of their then-current singles, with some of the other songs being of lesser quality—in short, material to fill up the album. Brian Wilson and the Beach Boys eventually moved into more musically adventurous territory in 1966 and 1967. The song "Good Vibrations," in particular, represented a type of impressionistic psychedelia, especially with its use of cello playing the repeated bass notes and the theremin, an electronic musical instrument most associated with science fiction movies of the 1940s and 1950s, playing an eerie, high pitched, vibrato-laden answer phrase.

The next major trend in 1960s pop music came from a place that few Americans probably expected: England. In the 1940s and 1950s British pop acts that became successful in the United States had been few and very far between. All that changed with the emergence of the Beatles in early 1964. The Beatles actually had been a highly successful group in Britain for two years. Their live appearance on the Ed Sullivan show in February 1964, however, found them taking America by storm. The Beatles featured remakes of older American songs by songwriters such as Chuck Berry, Carl Perkins, Smokey Robinson, and others, and material by group members John Lennon and Paul McCartney. (Although George Harrison later would emerge as an important songwriter, his songs were not issued as singles and he was allotted only a composition or two on each of the Beatles' early albums.)

Within a year, British bands like the Rolling Stones, the Dave Clark Five, the Kinks, the Who, the Zombies, Gerry and the Pacemakers, and others had hit records in the United States and appeared in America in concert and on popular television variety programs. The British groups that would endure the longest and have the greatest counterculture significance would include the Beatles, the Rolling Stones, the Who, the Animals, and the Kinks. The Rolling Stones, in particular, would be seen throughout the 1960s as being the great "dark" counterpart to the Beatles, who came to be seen as the loveable "moptops." By the early 1970s, the Rolling Stones had dealt frankly with such topics as drug addiction in their songs "Mother's Little Helper," "Gimme Shelter," and "Sister Morphine," and with youth street violence in "Street Fighting Man."

American musicians were greatly influenced by the so-called "British Invasion." While some groups openly imitated the style of the Beatles and the Rolling Stones, others created new musical styles that combined several influences. Among the latter was the Byrds. While the name of this Los Angeles–based band owed a debt of gratitude to the Beatles (animal names with unusual spellings), the group's musical style combined American folk revival music with the amplified, guitar-based style of the Beatles. This new hybrid, called folk rock, swept the United States in 1965. The Byrds recorded highly successful hit singles such as "Mr. Tambourine Man," a Bob Dylan composition, and "Turn! Turn! Turn! (To Everything There Is a Season)," a Pete Seeger composition. The instrumental sound of these Byrds recordings was characterized by Roger "Jim" McGuinn's electric twelve-string guitar. The instrument became one of the defining traits of folk rock. The Byrds went on to be one of the more interesting changling groups of the 1960s, moving between several different styles. Group member David Crosby would eventually become a member of Crosby, Stills, Nash & Young and several members of the Byrds would be early proponents of a country-rock style in the late 1960s.

Other folk rock acts also came into national prominence in 1965, including the Turtles. Even the Woody Guthrie disciple Bob Dylan embraced rock and roll and merged it with folk. Dylan created a controversy of major proportions when he appeared at the 1965 Newport Folk Festival backed by a rock band. Although Dylan never completely left his folk roots, he would be best known for the rest of the counterculture era for his folk rock and later country-based recordings. The most commercially successful singing duo of the 1960s, Paul Simon and Art Garfunkel, also merged folk and rock styles.

As young people increasingly turned to marijuana and LSD in the middle of the 1960s, drug-related music also emerged. Although perhaps the first pop song of the 1960s to deal with drugs, "Kicks," took a decidedly anti-drug stance, soon a wide range of groups, sometimes cryptically and sometimes overtly, sang the praises of psychedelic drugs. These included the Beatles, the Rolling Stones, the Grateful Dead, the Jefferson Airplane, and the Byrds.

The Beatles' *Rubber Soul* album of December 1965 marked an important turning point for the record album as an art form. Although previous albums by the Beatles and by most other important pop performers had been built around a collection of several singles, with some (sometimes) less-than-inspired filler, *Rubber Soul* did not rely on well-known singles for its structure. In fact, at the time no songs from the U.S. release of *Rubber Soul* had been issued or were subsequently issued as singles. Significantly, *Rubber Soul* also was the first Beatles album on which members of the group wrote every song.

The year 1966 saw several very important albums appear that followed the mold of *Rubber Soul*. The Beach Boys' *Pet Sounds* did include several singles, but was built around a theme that was carried throughout the entire package. The Beatles' *Revolver* found the group becoming increasingly experimental, largely a result of experimentation with LSD. By 1967, the album as an organic whole was on the minds of many pop musicians. Pink Floyd's *Piper at the Gates of Dawn*, the Jefferson Airplane's *Surrealistic Pillow*, the Jimi Hendrix Experience's *Are You Experienced?*, and the Doors' *Strange Days* were just a few of the significant albums that young people were interested in listening to all the way through—and not just picking out favorite hit-single tracks. Eventually, albums like *Piper at the Gates of Dawn* and the Beatles' *Sgt. Pepper's Lonely Hearts Club Band* would be known as concept albums. Concept albums generally featured a theme that linked some or all of the songs, as well as musical links between songs. The most highly developed concept albums of the late 1960s and into the 1970s, works like *Jesus Christ Superstar*, the Who's *Tommy*, and Frank Zappa's *Joe's Garage*, had such a high degree of structural integrity that they are described as rock operas.

As lyrics inspired by psychedelic drugs and music meant to enhance the drug trip became increasingly common in 1967, artists turned to unusual studio techniques, emphasizing the use of special effects, electronically altered voices and instruments, and rapid panning between the stereo channels. Much of the 1967 and 1968 work of Jimi Hendrix, including the songs on his album *Are You Experienced?*, are notable examples of these studio techniques. In addition to his own compositions, Hendrix treated a few songs by other composers to his unique sonic style. For example, one of Hendrix's best-known recordings is of Bob Dylan's apocalyptic song "All Along the Watchtower." Hendrix uses the wah-wah pedal, channel panning, distortion, and other techniques to heighten Dylan's text. Hendrix's multitracked guitar playing on the song represents a compendium of rock-blues-funk-soul styles of the late 1960s.

Some psychedelic musicians made specific references to drugs in their song lyrics. The Jefferson Airplane's "White Rabbit," for example, uses imagery from Lewis Carroll, but also references to drugs. The implication is that the drugs are responsible for the dream-like images evoked in the song. Drugs inspired even the names of some of the psychedelic bands. The San Francisco Bay area band fronted by singer Janis Joplin, Big Brother and the Holding Company, derived their name from references to George Orwell's character Big Brother in his novel *1984*, and from the slang term "holding," meaning to be in possession of drugs.

Other drug-inspired musicians recorded longer tracks that included extensive instrumental improvisations. For example, the full-length version of the Doors' song "Light My Fire" ran to nearly seven minutes on their self-titled first album. Another track on the same album, "The End," lasted over eleven minutes. Other musicians turned to unusual musical scales, including the *raga* (scale-melodic patterns) of Hindustani music, which became popular, especially among young people who were experimenting with psychedelics. This was especially ironic, given that the prominent Indian musicians and gurus of the day preached strict abstinence from mind-altering drugs. The Indian sitarist Ravi Shankar became an influence on Western pop musicians and something of a Western pop star himself, eventually performing at the 1969 Woodstock Music and Art Fair and at by-then-former-Beatle George Harrison's historically important Concert for Bangla Desh in 1971. Several rock musicians, in addition to being musically influenced by India, sought spiritual solace in Indian religious practices. George Harrison, Michael Love of the Beach Boys, and Pete Townshend of the Who were three of the more prominent rock musicians who followed Indian gurus beginning in the 1960s.

The rock music festival essentially began life in 1967 in Monterey, California. The Monterey International Pop Music Festival drew approximately 60,000 rock fans during June 16–18, 1967. This first of the great rock festivals featured performances by the Jimi Hendrix Experience, the Byrds, Eric Burdon and the Animals, Electric Flag, the Paul Butterfield Blues Band, the Mamas and the Papas, the Steve Miller Band, Moby Grape, the Jefferson Airplane, the Grateful Dead, Big Brother and the Holding Company (which featured Janis Joplin), Quicksilver Messenger Service, Country Joe & the Fish, the Who, Otis Redding, Booker T. and the MGs, and Ravi Shankar. The majority of these performers had been part of a thriving rock scene in the San Francisco Bay area for a couple of years. The Monterey festival enabled them to gain national exposure during the "Summer of Love." That new musical styles were emerging in 1967 is evidenced by Jimi Hendrix's famous proclamation on stage that the Monterey Pop Festival represented the death of surf music. Significantly, Hendrix's Monterey performance culminated in the musician setting his guitar on fire using lighter fluid. Hendrix's actions reflected a growing sense of theatrical spectacle that was increasingly characterizing rock music in 1967.

AM radio had been the standard music band, at least for pop music up to this point in time. Just as the album grew in importance, so did the desire of radio listeners to hear album cuts and entire albums. The commercial constraints of AM radio, however, generally discouraged the broadcast of long songs, and AM stations were more apt to be more sensitive to potentially controversial lyrics (such as those that openly promoted drug use) than FM radio. In addition, FM radio was capable of greater audio fidelity than the AM band. FM radio moved in to meet the need of the pop music listening public. Commercial FM stations of the late 1960s became of interest to the youth counterculture because of the freedom of programming the FM disc jockeys developed.

The psychedelic haze in pop music seemed to clear in 1968 when several highly influential rock bands returned to the roots, the essence of rock. The highly orchestrated music of the Beatles' *Sgt. Pepper's Lonely Hearts Club Band* gave way to the relative starkness of the group's 1968 album, *The Beatles* (more generally known as the "White Album"). The Rolling Stones and other groups, as well, turned to a harder-edged rock sound. Some of the newer bands that emerged in 1968 and 1969, like Steppenwolf and Creedence Clearwater Revival, quickly became popular performing in styles that owed little or nothing to the psychedelic music of the previous two years. The harder rock of 1968 and 1969 would also inspire the development of a new rock variant, heavy metal.

The years 1968 and 1969 also saw the development of a hybrid country-rock style. This movement was led by such diverse musicians as Gram Parsons of the Byrds, Michael Nesmith of the Monkees, the Grateful Dead, Bob Dylan, and Rick Nelson. Another hybrid, jazz-rock, had been hinted at in the Beatles' song "Got to Get You into My Life" in 1966, but emerged in full swing in 1968 and 1969. This style also owed a huge debt of gratitude to the great horn-based rhythm and blues bands of the 1940s and 1950s. Leading proponents of jazz-rock included Chicago, Chase, and Blood, Sweat & Tears. A number of cutting-edge jazz musicians also combined jazz and rock, but in less commercially accessible ways. Jazz trumpeter and composer Miles Davis, with his ground-breaking 1970 album *Bitches Brew*, merged jazz and rock and in the process made the *Billboard* pop top 40, received a Grammy nomination for Best Instrumental Arrangement, and won a Grammy award for Best Large-Group Jazz Performance. *Bitches Brew* was also Davis's first gold record, despite the fact that he had produced some of the best-selling and critically acclaimed jazz albums of the 1950s and early

1960s. Electric guitar virtuoso Mahavishnu John McLaughlin formed his Mahavishnu Orchestra and created a hybrid jazz-rock style that featured metrically complex music and scorching guitar solos. Jeff Beck, who had once been a member of the Yardbirds, also stressed guitar virtuosity in his combination of jazz and rock influences.

As the Black Power movement grew in strength in the late 1960s, African-American musicians began exploring musical styles that (consciously or unconsciously) differentiated them from both Motown and rock. James Brown had been developing his sound already for several years, but became a much more visible force in the soul music of the last two years of the 1960s. Similarly, Aretha Franklin, whose style merged gospel music and rhythm and blues, had no fewer than twenty top-40 pop singles between 1967 and 1970. Sly Stone took on issues like ghetto life, drug addiction, and racial discrimination, while developing his funk style in 1968 through the early 1970s. In fact, Sly & the Family Stone laid some of the cornerstones for mid-1970s disco music with their recordings at the start of the 1970s.

Drawing on the combination of classical musical instruments and structures, which were directly influenced by the production and orchestration work George Martin had done on the Beatles' *Sgt. Pepper's Lonely Hearts Club Band*, some late 1960s rock groups emphasized what came to be known as art rock. The Moody Blues, in particular, had hinted at this as early as their 1967 album *Days of Future Passed*, which juxtaposed singer-guitarist Justin Hayward and singer-bassist John Lodge's songs ("Tuesday Afternoon" and "Nights in White Satin," are the two best remembered songs from the album) with orchestral fantasies on their themes, composed by conductor Peter Knight. The London Festival Orchestra backed up the Moody Blues on the album. By the late 1960s and early 1970s, Emerson, Lake and Palmer, Yes, King Crimson, and other groups were following suit in creating rock music that was taken seriously as high art. Due to the fact that these groups tended to feature longish compositions that required a high level of audio fidelity for full effect, their music was most frequently heard on FM radio and on the groups' albums. These art rock or progressive rock bands also tended to place a great deal of emphasis on elaborate album cover art. An intriguing combination of artistic fascination with the medieval period and with the space age seemed to dominate both the music and the visual art associated with the progressive rock bands of the late 1960s and early 1970s.

The late 1960s and early 1970s also witnessed the development of heavy metal. Although the term "heavy metal" was inspired by a phrase in the

Steppenwolf song "Born to Be Wild," most of the early well-remembered heavy metal groups were British. Black Sabbath, the band fronted by Ozzy Osbourne, recorded one of the most important early heavy metal albums, *Paranoid*, in 1970. Songs on *Paranoid*, including the lengthy anti-war song "War Pigs," are defined by elaborate, virtuosic, unison electric guitar and electric bass lines and lyrics that suggest a fascination with wizards, witches, warlocks, and other medieval period lore. (This lyrical reference to European medieval period legend is shared with some of the progressive rock bands of the era.) The Jimmy Page–led band Led Zeppelin, also emerged as an important force at the end of the 1960s and the dawn of the 1970s. Like Black Sabbath, Led Zeppelin emphasized mythology and references to medieval lore. Music critic Stephen Thomas Erlewine also credits the band with establishing "the concept of album-oriented rock, refusing to release popular songs from their albums as singles. In doing so, they established the dominant format [the album] for heavy metal, as well as the genre's actual sound" (Erlewine 2003). Although several of Led Zeppelin's early albums sold well and made an impact on the world of rock, *Led Zeppelin IV* (1971) enjoyed the greatest commercial success of all of the band's albums in the United States. The album features songs such as "Black Dog" (notable for the use of the unison bass and lead guitar lines), "Rock and Roll" (which, curiously, in the early twenty-first century can be heard in television advertisements for Cadillac automobiles and SUVs), and Led Zeppelin's best-known recording, "Stairway to Heaven."

The frequent references to witchcraft and other "pagan" imagery in some heavy metal music and some progressive rock led to the genres generating suspicion among some members of conservative mainstream society. Led Zeppelin's "Stairway to Heaven," for example, received considerable scrutiny for hidden satanic messages. For many years, rumor had it that songwriters Jimmy Page and Robert Plant had placed phrases praising Satan in the recording using the technique of backwards masking. This technique involves the use of speaking or singing backwards, either phonetically, or through the use of tape recordings that are played backwards. Even some of the elaborate album cover art of Led Zeppelin and some of the progressive rock bands have been seen as representative of a new type of religious iconography by some writers. Edward Macan's book *Rocking the Classics: English Progressive Rock and the Counterculture* (1996) explores the religious implications of the music and visual art of Led Zeppelin, Yes, King Crimson, Pink Floyd, and other groups.

The year 1969 was the year of the rock music festival. Although the Monterey International Pop Festival had established the multiday rock festival as a viable undertaking in 1967, and the Miami Pop Music Festival of 1968 had drawn approximately 60,000 fans, the year 1969 witnessed festival after festival. The Newport Jazz Festival included rock acts for the first time. The jazz-rock group Blood, Sweat & Tears, virtuoso rock guitarist Jeff Beck, Savage Rose, soul superstar James Brown, blues-rock guitar virtuoso Johnny Winter, soul and pop chart favorites Sly & the Family Stone, and the blues–heavy metal superstars Led Zeppelin all graced the stage at Newport. The Newport Folk Festival also saw a greater than usual emphasis on blues and electric music. Later in the year, the Atlantic City Pop Festival drew over 100,000 people to hear Johnny Winter; Crosby, Stills, Nash & Young; Joni Mitchell; Santana; Jefferson Airplane; Creedence Clearwater Revival; the Paul Butterfield Blues Band; Janis Joplin; Canned Heat; Joe Cocker; and the Buddy Rich Big Band. The Atlantic City festival included sets by many other performers as well, including Chicago, Procol Harum, Booker T. & the MG's, Frank Zappa and the Mothers of Invention, the Sir Douglas Quintet, Little Richard, Dr. John, the Crazy World of Arthur Brown, Tim Buckley, Mother Earth, the Moody Blues, the Buddy Miles Express, and African musician Hugh Masekela.

The largest and most culturally significant rock festival, however, was the Woodstock Music and Art Fair, which took place August 15–18, 1969 near Bethel, New York. The organizers of the festival, Michael Lang, John Roberts, Artie Kornfeld, and Joel Rosenman, expected approximately 50,000 rock fans to come to the festival. When over 400,000 people showed up and overran the ticket gates, Woodstock was declared a free festival. Medical staff, transportation, sanitation, food concessions, and other services at the festival were inadequate, mostly due to the huge crowd. Rain also became a major problem. The festival personnel, musicians, and audience members, however, pulled together as a near-communal whole and what easily could have been a disaster, turned into perhaps the most important validation of the hippie lifestyle of the entire counterculture era. Many of the groups that performed at Woodstock had appeared at Monterey, Newport, and Atlantic City. The festival was captured in a documentary film and in audio recordings that have been reissued on compact disc. The Who's performance of their rock opera *Tommy*, Jimi Hendrix's set, which included his solo electric guitar arrangement of "The Star-Spangled Banner," Crosby, Stills, Nash & Young's lengthy set, and Country Joe McDonald's profane version of his "Fish" cheer

were all highlights of the festival and the subsequent film and audio recording.

If Woodstock represented the highpoint of the 1960s counterculture in
terms of putting into practice the philosophy of peace, love, and understanding, then the Rolling Stones' disastrous December 9, 1969 concert at California's Altamont Speedway represents one of the low points. The famed
British band had been on a North American tour, but had been passed over
by the organizers of the Woodstock festival. The Woodstock principals were
afraid that the Rolling Stones might incite violence with songs like "Street
Fighting Man" and "Sympathy for the Devil" and would require so much
extra security and command such a high performance fee that a Rolling
Stones appearance at Woodstock would not be worth the cost or the potential
problems. The band decided to stage their version of Woodstock at Altamont.
Since the band and their management team were not familiar with making
independent concert arrangements in California, the advice of California
groups was sought. The Grateful Dead suggested that members of the Hell's
Angels motorcycle gang be hired to work security. Ultimately, Altamont was
the scene of the killing of one concertgoer by the Hell's Angels and of numerous drug overdoses and bad trips.

The 1970s began with a new emphasis on the singer-songwriter. These
musicians, who would include James Taylor, Carly Simon, Paul Simon, Carole King, and Harry Chapin wrote and sang highly personal, introspective
songs. The recordings and the live performances of these singer-songwriters
tended to be free from studio effects and emphasized instruments like the
acoustic guitar and piano. James Taylor and Paul Simon, in particular, continued to enjoy hit after hit throughout the 1970s. Carole King, who had
been a hit songwriter ever since the late 1950s, recorded her album *Tapestry*
in 1971, just as the women's movement was hitting its stride. Although
Tapestry was anything but political in nature, it was in many respects the
perfect album for the time. The rich emotional content of the songs struck
a strong chord with young women like few, if any, previous works in the
rock genre, and *Tapestry* highlighted King's instrumental accomplishments
as a pianist, making her one of the first female pop stars that was taken
seriously as a vocalist, composer, and instrumentalist.

In complete contrast to the folk-like clarity and near-simplicity of the musical settings of some of the singer-songwriters, notably James Taylor, the
early 1970s also saw the development of glam rock. This highly amplified,
flamboyant style featured male bands that used stage makeup and dressed

in an androgynous style so as to raise questions about their sexual orientation. The New York Dolls, an American group that featured biting lyrics about life on the streets, and T. Rex, a British band fronted by Marc Bolan, were two of the most notable examples of glam-rock acts. David Bowie went through a glam-rock phase in the early 1970s, although his longevity as an important rock artist outlived the fairly short-lived glam-rock style.

After the fiasco of the Rolling Stones' Altamont concert, the rock world needed a positive rock festival to put the genre back on track. Alerted to the plight of the people of Bangla Desh by Ravi Shankar, former Beatle George Harrison mounted a massive Concert for Bangla Desh. New York City's Madison Square Garden was the site for this August 1, 1971 event. Harrison was joined on stage by Shankar and his group of Hindustani musicians, former Beatles drummer Ringo Starr, Leon Russell, members of the group Badfinger, Billy Preston, Jesse Ed Davis, and a host of prominent studio musicians. To cap off the evening, Bob Dylan made a surprise appearance. Although the Concert for Bangla Desh failed to raise as much money for the refugees of the war-torn nation as had been hoped due to various legal intrigues, Harrison's event represented the first of the great philanthropic popular music festivals. It set the stage for Farm Aid, Rock against Racism, and other socially conscious concerts and festivals of the 1970s through the present. In doing so, the Concert for Bangla Desh represented a return to the idealism of the pre-Altamont days of the 1960s.

The end of the counterculture era was marked coincidentally by the development of disco music and an entire disco culture. James Brown, Sly Stone, and George Clinton all helped to establish the musical basis for disco with their compositions and arrangements in the 1960s and early 1970s. Disco featured elaborate orchestrations and a similarity of beat (the similarity of beat made it easier for dance club disc jockeys to segue from one song to the next). Members of the gay community, in particular, became an important and highly visible part of the disco culture. Artists such as Grace Jones, Donna Summer, Village People, Sylvester, and others were favorites of the male homosexual community. Although the gay rights movement then was tied in a somewhat peripheral way to disco music, the style was notable for its general lack of connection with most of the other social issues of the mid-1970s. The fact that much disco music represented a sort of escapism contradicted the tendency of much of the music of the counterculture to address social issues head-on.

Although disco provided the most widespread national exposure for homosexual-related music, a subgenre of singer-songwriter, folk-influenced gay and lesbian music also emerged in the mid-1970s. Holly Near, Meg Christian, and Cris Williamson were three of the leading artists in this subgenre of music. They combined a feminist and lesbian stance in their songs and all three were active as performers, composers, and as owners of recording and publishing companies. Near, in particular, was also heavily active and visible in various progressive political movements (anti-nuclear, anti-multinational corporation, and pro–women's rights movements among them) throughout the 1970s and beyond.

Perhaps in response to the glitziness of disco, the mid-1970s also witnessed the re-emergence of straight-ahead rock and roll with lyrics that reflected a working-class mindset in the person of Bruce Springsteen. After working at many clubs in his native New Jersey in the late 1960s and forming his band in 1973, singer-guitarist-songwriter Springsteen burst on the American musical scene with albums like *Greetings from Asbury Park* and the mega-hit, *Born to Run*. The latter album marked Springsteen as a major figure in 1975. The song "Born to Run" became an anthem of disenfranchised, blue-collar male youth who saw rock and roll as their only salvation from the drudgery of a future living from paycheck to paycheck. Although legal difficulties made it impossible for Springsteen to release any new material on albums for a couple of years after the impact of *Born to Run*, his career was revitalized by 1978. He continued to explore similar themes in his work of the 1980s and 1990s, including his well-known "Born in the U.S.A.," a song that deals with the plight of Vietnam veterans.

Although the popular music changed a great deal from 1960 to 1975, all of the styles were primarily youth-based, and to a certain extent musically and/or lyrically reflected the spirit of rebellion against the prevailing society that defined the counterculture and "the movement."

3

Music and the Anti-War Movement

At the start of the counterculture era, the United States had military advisors stationed in South Vietnam, but no actual ground troops; the first U.S. bombings of North Vietnam would commence in late summer 1964, with ground troops being deployed in spring 1965. The anti-war music of the first several years of the era tended to focus on war in the abstract and on the possibility of nuclear annihilation; this very much was at the height of the Cold War. Some of these songs, associated with the anti-war movement from the beginning of the counterculture era through the period's conclusion, were newly revived folk songs, such as the "We shall live in peace someday" stanza of "We Shall Overcome" and the familiar "Down by the Riverside," with its "I ain't going to study war no more" text. The newly composed, somewhat generic anti-war songs followed in the tradition of Ed McCurdy's Korean War-era song "Last Night I Had the Strangest Dream," in which the singer describes a dream in which war has been banned. Among the more general, newly composed anti-war songs of the beginning of the counter-culture era are "Blowin' in the Wind," "I Ain't Marching Anymore," and "Where Have All the Flowers Gone?"

The first commercially successful anti-war protest song of the era was Pete Seeger's 1961 composition "Where Have All the Flowers Gone?" The song provides a valuable link to the nineteenth-century American folk music tradition, in the use of a cycle-of-life narrative that points out the inevitability

of death in the face of war, and a tune apparently derived from a Civil War–
era song. Seeger wrote in a general-enough manner so as to make the song
applicable to war in general or any specific war. Interestingly, writer Neil
Sheehan has referred to it as "perhaps the best-known song of Vietnam"
(Sheehan 1988), impressive considering that the song is so general in nature.
Making its *Billboard* pop singles chart debut in January 1962, the Kingston
Trio's recording of the song rose to #21 on the charts, remaining among the
top 100 for over three months. This recording was largely responsible for
the impact described by Sheehan. At the time of the recording's first chart
appearance, the Kennedy administration had just increased the number of
U.S. military advisors stationed in South Vietnam to 4,000.

After the Gulf of Tonkin Resolution and the subsequent introduction of
U.S. ground troops into Southeast Asia in 1965, pop/rock singer Johnny
Rivers, probably best known for his recordings of the songs "Poor Side of
Town" and "Secret Agent Man," took the Seeger opus to #26 on the *Billboard*
pop singles charts and included the song on his album *Johnny Rivers Rocks
the Folk*. The Rivers recording, although not as easily available today as that
of the Kingston Trio, makes for interesting study. The singer goes a step
beyond the early recording by bringing the cycle-of-life narrative to more
obvious conclusion by repeating the first stanza at the end of the song. Then,
during his vocal improvisation in the studio fade out, Rivers specifically links
soldiers with their inevitable death and asks a final time when the soldiers
will ever learn the lesson. This certainly represents a more direct approach
than in the earliest published version of the song or in the Kingston Trio
recording, but by the time of the Rivers recording, the anti-war movement
was gaining intensity.

Although many might equate the counterculture anti-war movement solely
with those not in the military, "Where Have All the Flowers Gone?" found
its way into the jungles of Southeast Asia. According to a February 1968
report in the *New York Times*, in the midst of a night "when more than 1,000
rounds hit Khesanh," officers in charge ordered soldiers to sing songs to
pass the time. Lance Corporal Richard Morris played the guitar for some of
his favorite songs, including the Seeger composition. According to the report, "a hard emphasis accompanied the part that went: 'Where have all the
soldiers gone? To the graveyard every one. Oh, when will they ever learn?
Oh, when will they ever learn?' " (Folk Music in Vietnam 1968). And what
of other songs appreciated by U.S. troops for what they heard as an implied
anti-war stance? Curiously, the non-war-related records "We Gotta Get out

of This Place" by the Animals and "Time Is on My Side" by the Rolling Stones were two early hits among the G.I.'s, mostly because of the sentiments expressed in their titles!

Pete Seeger was not the only leftist folk revival singer-songwriter to protest war in the early days of the Vietnam Conflict. Others, whose songs were not as widely recorded commercially, had their material published in such sources as the protest song magazine, *Broadside*, and the topical folk song magazine, *Sing Out!* In fact, Seeger, Bob Dylan, Tom Paxton and others of the more commercially available songwriters also had their works published in the two left-leaning magazines. Anti-war material found in the magazines in the first several years of the counterculture era include Dylan's "Blowin' in the Wind," which appeared in *Broadside* #6 (late May 1962) and *Sing Out!* 12/4 (October–November 1962); Ewan MacColl's "The Dove," published in *Sing Out!* 10/4 (December–January 1960–1961), and Pete Seeger's "The Flowers of Peace," which appeared in *Broadside* #3 (April 1962) and *Sing Out!* 12/3 (Summer 1962). It should be noted that, although the anti-war songs of many of the *Broadside* songwriters such as Phil Ochs, Malvina Reynolds, and others, made few gains in the commercial marketplace of radio airplay and record sales, the works were performed by folk revival musicians at coffeehouses and in concerts, and frequently, and sometimes quite spontaneously, by protesters at rallies.

As previously mentioned, Bob Dylan's "Blowin' in the Wind" appeared in lead sheet form in *Broadside* and *Sing Out!* in 1962. Unlike many of the works of the *Broadside/Sing Out!* crowd, this song would make tremendous commercial impact more than once during the course of the Vietnam Conflict. Although the best-known recording of the song was by the folk revival trio Peter, Paul & Mary, let us consider Dylan's own recording of the song, found on his 1963 album *The Freewheelin' Bob Dylan*. Since this is the composer's own performance, we might consider it to be the definitive example of what Dylan had in mind for the song.

Dylan's performance, in which he sings and accompanies himself on guitar, providing harmonic solos to answer the *b* phrases in each stanza, remains firmly in the no-nonsense style of the acoustic American folk tradition. Highly unusual in common-practice concert music and American popular song, however, is the asymmetrical phrase structure of the song in this definitive version (*a* [eight measures], *a¹* [eight measures], *a* [eight measures], *b* [seven measures], *b¹* [eight-measure harmonica answer]). Readers familiar with music of the true country folk and rural blues traditions, such as the music of Jimmie Rodgers or Robert Johnson, will recognize that this type of unexpected structure is not uncommon in older American musical traditions. The melody of the song, as it is based on an old anti-slavery song from the nineteenth century, also maintains the connection to earlier tradition.

Although even at this early point in Bob Dylan's career young people were listening to his music, his every word, with keen seriousness, as especially well documented by writer Wilfred Mellers, one of the first musicologists to give serious attention to music of the rock era (Mellers 1969, 185), in the case of "Blowin' in the Wind" it was not the composer's recording that had the greatest impact or reached the greatest number of people. Folk artists Peter, Paul & Mary took their single release of the Dylan song to #2 on the *Billboard* pop charts, and the album on which the song appeared, *In the Wind*, held the #1 position on the magazine's pop album charts for five weeks. Incidentally, the Peter, Paul & Mary album stayed on the *Billboard* charts for some eighty weeks. Sales success like this brought Dylan's subtle anti-war, anti-discrimination, anti-apathy message to millions. Aside from their beautiful vocal harmonies, Peter, Paul & Mary also increased the commercial potential of the Dylan song by smoothing out the phrase structure and eliminating the (what some listeners might find to be) irritating harmonica breaks.

In mid-1966, when the war was fully underway, singer-multi-instrumentalist (and possibly the greatest child prodigy in the history of American popular music) Stevie Wonder took the Dylan song to #9 on the *Billboard* pop charts. Although Wonder would later record in various styles ranging from gentle ballads to heavy, hard-core funk, to Latin rock, at this point in his career he generally did not stray too far from the style of other Motown-Tamla acts like the Temptations and the Supremes. Wonder's recording of "Blowin' in the Wind" features the Motown swing of the era and is an effective counterpoint to much of the extremely hot rhetoric of many of the anti-war songs of the time. Interestingly, Stevie Wonder's recording of "Blowin' in the Wind" represented a rare political (mild though it is) stance against the war for Motown. As we shall later see, when the record label's songwriters finally got around to dealing with social issues in a significant way in the late 1960s, they were accused of jumping on by-then-long-established trends simply to sell records.

And what of the rhetorical style of "Blowin' in the Wind?" As an example of counterculture protest music, it is gentle in style. The composer asks a series of rhetorical questions concerning the various injustices he sees in the world, with an apparent focus on U.S. society, and concludes that the answers to these problems are, as the title suggests, blowing around in the wind. In other words, the answers are there, but, like the wind, they are difficult, if not impossible, to grab in one's hands. In terms of its gentle rhetoric, the song resembles Pete Seeger's "Where Have all the Flowers Gone?"

Dylan's "Masters of War" makes a significantly stronger, even accusatory, anti-war statement. A near contemporary of "Blowin' in the Wind," the song was published in *Broadside* #20 (February 1963) and *Sing Out!* 13/3 (Summer 1963). Writer Ray Pratt suggests that "while critical minorities on the left might have given voice to similar sentiments [as those expressed in "Masters of War" and the slightly later "With God on Our Side"], Americans had never heard anything like these bitter comments on aspects of their nation's history and wars issued on commercial recordings" (Pratt 1998, 17). While Dylan based the melodic and harmonic structure on the Appalachian folk song "Nottamun Town," as he had learned it during his travels before settling into the New York City folk revival scene, the text is entirely his own. The writer takes on generals who plot battles far away from the battlefield, heads of corporations who knowingly manufacture weapons and other products whose sole purpose is destruction of life, in short, the entire military-industrial complex. He compares the masters of war to Judas Iscariot, Jesus's betrayer, and suggests that they should be stopped by all means necessary. "Masters of War" was issued on the 1963 album *The Freewheelin' Bob Dylan*.

The Freewheelin' Bob Dylan also included "Talkin' World War III Blues," another Dylan anti-war song in which Dylan recounts for his psychiatrist a post-apocalyptical dream he has had. In the dream Dylan tries to converse with various people he encounters as he wanders through the city after a nuclear war. He finds paranoia in abundance and he has difficulty making human connections with any of the other survivors. When the dream finally ends, Dylan and the doctor discuss similar dreams that the doctor has been having. In fact, it seems that many of the doctor's patients seem to be having similar dreams in which the dreamer finds himself or herself alone, isolated. Indeed, at the time of the Cuban missile crisis, paranoia, general disorientation, and alienation were serious problems and received a great deal of media attention.

Bob Dylan was quoted as telling topical songwriter Phil Ochs, "The stuff you're writing is bullshit, because politics is bullshit. Just look at the world you're writing about and you'll see that you're just wasting your time" (Scaduto 1971). Dylan actually stopped writing explicitly political material by 1964; however, his 1964 song "It Ain't Me, Babe," from his album *The Times They Are A-Changin'*, was widely interpreted as an anti-war statement. Like so many Dylan works, the song could be, and was, interpreted on several levels. Dylan could be rejecting a former lover in a relationship that had gone bad, or he could, as *Broadside* writer Paul Wolfe so aptly put it, be telling "his thousands of worshippers to look elsewhere for someone to walk on water" (Wolfe 1964, 11). Many listeners, however, heard Dylan telling the military to draft not him, but someone else. The surface message, that of the rejection of a former lover, is worded in such a way, with references to strength, protection, and so forth, that it easily can allow the deeper, anti-war interpretation to come through. That this interpretation quickly became widespread, at least among those active in the anti-war movement, is evidenced by the fact that the chorus, which includes the song's title in its lyrics, was sung at numerous anti-war rallies.

When the Turtles covered "It Ain't Me, Babe" in 1965 as the title song for their first album, context played a significant role. *It Ain't Me, Babe* features much in the way of folk-rock material, no pro-U.S.-involvement-in-Vietnam songs, and includes the notorious anti-war song "Eve of Destruction," a work previously discussed. In *this* context, Dylan's composition can easily be understood as a thinly veiled anti-draft anthem. Numerous other acts covered the song, including Johnny Cash and June Carter, and the Spokesmen. The Spokesmen's recording of the song suggests that context can be highly influential in determining whether or not an audience reads any hidden meaning into an intentionally vague song like "It Ain't Me, Babe." The group included the Dylan song on their 1965 album *The Dawn of Correction*, a package that included the group's self-penned song "The Dawn of Correction," which supported the U.S. involvement in Vietnam and was a centrist/slightly right-wing response to "Eve of Destruction." In this context, Dylan's song could only be understood as a trendy folk-rock song about the breakup of a relationship.

The left-leaning folk revival musicians protested the war in ways other than writing new songs as well. Joan Baez, in late 1964 even before "official" U.S. ground forces were in place in Southeast Asia, fired off a letter to the Internal Revenue Service, with copies strategically sent to the press, indicating that she would withhold the estimated 60 percent of her income tax that would ordinarily go toward funding the military. That letter, reprinted in *Daybreak* (1969), made headlines throughout the country.

Among the *Broadside* and *Sing Out!* protest songwriters, an entire sub-genre of songs mocked the repressive politics of the rulers of South Vietnam in the days leading up to the outbreak of an "official" ground war. Examples of these include Bonnie Day's "What Can We Do for Madame Nhu" and Bill Frederick's "Two Brothers—A Nhu Version." Incidentally, lest it seem that many of these *Broadside* songs are obscure and unavailable, the reader should note that many of the original 1960s recordings that were transcribed for publication in the magazine recently have been reissued on compact disc on the Smithsonian/Folkways label.

Other protest singers focused on the bitter irony that entire villages were being destroyed in an already-established air war by bombing them with napalm, a jellied form of gasoline that would incinerate everything in the area. Malvina Reynolds set new words to an older Woody Guthrie song to produce the *Broadside* song "Napalm," and songwriter Jimmy Collier took on the completeness of the destruction caused by this type of bombing in his "Fires of Napalm." Some of the songs did not have titles that were quite as obvious, including Richard Kohler's "Beware: Here Come Friends," which dealt specifically with the irony that the United States was destroying not only North Vietnamese villages, but South Vietnamese villages as well.

Some of the left-leaning protest singers created new songs at rallies or on the way to rallies. Most frequently, a pre-existing melody would be fitted with new words to create a song addressing a particular current event. On the way to one such anti-war rally, folk musicians Judy Halperin, Joan Halperin, Susan Perkis, Susan Warshau, George Phillips, and Happy Traum created a topical song about U.S. Secretary of Defense Robert S. McNamara entitled "The New 'MacNamara's' Band." They based their song on the traditional folk melody "MacNamara's Band," but addressed what they saw as an unacceptable pro-war stance by the U.S. administration.

Several of the singers, notably Judy Collins, Phil Ochs, and Joan Baez, appeared frequently at anti-war protests, and apparently to good effect. Writer James Miller describes the first major anti-war rally to take place in Washington, D.C. in spring 1965. He mentions that Judy Collins sang Bob Dylan's "The Times They Are A-Changin' " and quotes the famous Yale historian who was a vocal opponent of the war, Staughton Lynd, as saying "It was unbearably moving to watch the sea of banners and signs move out from the Sylvan Theater toward the Capitol as Joan Baez, Judy Collins and others sang 'We Shall Overcome' " (Miller 2001, 66). This spring 1965 "performance" is notable in that it demonstrates that the anti-war movement had adopted "We Shall Overcome," a song that wholeheartedly had been the near-official song of the Civil Rights movement just two years before. While this may have diluted the effectiveness of the song in one sense—taking it away from its traditional role as a song of racial struggle—it also shows the universality of this prevailing song of protest against the prevailing power structure.

With Bob Dylan's retreat from the protest music scene, Phil Ochs became the most successful of the male protest singer–songwriters in the 1964–1965 era. Although Ochs wrote, frequently performed, published, and recorded numerous anti-war songs, his "Draft Dodger Rag" and "I Ain't Marching Anymore" were the most notable. Historian Ray Pratt describes the two songs as quickly having achieved "anthem status" in the peace movement. Pratt also writes that Och's albums *All the News That's Fit to Sing*, containing "One More Parade," and *I Ain't Marching Anymore*, containing both "Draft Dodger Rag" and the title song, became "essentials of the record libraries of activist students and early opponents of the war" (Pratt 1998, 176).

"Draft Dodger Rag" consists of several stanzas, each constructed of two identical eight-measure phrases, in which the singer details a litany of ailments and perversions he has that, he hopes, will make him unfit for military service. The "Rag" is actually misnamed; it contains no classical ragtime syncopations at all. What it does contain is a boom-chuck style guitar accompaniment (in Ochs's recordings of the song) suggesting the left hand part of a piano rag, and the type of dotted rhythms found in the post-ragtime, early jazz piano work of Jelly Roll Morton. In terms of the anti-war movement and the war resistance movement, the song's appearance coincides with the first of the publicized draft-card burnings related to Vietnam and the start of mass attempts to avoid the draft by seeking conscientious objector status and various types of deferments. The history of this resistance movement is detailed in journalist/draft resister Roger Neville Williams' book *The New Exiles: American War Resisters in Canada* (1971).

Easily Phil Ochs's best-known and best-remembered composition on the subject of the Vietnam Conflict, "I Ain't Marching Anymore" found a home at numerous anti-war rallies from 1965 through the end of the war. Ochs's magnum opus was printed in *Broadside* #54 (January 20, 1965) and *Sing Out!* 16/1 (February–March 1966). While right-wing writers called the song

Sisters and folksingers Mimi Fariña (left) and Joan Baez (right). Photography by Henry Diltz.

One of the leading protest singer–songwriters, Phil Ochs, performed at anti-war rallies through-out the Vietnam Conflict. Photography by Henry Diltz.

"notorious," "un-American propaganda" (Noebel 1966, 225, 226), and "sub-versive" (Allen 1969), a presumably left-wing writer in a letter to *Broadside* stated, "Phil Ochs speaks more than any other American I know of today for a segment of American youth which is discontented and restless and can not find the channels through which to register their discontent and bring about needed changes" (O.S. 1965, 12). Ironically, at about the time of the publication of "I Ain't Marching Anymore," Ochs himself told a *Village Voice* interviewer, "I'm writing to make money. I write about Cuba and Mississippi [and presumably Vietnam] out of an inner need for expression, not to change the world. The roots of my songs are psychological, not political" (Eliot 1979, 93). Sadly, Ochs never achieved the commercial success of some of his col-leagues and, perhaps convinced that the movement that had so consumed his musical energies during the 1960s was for naught, took his own life in 1974.

Although Tom Paxton would later be known as an important composer of children's songs, he contributed several rhetorically potent anti-war songs to the movement's repertoire. Unlike Dylan, who used little humor in most of his anti-war songs, many of Paxton's songs relied heavily on satire and sometimes a firmly-tongue-in-cheek sense of humor. "Lyndon Johnson Told the Nation" picked on the hypocrisy of President Lyndon Johnson telling Americans (and the world) that he sought no wider war, while simultane-ously ratcheting up U.S. military activity in Vietnam. "Buy a Gun for Your Son" found Paxton playfully espousing the benefits of giving children toy guns so that they might better kill later in life. "The Willing Conscript" features a sing-song tune and lyrics that find a young soldier-to-be begging his superior to teach him to kill, as he has no previous work experience in the area. Finally, Paxton's "Talking Vietnam Pot Luck Blues" concerns a hilarious, and apparently true incident in which American soldiers and Viet Cong soldiers pass the hashish pipe back and forth, finding peace through "pot." It should be noted that the sly humor of Paxton's anti-war songs, as well as Phil Ochs's "Draft Dodger Rag," suggests the social satire of the 1950s and 1960s singer-songwriter-humorist Tom Lehrer.

As folk and rock started to merge in 1965, one might assume that a great number of rock recordings addressed issues of war and peace. In actuality, less than 2 percent of the songs of the *Billboard* top 100 singles sales charts during the Vietnam Conflict made any comment at all about the war; this, despite the fact that many of the musicians undoubtedly held anti-war beliefs (Bindas and Houston 1989). Many chose to express their feelings in a much more universal, subtle way than many of the folk revival musicians. For example, when John Lennon was asked at a 1965 press conference why his group, the Beatles, had not recorded any anti-war songs, the musician responded in a widely aired quote, "All our songs are anti-war." Indeed, Lennon's statement reflects the very general nature of what made up the counterculture, or the movement, in the 1960–1975 period. The movement was a collection of causes, but could not, despite the efforts of many in the established power structure of the United States, be defined in terms of hair length, age, or lifestyle; the counterculture was too amorphous. Lennon's statement suggests that, by dealing with love in male/female relationships, as well as a sort of universal, agape-type love, and by dealing with the complexity of relationships between those of different generations, as in Paul McCartney's "She's Leaving Home," the Beatles were supporting peace, love, and understanding, thereby taking a stand against war in the most general of terms.

Over the next couple of years, others would compose and perform equally inflammatory anti-war songs as Bob Dylan's previously discussed "Masters of War," but none stands out quite like "Kill for Peace," written by Tuli Kupferberg and performed by his group, the Fugs. *Sing Out!* published the song in its April–May 1966 issue and the Fugs issued a barely commercial recording of it the same year. The tune for the chorus of the song, the only part actually published in *Sing Out!*, is a simple, four-note tune, consisting of the solfege syllables mi-fa-sol-fa (on the piano, these notes could be played as E-F-G-F). One should note that the same tune is used over and over for each stanza as well. As I wrote in my book *Songs of the Vietnam Conflict,*

> The recording has a raw quality, from the simple, somewhat
> unprepared-sounding instrumental work to the brittle recording
> quality itself. Accompanying this is an *audio vérité* [*musique con-
> crète*] collage of machine guns shooting and bombs exploding. The
> black and white album cover art, too, exudes rawness, looking like
> a major source of inspiration for the cover art used by British punk
> rock bands . . . a decade later. The photographs of the band mem-
> bers show them looking dangerous, with angry expressions. (Per-
> one 2001, 42)

The great Beat poet Allen Ginsberg wrote, "when they [the Fugs] scream 'Kill for Peace' they're announcing publicly the madness of our white haired crazy governments" (Ginsberg 1966). The Fugs' lyrics are satirical, even sarcastic, and refer to the Vietnamese by the offensive, racist term "gooks," (pointing out what they see as the racism of the United States military) and suggest that the rush one feels when killing is similar to the ecstasy of sexual orgasm. Even the name of the band—the Fugs—is a counterculture statement, as the word "fug" is a thinly veiled mutilation of the word "fuck." To publicly utter that particular obscenity in 1965 was against the law in many municipalities, and was seen by members of the counterculture as being just one small way of defying the power structure of the United States. The Fugs attempted to point out the hypocrisy of U.S. actions in Southeast Asia by trying to offend and prod into action with great force. Yes, the Fugs were truly the stuff of counterculture, and with strong ties to the tactics used by the radical politicos (like Abbie Hoffman and Jerry Rubin) of the era.

Throughout the Vietnam Conflict topical protest singers dealt with current events related to the war and the protest against it. Sometimes singer-songwriters would use popular pro-government songs and change the lyrics to give the song a rhetorical slant that clearly opposed what the U.S. government was doing in Southeast Asia. For example, Grace Mora Newman set her text, "The Fort Hood Three's Answer to the Green Berets" to the tune of SSgt. Barry Sadler and Robin Moore's popular hit "The Ballad of the Green Berets." ("The Ballad of the Green Berets," a song that celebrates the bravery, commitment, and skill of this elite group of special-forces troops, was the biggest-selling Vietnam-related single record ever.) Grace Mora Newman was the sister of one of the "Fort Hood Three," a group of soldiers stationed at Fort Hood who made headlines across the United States for their refusal to kill. The three soldiers were jailed for their protest against the killing. Newman's text, which was published in *Broadside* #76 (November 1966) chronicles the bravery and commitment to values of peace exhibited by her brother and his comrades (The text is also included in Dane and Silber 1969). Pete Seeger also wrote a song about the Fort Hood Three. He used the traditional folk melody "Peter Amberly" to set his text "The Ballad of the Fort Hood Three." *Sing Out!* 16/6 (January 1967) included Seeger's lyrics. By the way, other protest songwriters of the era also parodied "The Ballad of the Green Berets," including Leda Randolph whose song "Green Berets" sarcastically portrays the U.S. troops as a superior race—in a way equating them with Hitler's elite troops in Nazi Germany–trained to scorn and kill those with darker skin.

By 1966, some of the references to the war and the military were sufficiently veiled, that the listener who "got it," that is, who understood the subtext of the song, felt himself or herself truly to be part of the counter-culture. Even the (apparently) most innocuous of top-40 pop songs could hide these subtexts. Tommy Boyce and Bobby Hart's composition "The Last Train to Clarksville" was a perfect example. The song, popularized by the Monkees, finds the singer asking his sweetheart to take the last train to Clarksville to meet him. Apparently, the two will be away from each other for some time, but the reason is never explicitly given. Those "in the know" would have realized, so the songwriters hoped, that the military base at Clarksville, Tennessee was one of the primary first stops for troops on their way to South Vietnam. Since Boyce and Hart do not mention war of any kind, it would be difficult to consider "The Last Train to Clarksville" an anti-war song. A song like this served more of a "wink, wink, nudge, nudge" function for those involved in the movement, proving that one could pull the wool over the eyes of the older generation and encode a song seemingly devoid of any reference to contemporary events of a politically controversial nature with a hidden meaning.

Future episodes of *The Monkees* (a series that lasted only two seasons) would feature increasingly blatant anti-war statements. In particular, the last episode of the second season of the program, as well as the group's album *The Birds, the Bees & The Monkees*, featured Bill and John Chadwick's "Zor and Zam." On the Monkees' recording singer Micky Dolenz seemingly imitates the Jefferson Airplane's Grace Slick in the phrasing, timbre, and intonation of his lead vocal. Musically, the song refers to folk rock in its guitar parts and includes a military-style drum part. The lyrics deal with the preparations for war by the mythical lands of Zor and Zam; the war never takes place, answering that rhetorical question of the time, "What if they gave a war and nobody came?" This rhetorical question suggests the slightly absurdist declarations of the end of the war that I will discuss later. The Monkees recorded another anti-war song, "War Games," written by group member David Jones and collaborator Steve Pitts. The song was not issued at the time of its 1968 or 1969 recording, not appearing until years later; however, it is interesting to note that it is one of the few songs from the Vietnam era to deal with the extensive media coverage given to the war.

As the 1960s progressed, folk revival singers like Judy Collins, Phil Ochs, and Joan Baez continued to appear at anti-war rally after anti-war rally; however, some of the earlier focus of these singers seemed to be fading. An article by Israel G. Young in the April–May 1967 issue of *Sing Out!* mentioned that Scottish folk and later psychedelic musician Donovan had given up protest music for the time being and that Phil Ochs now "makes fun of those madcap Free Speech things and Mississippi peace marches he made a reputation on" (Young 1967, 35). An article by Larry McCombs in the same issue of the magazine details a reportedly "lost" Joan Baez album, a recording unreleased by the musician because, as she said, "I'm trying to grow up. That involves eliminating, not adding to, what's in your head." She goes on to explain that instead of protesting and complaining, she now wants to "elevate the spirit"; apparently the songs on the album did not accomplish that goal (McCombs 1967, 49).

The anti-war recordings after 1966, in sharp contrast to work of the Fugs, grew increasingly commercial and polished, for the most part. There were, however, a few highly notable exceptions, music that for one reason or another truly "feels" counterculture and not part of the general American popular culture. Let us now briefly examine several of these songs.

Carrying a 1966 copyright, Arlo Guthrie's "Alice's Restaurant" made its print debut in *Broadside* #80 (April–May 1967) and was expanded in *Broadside* #81 (June 1967), at which time the title was also expanded to "Alice's Restaurant Massacree." That Guthrie would end up writing one of the best-known works of 1960s anti-war, counterculture movement probably came as no surprise. The son of folk/protest legend, singer-songwriter Woody Guthrie, Arlo had been exposed to protest music for literally all of his life, hearing the songs of his father and the major figures in folk and protest music at his home in New York City, traveling as a teen to the Newport Folk Festival with Phil and Michael Ochs, and so on.

The 18½-minute song consists of a catchy chorus that recurs from time to time and a long, rambling monologue spoken over the chord progression of the chorus. The chorus was originally an advertising jingle for Guthrie's friend Alice's eating establishment, while the spoken monologue tells the story of Guthrie's misadventures trying to dispose of the restaurant's trash on Thanksgiving. The incident eventually leads to Guthrie's arrest and his being judged unfit to serve in the military in Vietnam. The anti-war aspect of the song is slow to evolve, but clearly emerges at the end; what one hears throughout the song is a tale of the polarization of young versus old, status quo versus the counterculture.

Arlo Guthrie's album *Alice's Restaurant* made its chart debut in *Cash Box* in November 1967, and graced the charts for twenty-five weeks. It returned to the charts in October 1969 for twenty-three more weeks following the release of a film based on the song "Alice's Restaurant Massacree." Although numerous other albums sold more copies than Guthrie's magnum opus, *Alice's Restaurant* was a staple of the counterculture in the last few years of the 1960s.

Incidentally, "Alice's Restaurant Massacree" was first performed at a song-writing workshop. In the folk revival/protest song movement, established performer-composers assisted younger artists one on one, and a mixture of established and up-and-coming songwriters helped each other at more formal workshops. There was a true sense of community among these musicians, most of whom fought for the same political and social causes in their songs and in their lives. The songwriting workshops were essential components of the various festivals, including the important Newport Folk Festival. Workshops, such as the Newport happening at which Arlo Guthrie first performed his masterpiece, provided composers with instant feedback and suggestions from colleagues. The story behind the Guthrie song is that it was so well received at the workshop that the singer was invited to perform it at an afternoon concert for an audience of 3,500. That afternoon performance proved so successful that Guthrie was invited back for the featured concert that same evening, at which time he performed "Alice's Restaurant Massacree" for over 9,000 people.

Probably recorded around 1967, J. B. Lenoir's "Vietnam Blues" may have had little real impact in the United States. The Black, blues singer-songwriter was better known in Europe, especially among heavy-duty blues aficionados (Pratt 1998, 181). Lenoir had been fairly well-known among some of the leftist counterculture in the 1950s, when his Korean War–era song "Eisenhower Blues" gained notoriety. "Vietnam Blues" articulates observations and beliefs probably on the minds of many African-Americans, but not articulated by earlier music. The basic feeling, which can be supported by or refuted by statistics, depending upon which set of statistics one chooses to believe, was that Blacks were over-represented numerically among the U.S. forces stationed in South Vietnam. While African-American songwriters would grow more openly critical of the war in 1969 and 1970, Lenoir anticipated this trend. Among the anti-war blues songs to follow Lenoir's composition were Johnny Shines's "So Cold in Vietnam," Bob Thiele's "Vietnam" (which was recorded by T-Bone Walker backed by members of what would later be known as the L.A. Express), and Junior Wells's "Viet Cong Blues."

Black folksinger-songwriter Richie Havens, in his "Handsome Johnny" (co-written with the later famous actor Louis Gossett, Jr.), was one of the few counterparts to Lenoir who was actively protesting the war through music. Although the song would become much more widely known due to its inclusion as part of Havens's set at the Woodstock festival in 1969, the musician performed it frequently for a couple of years before that mammoth festival. The lyrics of "Handsome Johnny" resemble the earlier Phil Ochs song "I Ain't Marching Anymore" in that Havens and Gossett take the listener chronologically through a succession of wars in which Handsome Johnny, a sort of universal soldier, finds himself. Following Johnny's appearance in Vietnam, Havens sings about the character fighting in the streets of Birmingham, thereby tying together war and the Civil Rights movement. The final stanza of the number, however, is the real clincher, when the singer asks what it will take for Americans to listen to and understand the message of the song, perhaps nothing short of the dropping of a hydrogen bomb? As I wrote in my *Songs of the Vietnam Conflict*, Havens and Gossett seem ultimately to be asking,

> "With all of the millions of anti-war protest records that have been purchased, and with all of the performances by protest singers at peace rallies and concerts, what will it take for you [the American public] to listen, really pay attention, and take action based on what we sing?" (Perone 2001, 49)

The year 1967 also continued to find protest singer–songwriters publishing their works in *Broadside* and *Sing Out!* Norman A. Ross's "Who Killed Vietnam?" is just one example. The lead sheet for the song appeared in *Broadside* #88 (January 1968). Interestingly, Ross presents a set of notes, E, G, A, B, C, and D as asks the performer to freely improvise on the notes, or "make up [their] own tune." Stanza by stanza the song places the blame for the killing of Vietnamese on each of the following: the eighteen-year-old soldier, President Lyndon Johnson, General William Westmoreland, U.S. Secretary of Defense Robert McNamara, Secretary of State Dean Rusk, and the so-called silent majority, represented in the song by the writer's next-door neighbor. In spreading the blame around to include the bulk of the population of the United States, this is one of the blunter counterculture anti-war songs of the era.

Backed by acoustic guitars and brass ensemble playing arranger-conductor Peter Schickele's funeral-like, minimalist dirge, singer-songwriter Joan Baez included the song "Saigon Bride" on her 1967 album *Joan*. The song, a collaboration between Baez and Nina Dusheck, portrays a soldier saying goodbye to his Saigon bride as he ventures off into battle; Baez takes the role of the soldier in her performance of the song, following an Anglo-American folk music practice of stripping characters of their gender by allowing women to sing material associated with male characters and vice versa. The composers base the melody on the repeated expansion of a short ascending motive contrasted by a static final phrase in each stanza and use the metaphors of time and of a wave in the soldier's explanation for why he must fight in Vietnam. The songwriters also hint at the inherent racism in the war in their use of color metaphors. To me, "Saigon Bride" symbolizes in an anecdotal way the extent to which album tracks, and even songs known primarily through their live performance by singer-songwriters, could greatly impact the lives of Americans during the Vietnam Conflict. One of my colleagues at Mount Union College mentioned this song as among the most meaningful anti-war ballads of the era for him, significant to note due to the relative lack of commercial popularity of the song compared with, say, a "Eve of Destruction" or "Where Have All the Flowers Gone?"

The reader undoubtedly will have noticed that the vast majority of anti-war songs focus on the immorality of war in general, the immorality of the Vietnam Conflict in particular, and the tremendous amount of killing that was going on in Southeast Asia. Those anti-war songs that dealt with particular groups of people naturally focused on soldiers, civilians killed by soldiers, and the loved ones, friends, and relatives of soldiers. "Saigon Bar-Girl," which was printed in *Broadside* #87 (December 1967), chronicles the problems faced by a young woman with hungry children at home, whose only hope for survival is to serve, or perhaps to service, American soldiers. Composers Gail Dorsey and Emilie Gould point out that the United States has not provided anything tangible, like food, that the woman needs, and that the only advantage she can get from U.S. involvement in her land is what she obtains by prostituting herself, if not in the physical sense, then at least in the emotional sense.

An almost absurdist approach to the anti-war movement also became fashionable among musicians beginning in 1967. The trend, probably enunciated as well as anywhere else by the very title of Phil Ochs's June 1967 *Los Angeles Free Press* article "Have You Heard? The War Is Over!" (later reprinted in November 1967 in *Village Voice*), fit in with the rhetorical question of the day, "What if they gave a war and nobody came?" Ochs's article basically rejects the very notion of war and eagerly anticipates a day when the conflict has ended. Phil Ochs composed a song, "The War Is Over," on the same theme. The music and lyrics proclaim the end of the war and the glory of peace. Ochs's own recording of the song features a full orchestral arrangement backing him up. Fragments from such patriotic compositions as John Philip Sousa's *The Stars and Stripes Forever* are woven into the texture, the implication being that peace can be patriotic. Incidentally, Jonna Gault's song "What If They Gave a War and No One Came?," a work first published in *Broadside*, takes up the same theme, but without the elaborate studio effects of the Phil Ochs song.

Spring 1968 saw the release of the Doors' song "The Unknown Soldier" as a single. The recording reached #39 on the *Billboard* pop charts during its eight-week run, but made it to #22 on *Cash Box*'s charts, remaining on the *Cash Box* charts for ten weeks. Relatively few singles expressing an anti-war stance exhibited this degree of difference between their chart standings in these two magazines. Since *Cash Box* dealt more with jukebox play than the more-consumer-sales-oriented *Billboard*, it would appear that listeners were more willing to use their coins to hear the song than to buy the record. The song reappeared in August 1968 on the album *Waiting for the Sun*, the group's biggest-selling collection, which held onto the #1 spot in *Billboard's* pop album charts for four weeks.

"The Unknown Soldier" is highly sectional, exhibiting much textural, tempo, dynamic, and lyrical mood contrast. Like many of the Doors' pieces, particularly those written by singer Jim Morrison, it is highly theatrical in nature. The work begins as a mysterious, impressionistic, slow-paced tribute to the unknown soldier, that nameless, faceless individual who has made the ultimate sacrifice for his country. While each stanza of the song uses the same melody, the setting changes dramatically to alter the mood. The use of electronically manipulated keyboard, electric guitar, and voice in particular gives "The Unknown Soldier" its mysterious, eerie quality. Although the entire song, with its eerie, even grotesque portrayal of the outcome of war, delivers an anti-war message, what perhaps heightens this statement the most is the triumphant celebration at the end, complete with a faster tempo, tolling church bells, and a cheering crowd, as singer Morrison proclaims that war is over.

The power of television as a means of disseminating music can be seen in the success of groups like the Monkees and Paul Revere and the Raiders, ensembles that had a huge presence on television in 1966–1968. Easily the most politically oriented musical variety series of the counterculture era, *The*

The Doors, in an outtake from the photography session for their 1970 *Morrison Hotel* album. Photography by Henry Diltz.

Smothers Brothers Comedy Hour featured performances of a number of antiwar songs including Phil Ochs's "Draft Dodger Rag." Another political highpoint for the program was Pete Seeger's performance of "Waist Deep in the Big Muddy"; this after years of having been blacklisted from television for his leftist political activities. It should be noted that network censors refused to let the singer perform the last stanza of the song, the one that identified the U.S. president as the "big fool" who pushes the soldiers forward despite warnings of the possible dire consequences of his actions. In Tom and Dick Smothers the counterculture found spokespersons who were clean-cut, and, therefore, capable of greater acceptance from older audiences than rock musicians. The duo also flirted with music and comedy sketches that could be taken as endorsing or at least condoning psychedelic drugs. By 1969, the appeal to a pluralistic audience disappeared as the duo become increasingly outspoken and confrontational (Bodroghkozy 2001).

Although he would later become widely known as a solo artist backed by his Silver Bullet Band, Bob Seger fronted the Bob Seger System in the late 1960s. Seger composed the oddly titled " '2+2=?'," another of the large number of rock songs taking a stand against the war in Vietnam recorded in 1968. A theme previously taken up in "Eve of Destruction" and several folk revival protest songs, the basic idea of " '2+2=?' " is confusion over how someone can be old enough to kill but not old enough to vote. Singer-songwriter Seger also does not understand why one of his friends had to leave his girlfriend and go to Vietnam where he was killed. The curious title of the song refers to Seger's desire to have a simple answer to his questions. He wants to question the war, but is scared to ask the question. He wants simple, black and white answers, but seems to conclude that such answers are difficult to come by. The riff-oriented structure of the song, the "freak out" style arrangement on Seger's recording, which finds the rock band's various instruments moving through the aural space from channel to channel, the fuzz-tone electric guitar, and the unison backing vocals from Seger's bandmates all call to mind early Jimi Hendrix Experience material. In fact, the style of the song strongly suggests Hendrix's song "Fire." A listener familiar with Hendrix's work with the Experience might say that " '2+2=?' " sounds very derivative. As a stand-alone expression of the Seger's character's confusion over the reasons behind the war (and ignoring the close resemblance between the song and Hendrix's work), " '2+2=?' " is highly effective.

Although the Boston, Massachusetts, rock/jazz/country/bluegrass group Earth Opera made virtually no impact on American radio in the late 1960s and early 1970s, they did record the nearly eleven-minute opus "American Eagle Tragedy" in 1968. It has been suggested by sociologist R. Serge Denisoff that perhaps because of the length of the song, "American Eagle Tragedy" received virtually no AM radio airplay, although it was heard on some progressive FM radio stations (Denisoff 1972a). Musically, the song mixes somewhat avant-garde jazz reminiscent of Rahsaan Roland Kirk, references to bluegrass, frequent tempo changes, and screeching lead fuzz-tone guitar. You might be familiar with bluegrass, a traditional country music form that features virtuosic playing of acoustic string instruments such as the mandolin, fiddle, and banjo, and you may have experienced the song's guitar style in heavy metal or punk rock. Earth Opera's references to avant-garde jazz probably require a bit more explanation. Rahsaan Roland Kirk, a blind African-American jazz woodwind player who would sometimes play two or even three instruments simultaneously, was well-known among jazz fans of the 1960s for his long, highly technical solos that mixed traditional blues-influenced licks with material that sometimes stretched the bounds of tonality. That Earth Opera could manage to successfully mix these diverse styles in one anti-war song was truly remarkable. The lyrics suggest the impressionistic, metaphor-laden Bob Dylan of "All Along the Watchtower" and recount the ironic discrepancies between the public lives of President and Mrs. Johnson and the reality of young men being sent off to the jungles of Southeast Asia. "American Eagle Tragedy" paints a picture of the near chaos that defined the United States in 1968. Peter Rowan, guitarist, vocalist, and tenor saxophonist of Earth Opera, composed the piece, which in its complex structure and use of metaphor also recalls some of the contemporary works of Jim Morrison of the Doors. In his *All Music Guide* review of the album, Jason Ankeny refers to *The Great American Eagle Tragedy* as "an intriguing experiment which has stood the test of time" (Ankeny 2000).

David Crosby, Chris Hillman, and Roger McGuinn of the Byrds composed "Draft Morning," a song that is included on the group's 1968 album *The Notorious Byrd Brothers*. The song juxtaposes gentle folk-rock stanzas in which the singer indicates that he is going to take his time rising on this particular morning, as it is the day he will have to go and learn to kill, with a more aggressive, slightly distorted electric guitar-based instrumental section that is introduced by a bugle call in a dissonant key area. This more aggressive section also contains *musique concrète* recordings of the sounds of combat. The anti-draft message of the song takes on added significance when the song segues into the Gerry Goffin and Carole King song "Wasn't Born to Follow"; the implication of the juxtaposition of the two songs being that the singer was not born to follow the sheep (draftees) into slaughter. Incidentally, the Goffin and King song was also included in the soundtrack of the hit counterculture film *Easy Rider*. Filmmaker-actor Dennis Hopper, who selected music for the soundtrack as he was editing the film, placed "Wasn't Born to Follow" into a similar context.

Eric Burdon and the Animals' "Sky Pilot" was probably the best known of the 1968 anti-war rock songs to incorporate *musique concrète* sounds of battle. This double-sided single made its chart debut on June 1, 1968, and spent sixteen weeks on *Cash Box*'s pop charts, reaching #16, and fourteen weeks on the *Billboard* pop singles charts, where it hit #14. We know that today compact disc players read only the bottom side of the disc; no information is encoded on the label side. In the pre-CD counterculture era, vinyl 45-rpm singles usually contained one song on each side. A long song, like "Sky Pilot," would have to be split in two, requiring the listener to flip the record over to hear the second half. According to Denisoff (1972a), the record received relatively little AM radio airplay due to its length, making its chart success all the more significant: the record industry of the 1960s considered radio airplay to be essential for ensuring sales.

The overriding theme of "Sky Pilot" is the exposure of the active and tacit support of war by organized religion. Throughout the song Burdon and the Animals use a variety of musical effects to support the lyrics. The title character of the song, a military chaplain, blesses soldiers as they prepare their weapons for battle in the song's first stanza. During the following chorus the electric guitars and voices are treated using a phase shifter, giving them an otherworldly quality. In the second stanza the chaplain recognizes the fears of the soldiers and comes to the realization that those waiting for them back home will feel much anguish should the soldiers die. In the third stanza the chaplain says a prayer and smiles. The soldiers receive their orders to go into battle as the chaplain stays behind meditating. Here the implication is that the chaplain's prayers alone cannot protect the troops, nor can his meditation end the war. The chaplain's lack of action to stop the war, and his blessing of the troops, then, supports war as a means to achieve an end. This issue returns at the end of the song.

The troops go into battle in the fourth stanza while the chaplain feels satisfied that he has helped provide them with courage through his words. The fourth stanza is followed by a repeat of the chorus. The conclusion of the chorus is signaled by an electric guitar solo, which itself leads into the *musique concrète* sounds of battle. In addition to recordings of explosions, machine gunfire, and horrible screams, the electric guitar provides an imitation of an air-raid siren in its distortion-drenched glissandi. After the fighting grows in intensity, bagpipes and their attendant drums overtake the sounds of battle; the sounds of a hard rock band have completely faded out.

The bagpipes effectively split the song into its two parts. The fadeout of the pipes and drums leads to the electric bass guitar introducing the second part of the song: the aftermath of the battle. Part 2 of "Sky Pilot" is distinguished by a much cleaner timbre in the electric guitar parts and string orchestra accompaniment. In the fifth stanza the chaplain places the fate of the country in the hands of the soldiers, telling them that God is on their side and that only time will tell if their sacrifice was worth the cost. In other words, only by winning the war can the soldiers validate the sacrifice of their comrades. In the sixth stanza one young wounded soldier looks at the chaplain after his return and remembers the Old Testament commandment "Thou shall not kill." It is the soldier's questioning look at the Sky Pilot that points out the hypocrisy of this man of God: the soldier realizes that in stark contrast to the Old Testament teaching, the chaplain has actively encouraged the killing in which he, the soldier, has just participated.

After the young soldier's questions bring home the meaning of the entire song, a final statement of the chorus is heard. This time, no effects pedals are used in the guitar parts, the voices are free from electronic manipulation, and woodwinds, brass, and strings accompany Eric Burdon and the Animals for the first time. This orchestration is reminiscent of the work of George Martin in his 1967–1968-era work with the Beatles. In fact, "Sky Pilot" is one of the few songs from the period to effectively juxtapose Jimi Hendrix–influenced electric-guitar-based, American-style acid rock (part 1 of the song) and *Sgt. Pepper Lonely Hearts Club Band*, British-style acid rock, featuring elaborate orchestrations (part 2 of the song).

The stanzas of "Sky Pilot" have a notably simple melodic structure, being essentially $aaaa^1$ with each being a two-measure phrase. Interestingly, the harmony of the a^1 phrase ends with a half-cadence (on the dominant chord, rather than on the main, or tonic, chord of the key), which leads into either the next stanza or a statement of the chorus. The simplicity of the melody allows, or perhaps forces, the listener to pay attention to the progression of the story: one would not listen to "Sky Pilot" for the beauty of its melodic line. Likewise, the open nature of the harmony at the end of each stanza pulls the listener into the next chorus section. Although the text does not specifically mention Vietnam (which would tend to make a pop song more of a period piece), this is one commercially successful single that has not found a place on oldies radio stations, any more than it found a place on top-40 stations at the time of its popularity. It has become a memory, but one still vivid in the minds of those in the anti-war movement and those concerned about loved ones stationed in Southeast Asia. "Sky Pilot" was reissued on the 1991 Rhino Records compact disc compilation *Songs of Protest*, one of the few present-day sources for the song.

While our focus has been on songs that deal extensively or even exclusively with an anti-war message, it should be mentioned that there were several pop songs of the late 1960s that carried a subtle anti-war sentiment. Tommy James and the Shondells' hit single "Sweet Cherry Wine" is one of those songs. The Vietnam Conflict is mentioned in one stanza of the song, in which the protagonist sings about a friend of his who has fought in the war. While the song deals briefly with the issue of who decides who should live and who should die and the destruction and suffering caused by warfare, the whole gestalt of the song basically is that peace, love, and understanding will carry humanity through anything. The record reached #7 on the *Billboard* pop singles charts in 1969.

John Lennon and Yoko Ono picked up on the earlier "The War Is Over" sentiment in 1969 and 1970 staging their rather infamous "bed-ins" for peace, using the theme "War Is Over, If You Want It." Lennon and Ono's activities also may have appeared to be somewhat absurdist, but they certainly drew attention to the peace movement, especially from members of the media, who were eager to find out just what the couple was doing in bed; the media types would generally be disappointed. At this stage, a fair number of songs were being recorded that proclaimed a gentle pro-peace message. Lennon's "Give Peace a Chance" and Cat Stevens's "Peace Train" delivered a message that really no one could argue with (even those who supported the U.S. role in the Vietnam Conflict generally were not pro-war, they simply believed that only through winning this particular war could future peace be secured), demonstrating the extent to which objection to the Vietnam Conflict had become part of general American popular culture, as opposed to a strictly counterculture movement.

Melanie Safka, who used just her first name professionally, wrote and recorded the spring 1970 pro-peace hit "Lay Down (Candles in the Rain)." The song is the thematic centerpiece of the album *Candles in the Rain* and was issued as a 45-rpm single. The single reached #6 on the *Billboard* pop charts and, due to its jukebox popularity, hit #3 during its seventeen-week run in the *Cash Box* charts. "Lay Down (Candles in the Rain)" exhibits an impressionistic quality in its lyrics, which best can be experienced by listening to the song on the *Candles in the Rain* album, where the song is preceded by the spoken prelude/poem "Candles in the Rain." The singer-songwriter uses the metaphor of catching a disease for the need of those in the peace movement to be activists. By using this particular word (disease), Melanie cleverly shows both the infectious nature of activism and the dis-ease those in the movement feel with the ongoing war. The strongest metaphor in the song is that of holding a candle high in order to remain dry in the pouring rain, symbolizing keeping the hope for peace alive through activism. Melanie sings passionately throughout and the arrangement features a strong use of dynamic and stylistic contrast to highlight her lyrics. Although it tends toward the general and makes a greater use of metaphor than some listeners might have liked, this gospel-tinged song, with a religiosity imparted by the featured Edwin Hawkins Singers, remains one of the best songs of hope of the period.

Authors Joan and Robert K. Morrison quote musician Jason Zapator, who had attended the Woodstock Music and Art Fair, as saying,

> The music wasn't just something that you listened to. It was some-
> thing that you felt inside. It would be as though it could come out
> of you, out of everybody who was there. I remember the night
> when Melanie came out and sang that song, "Lay down, lay it all
> down." What is it? . . . "Let your white bird smile . . ." Something
> like that—a very peace-oriented song. It was beautiful. Everybody
> lit up candles, and the whole valley looked like a sea of stars in
> the dark. (Morrison and Morrison 1987, 199)

Although Zapator may have misheard or misremembered the lyrics, his rec-ollection makes for some interesting analysis. While my analysis of the song stressed Melanie's use of metaphor in both the verses and the chorus, ob-viously Zapator was most affected by the chorus. He does not mention the subtleties of the verses in his interview.

John Fogerty's "Who'll Stop the Rain," recorded by his group Creedence Clearwater Revival, a contemporary of the Melanie song, also used rain as a metaphor for war. "Who'll Stop the Rain?" deals in part with the sense of loss many who were part of the anti-war movement felt when Robert Ken-nedy was assassinated during his 1968 presidential campaign. Many people had felt that Kennedy would be the one who would be able to "stop the rain." U.S. military personnel who were serving in Southeast Asia counted the Creedence Clearwater Revival recording among their favorite songs that dealt with contemporary political issues (Pratt 1998, 179).

Melanie Safka would make the singles charts again in August 1970 with another parenthetically titled song, her "Peace Will Come (According to Plan)." The singer-songwriter, backed by acoustic guitar, bongo drums, elec-tronic organ, and bass, expresses the hope that peace will eventually come as part of God's plan. "Peace" as used by Melanie in this song is quite general in nature; she could be singing of the absence of war or of an in-dividual, inner peace.

Counterculture aspects of the anti-war movement's music remained; how-ever, they were not necessarily as well-known as the pop pro-peace songs like those of Melanie, Cat Stevens, John Lennon, and others. In particular, several songs emerged at the end of the 1960s and into the early 1970s in support of the draft resisters who had fled to Canada to avoid service in the U.S. military. Of these, the 1969 Steppenwolf album cut "Draft Resister" is probably the best example. The song, co-written by John Kay, Goldy McJohn, and Larry Byrom, all members of the rock band, featured a hard rock, nearly heavy metal electric guitar-based sound, and Kay's characteristic, rather harsh vocal style, probably more familiar to many listeners from Steppenwolf's best-known song, "Born to Be Wild." Incidentally, Steppenwolf's studio recording of "Draft Resister" also uses marimba, an unusual instrument to be found in a rock song; among the few other groups ever to incorporate the marimba into a rock context are the Doors and the Rolling Stones. "Draft Resister," featured on the studio album *Monster*, and later included on *Steppenwolf "Live,"* deals primarily with the loneliness of the life of those tens of thousands who had fled the United States to avoid the draft; these men are painted as brave souls who have given up their homes, their friends, their families, their loved ones, and their beloved country in order to protest the unjust actions of a government and military that had gone completely out of control. The song is a tribute to those exiles. Given the counterculture nature of much of the band's material and the look of the *Monster* cover art, it can be reasonably assumed that Steppenwolf's audience might have included both those who are toasted in "Draft Resister" as well as those who might have been on the verge of joining their ranks.

Coincidentally, at approximately the time the Steppenwolf song was making the rounds on the #17 *Monster* and #7 *Steppenwolf "Live"* albums (*Billboard* pop album chart data), *Broadside* published a talking blues by someone identified only by the initials K. C., a resister who had avoided the draft by escaping to Canada. His personal story of immigrating, having difficulties finding work as an immigrant, and the pain he felt in having to leave his friends and family, published as "Talking Draft Exile Blues" in *Broadside* #98 (May 1969), gives flesh and blood to the nameless draft resisters of John Kay and company's composition. The plight of "the new exiles," as writer Roger Neville Williams called them, draft resisters and deserters from the U.S. military, is well detailed in Williams's book *The New Exiles: American War Resisters in Canada* (1971). According to Williams, himself a draft resister, the election of Richard Nixon in 1968 and the 1968 Democratic National Convention debacle greatly increased the flow of American men of draft age into Canada and other countries: K. C.'s "Talking Draft Exile Blues" and Steppenwolf's "Draft Resister" were very much pieces of their time.

The anti-war movement featured a somewhat unlikely song, "The Star-Spangled Banner," due to Jimi Hendrix's performance of the national anthem of the United States of America on the last day of the Woodstock Music and Art Fair. The previously quoted Woodstock attendee Jason Zapator recalled that Hendrix's performance "was probably the truest rendition of that song I've ever heard, because Hendrix was using sound effects through the guitar to complement the lyrics." There was an irony, however, to the performance because Hendrix's "playing was reminding everybody that 'the rockets' red glare' and 'the bombs bursting in air' was really the napalming of the villages" (Morrison and Morrison 1987, 200). In Zapator's mind, then, the performance seems to at once be a strong patriotic statement, supporting the ideals of the United States, and an equally strong statement against the activities of the U.S. military in Southeast Asia.

The late 1960s and early 1970s saw the development of a new subgenre of rock: heavy metal. One of the original heavy metal bands, Black Sabbath, was fronted by Ozzy Osbourne, who remains a celebrity today by nature of the "reality" television program about his family. Black Sabbath included the vehemently anti-war song "War Pigs" on their landmark 1970 album *Paranoid*. As I wrote in my book on music of the Vietnam Conflict,

> "War Pigs" equates generals with witches, wizards, and even Satan; Black Sabbath suggests that military commanders control the minds of their soldiers and derive pleasure from the plotting of the taking of life. The song paints politicians who support war as cowards who start wars, but force others to do the dirty work involved. And, on the Judgment Day, Satan will laugh as all of these War Pigs shudder in the shadow of God and become consigned to Satan's nether kingdom. Every aspect of Black Sabbath's performance, including instrumental and vocal timbre, virtuosic lead guitar and drum work, the use of longish, twisting riffs, and the subject matter of the song itself make this a prototypical heavy metal performance—an early but fully mature example of the genre. (Perone 2001, 64)

In the years since Black Sabbath virtually defined heavy metal as a style on *Paranoid*, there have been countless albums in the genre. In his definitive book of heavy metal album ratings, critic Chuck Eddy lists Black Sabbath's *Paranoid* as the twenty-seventh best metal album of all time, suggesting its lasting impact (Eddy 1998, 26).

Although our primary focus has been on popular music as part of the anti-war movement, it should be noted that composers of serious concert music took up the cause as well. According to historian Ben Arnold,

> the Vietnam conflict was a new age war, a war with a culture of protest. Composers no longer wrote compositions to support war as had Aaron Copland, Samuel Barber, Roy Harris, Gail Kubrick, and dozens of others during World War II; they openly protested the war and expressed anti-government sentiments directly and to a degree unprecedented in history. (Arnold 1993, 317)

The author details over sixty works of the Vietnam era in his reference guide *Music and War: A Research and Information Guide*. Arnold notes, however, that "while a large educated public reads novels about the Vietnam conflict, few (if any) of the art compositions dealing with Vietnam are known even in the music/academic world that produced so many of them" (Arnold 1993, 324). Indeed, George Crumb's 1970 work *Black Angels* (13 *Images from the Dark Land: Images I*) for electric string quartet is the one work that has made it into the repertoire, and then only occasionally showing up on programs by quartets specializing in twentieth-century music.

Crumb structures his anti-war composition in three movements, each of which contains several well-defined sections. The first movement, "Departure," begins with music meant to depict electronic insects, representing the ever-present helicopters over the Vietnamese skies. The second section of the movement depicts the sounds of bones and flutes, and is followed by the sound of lost bells. Crumb then writes what he calls "Devil-music," for the entire first movement's purpose is meant to depict a fall from grace, a departure for the underworld of Hades. The movement concludes with a "Danse Macabre."

In the second movement of *Black Angels*, "Absence," Crumb fully explores the idea of the fallen angel, with sections entitled, "Pavana Lachrymae"; "Threnody II: Black Angels!"; "Sarabande de la Muerte Oscura"; and "Lost Bells (Echo)." "God Music" ushers in the final movement, entitled "Return." The promise of forgiveness presented by the solo cello in "God Music" leads to "Ancient Voices" and "Ancient Voices (Echo)." Ultimately, however, Crumb returns to the "Night of the Electronic Insects" music at the end of the piece, bringing the listener back to the reality of the ongoing Vietnam Conflict.

Although earlier anti-war rallies had sometimes turned violent, the events of early May 1970 at Kent State University and Jackson State University captured the nation's attention like no earlier rallies. In these cases, students were shot dead by National Guardsmen. Some writers have suggested that the fiasco at the 1968 Democratic National Convention and the Kent State shootings proved once and for all that new ways had to be created for changing society. It has also been suggested that the violence of these rallies strongly suggested that U.S. society was in great need of being changed. While I will deal with music related to the 1968 Democratic National Convention elsewhere—the events are tied in more fully with the larger radical political movement of the time than with the anti-war movement per se—I will deal with the best-known song related to the Kent State shootings here. Shortly after the shootings, Crosby, Stills, Nash & Young recorded and began performing in concerts Neil Young's composition "Ohio." The premiere of the song, at a June 1970 concert in Cleveland, was especially meaningful for Leone Keegan, who had been an eighteen-year-old freshman at Kent State University. She is quoted as having said,

> It was the first time they'd sung "Ohio" live, and it was chilling. People were on their feet, you know, clapping their hands, moving their bodies, crying. Everybody was sort of shaking. . . . You listen to the music now and it seems so candyish. . . . Then, it seemed to have a purpose. I'll never forget that night. (Morrison and Morrison 1987, 338)

Young's song portrays the Guardsmen as "tin soldiers" and points to President Richard Nixon as the one ultimately responsible for the murder of the four young people. His lyrics suggest, in a veiled manner, that the events should serve to galvanize the movement against the prevailing power structure, while simultaneously acknowledging that the situation in America has evolved to the point that the soldiers are now being used against the citizenry. On the studio recording of "Ohio" that Crosby, Stills, Nash & Young made, Young sings the song passionately, emphasizing his outrage at the true story he tells in his lyrics. CSN&Y's almost garage band–like approach to the electric guitar parts further emphasizes the "them" against "us" nature of the anti-war movement. The single release of "Ohio" reached #14 on the *Billboard* pop charts and, probably much to the chagrin of Ohio Governor James Rhodes and members of the Ohio National Guard, received significant radio airplay, either in spite of or because of the utter outrage Neil Young expresses in the lyrics and in his interpretation of them. In retrospect, the killings probably did little to galvanize the movement; if the events of 1968 disillusioned many in the movement, the events of 1970 probably caused them to seriously re-evaluate the way in which they were trying to change society. Despite that, Young's composition was a rallying cry at the time, serving a broadside-like purpose of commenting on and encouraging action related to current events.

According to historians Kenneth J. Bindas and Craig Houston,

> between 1970 and 1971 a majority [56 percent] of Americans viewed the war as a mistake and sixty-one percent advocated early withdrawal. Motown Records, the so-called "General Motors of rock" (both General Motors and Motown were based in Detroit, and both were factories, one whose products were automobiles and the other whose products were hit records), decided to cash in on the public's new outlook toward war and society. (Bindas and Houston 1989, 16)

Whatever songwriters Norman Whitfield and Barrett Strong's ultimate motivation—profit or the anti-war cause—their song "War," became "the first fully anti-war single record specifically dealing with the Vietnam Conflict to reach #1 on the *Billboard* pop charts" (Perone 2001, 63). The song had been issued by longtime Motown standouts the Temptations on their *Psychedelic Shack* album of April 1970. The most well-known recording, however, was by the relatively little-known Motown solo singer Edwin Starr; it was Starr's recording that made it to #1. Even if Bindas and Houston are correct in their assessment of "War" as a cash-in, the song certainly reflects the increasingly widespread dissatisfaction about the war among Blacks. In particular, many African-American leaders were pointing to statistics that suggested that a disproportionate number of Blacks were serving on the front lines (such as they were in this type of guerilla warfare) and suffering deaths in combat. I consider the Edwin Starr recording, which was produced by Norman Whitfield, to be potent and deserving of its smash hit status. The same could not be said of Whitfield and Strong's "Stop the War Now," which was also recorded by Edwin Starr. "Stop the War Now" reached #5 on the *Billboard* R&B charts, but only #26 on the pop charts. As I suggested in my book on music of the Vietnam Conflict, "the brass and saxophone lines, rhythmic style, and even some of the text sound so suspiciously like a 'War' outtake that one has to wonder if Whitfield and Strong would have sued for plagiarism had other writers composed 'Stop the War Now' " (Perone 2001, 63).

Despite the spring 1970 horrors of Kent State and Jackson State Universities, in which the anti-war movement was clearly at odds with the prevailing U.S. power structure to the point of young people being killed by National Guard troops, the 1970–1971 period exhibited signs that the anti-war movement was shifting from strictly being a counterculture phenomenon to becoming more a part of general American popular culture, at least insofar as the music went. We have already seen that Melanie, Cat Stevens, John Lennon, and other songwriters chose to tone down the rhetoric by issuing highly successful pro-peace songs. We have also seen that a potent anti-war single like Whitfield and Strong's "War" could rocket to the top of the charts. The emerging mass popular culture appeal of the anti-war movement was probably most evident, however, in the proliferation of lyrically tame anti-war songs like Gregory Perry, Angelo Bond, and General Johnson's "Bring the Boys Home." The song was recorded and released in 1971 by African-American singer Freda Payne, in a Philadelphia-Sound pop-soul arrangement. The Payne recording reached #3 on the *Billboard* R&B charts and #12 on the magazine's pop charts, suggesting that it was more popular with Black audiences than with the more general audience measured for the pop charts. Bindas and Houston 1989 describe "Bring the Boys Home" as one of the "slick" songs probably issued to take advantage of the changing view of the Vietnam Conflict throughout America. One of the complaints lodged against material like "Bring the Boys Home" is that the innocent, danceable settings, combined with an anemic rhetoric tended to underplay the seriousness of the movement. Although not many have done so, one could argue that this type of song actually could be more effective in delivering the anti-war message than an abrasive song that might appeal to the few while antagonizing the many.

Despite the growing commercialism of anti-war songs, some recordings with a more traditional counterculture appeal were still being made. Buffy Sainte-Marie included her composition "Moratorium" on her *She Used to Wanna Be a Ballerina* album. The song also was published in lead sheet form in *Broadside* #112 (March–April 1971). In contrast to the commercially successful pop songs of the period, Sainte-Marie's recording of "Moratorium" seems to be designed to avoid commercial appeal. She sings with a harsh, passionate, almost brutal voice, describing scenes of anti-war protesters encountering returned Vietnam veterans. Ultimately, the protesters affirm the humanity of the former soldiers and the singer-observer begs for the men stationed in Vietnam to be brought back because they are needed at home. Compared with the counterculture anti-war songs from early in the Vietnam Conflict that were published in the protest song magazine *Broadside*, "Moratorium" represents a huge shift in the type of anti-war rhetoric common in 1971. Many, if not most of the 1964 and 1965 songs portrayed U.S. military personnel as agents of genocide. Most interesting is the fact that one of Buffy Sainte-Marie's songs from that earlier era, "The Universal Soldier," had gone even further. "The Universal Soldier," which was recorded by Sainte-Marie, Glen Campbell, Donovan, and others, paints all soldiers from all cultures, religions, races, and nations as being the ones who have perpetuated war throughout history by means of the fallacy of "killing for peace." Sainte-Marie's 1971 *Broadside* opus, however, clearly paints the service personnel as victims. In doing so she reflects the fact that during the last few years of the war, many in the movement were embracing the veterans and increasingly were turning to anti-war veterans as spokespersons. One of the most vocal of these spokespersons, now-Senator John Kerry of Massachusetts, was a former naval officer, who had served with honor in Vietnam, but by the early 1970s was intent on exposing the atrocities of Vietnam and the futility of this particular war.

The atrocities of the war in Vietnam and the suggestion that Americans were not being told the whole story of the Vietnam Conflict by the U.S. government had been hinted at for years. The June 13, 1971 release of the first installment of the *Pentagon Papers* by the *New York Times* provided evidence strongly supporting those suspicions. The report represented over 3,000 pages of text and detailed the diplomatic and military failures of the United States in 1967 and 1968 (Graves 1972). People in the movement quickly jumped on the *Pentagon Papers*, along with the public statements of prominent anti-war Vietnam veterans, and found that they were being taken more seriously. In many respects, however, it was too late. Reductions in the number of U.S. troops were already well underway, to the extent that in less than two years all U.S. troops would be out of South Vietnam. The fact that those in the movement saw the release of the *Pentagon Papers* as a serious victory for truth and a serious blow for the prevailing power structure can be heard in Holly Near's song "No More Genocide." Near issued the song on her 1973 album *Hang in There*, but it was inspired by her 1971 travels to Southeast Asia with actors and anti-war activists Jane Fonda and Donald Sutherland, and her Indochina Peace Campaign tours of the United States in 1972 and 1973 with Fonda and progressive activist Tom Hayden. In "No More Genocide," Near asks why the United States is preventing the

Vietnamese from living in peace as one people. She also points out what she sees as the lies of history books. According to Near, official history all but ignores the slaughter of countless Native Americans and the expulsion of Chicanos from California. She then points to the *Pentagon Papers* as one of the few sources of the light of truth. Near's entire *Hang in There* album, in fact, serves as a sampler of the rhetoric of the last years of the anti-war movement. It is also a fine document of the various musical styles used for topical music of the early 1970s and times past: "Hang in There" resembles a nineteenth-century African-American spiritual in form and performance style, while "Oh America" owes a debt to traditional country music. Incidentally, "Oh America" also documents the effect that the truth of the *Pentagon Papers* had on ordinary citizens Near encountered in her 1972–1973 tours. Holly Near variously expresses rage, hope, sadness, empathy, resignation, and resolve—the entire range of emotions associated with the late stages of the anti-war movement. This all helps to make *Hang in There* an especially rich movement-related album, really almost like a classical song cycle. Unfortunately, like so much of the excellent music released on small, artist-owned, independent record labels, this album is out of print today.

Holly Near was not the only musician to write songs that dealt with the revelations of massacres by U.S. troops and the secrecy of the Pentagon. *Broadside* magazine published several such songs in the late 1960s and early 1970s. Tom Parrott was a prominent *Broadside* songwriter and the protest song magazine published his lament about the regrettable slayings of civilians at My Lai and Truong Am by American troops "The Massacres of My Lai (Song My) and Truong Am, March 1968."

As the Vietnam Conflict and the counterculture era neared their ends in the mid-1970s, music with an anti-war message became more and more difficult to find. In fact, it would take several years for songwriters to deal with the war again. When they did, in the late 1970s through the 1990s, the focus generally turned toward the plights of the veterans—those who had perished in action, or, more commonly, those who encountered problems returning to U.S. society. Since the United States has not been involved in a protracted and highly controversial war since Vietnam, it is difficult to compare post-counterculture era anti-war music to the music of 1960–1975. To date, the counterculture era stands apart from earlier periods and from the past quarter-century in the amount of and intensity of the music that took a direct stand against U.S. military policy.

Music and the Oppressed

4

Well before the counterculture era began, musicians had dealt with the plight of the oppressed. Topical songs related to the labor movement and labor strife in nineteenth-century America made the rounds. The plight of early twentieth-century African Americans was described in a number of songs, with "Black and Blue," as performed and recorded by Louis Armstrong, being one of the better-known examples. In the 1940s and 1950s other songs, like the famous Billie Holiday recording of Lewis Allan's (a pseudonym for Abel Meeropol) "Strange Fruit," would document the violence of racial discrimination in the southern United States. Other songs related to the plight of workers were widely performed and recorded by Pete Seeger, the Weavers, and other folk singers in the 1940s and 1950s. Music was an essential part of the civil rights marches that pre-dated the counterculture era and continued throughout it.

In all of the pre-counterculture era examples cited above and in the case of the counterculture-era music that documented and commented upon the plight of the oppressed, the songs generally elicited great controversy. While evidence exists that such things as gender, race, and sexual orientation played a role in hiring practices, in length of prison sentences, and in many other areas, not all Americans agreed that this oppression was real, or that it was wrong. Interestingly, while most members of the movement held certain similar core beliefs about the war in Vietnam, they seemed not to agree on the plight of the oppressed. We shall see that some songwriters, for example, took left-wing politicos to task for their treatment of women, who in many cases were marginalized from the movement. The issue of race divided many individuals who considered themselves to be part of the movement as they considered, say, guitarist-composer-singer Jimi Hendrix's role in the movement.

THE CIVIL RIGHTS AND BLACK POWER MOVEMENTS

Insofar as some historians date the start of the counterculture era as the February 1, 1960 lunch counter protest in Greensboro, North Carolina, and since music frequently is part of every social movement, one might reasonably assume that music had been part of the Civil Rights and Black Power movements since the beginning of the 1960s. Indeed, music was a part of the struggle of African Americans for equal rights and equal treatment, with the folk standard "We Shall Overcome" becoming the unofficial song of the early days of the movement. What would take a surprisingly long amount of time to develop, however, would be songs of the movement to come from commercial songwriters.

Originally known in black churches as "I'll Overcome Someday," the song eventually known as "We Shall Overcome" was used by the predominantly black union members in a 1945 strike. White folk musician Pete Seeger later changed the line "We will overcome" to "We shall overcome," and added extra stanzas of text. By 1963, the song, in its updated form, had become an unofficial song of the Student Nonviolent Coordinating Committee's civil rights activities (Martin 2001, 167–68). Writer Bradford Martin also points to the song "We Shall Not Be Moved" as having been an important song early in the movement. "We Shall Not Be Moved" was used primarily to allay the fears of participants in civil rights demonstrations.

One of the more notable events organized by the Student Nonviolent Coordinating Committee was a June 1963 benefit concert at New York's Carnegie Hall. The SNCC Freedom Singers and Mahalia Jackson performed. According to Bradford Martin, whose dissertation work included study of the Freedom Singers, the singing group, who also had performed with Pete Seeger, sought

> to advance the movement's integrationist and egalitarian goals of
> helping African Americans attain the privileges of full citizenship

and inclusion in mainstream American society. While freedom
singers created a rich and unique array of songs, their artistic purpose remained secondary to their reality as activists in a mass
democratic movement. (Martin 2001, 160)

Singing as part of the Civil Rights movement helped to maintain a black
cultural identity. In addition, the use of numerous hymns from the mainstream black Christian tradition bridged the gap between the activists involved directly in the movement and the masses of Black Americans.

A number of jazz artists exhibited an anti-discrimination and even an
Afrocentric view in their compositions prior to the counterculture era.
Bassist-composer Charles Mingus was probably the most overtly political jazz
musician of the 1950s and 1960s. Charles B. Hersch writes that

One does not have to probe beneath the surface to see Charles
Mingus' music as political commentary. The most obvious starting
place is his song [sic—the pieces are, for the most part instrumental compositions and therefore not technically songs] titles: "Work
Song" (1955), "Haitian Fight Song" (1957) (which he said could be
titled "Afro-American Fight Song"), "Fables of Faubus" (referring
to the segregationist governor of Arkansas) (1959), "Prayer for Pas-
sive Resistance" (1960), and "Meditations on Integration" (1964).
(Hersch 1998, 109)

Hersch suggests that the dissonance and emotion in Mingus's music reflect
the cultural dissonance of racism that Mingus saw all around him (Hersch
1998, 110). Interestingly, as the counterculture era began, the texture of some
of Mingus's compositions reached back to the polyphonic jazz of early-
twentieth-century New Orleans. This can be seen as a deliberate return to
what had been a vital roots-based African-American musical style, and not
a nostalgic, rose-colored-glasses look at the past.

Around the same time as Mingus was exploring polyphony, the free jazz
movement, spearheaded by alto saxophonist–composer Ornette Coleman,
gained notoriety. Hersch writes that "Although Ornette Coleman, unlike
Mingus, did not express political sentiments through song [sic] titles and
lyrics, his music represents a radical musical freedom that in the context of
its time [the early 1960s] embodied the positive and negative freedom civil
rights activists were fighting for" (Hersch 1998, 116). Certainly more than
the compositions of Charles Mingus, whose inspiration could more obvi-

ously be traced from earlier jazz and blues styles, the more open forms and less-tonality-oriented music of Coleman and trumpeter Don Cherry *was* a counterculture music, in the respect that few understood, appreciated, or liked it. According to noted author, musicologist, and sociologist LeRoi Jones, writing at the time of the heat of the Black consciousness movement, Ornette Coleman and the freedom of his music represented the rebirth of Black cultural consciousness in the early 1960s (Jones 1968; although Jones later changed his name to Amiri Baraka, the works I cite were written under his given name). Interestingly, free jazz, frequently pointed to as a symbol of the growing Black consciousness of the 1960s (by numerous writers in addition to Jones and Hersch), also played a central, yet relatively unacknowledged, role in the early days of psychedelic drug use. Ornette Coleman and multi-instrumentalist Rahsaan Roland Kirk were both favorites of Ken Kesey and his Merry Pranksters. Free jazz also greatly influenced the MC5, a rock band associated with the radical White Panther Party in the late 1960s. In the 1970s and beyond, musicians associated to some degree with the group improvisation of the free jazz style, such as the Art Ensemble of Chicago (a group associated with Chicago's highly influential, Afrocentric Association for the Advancement of Creative Musicians), would create an overall Afrocentric gestalt, from their musical style, to the clothing that they wore, and the way in which they would live their lives.

Much better known than the music of Ornette Coleman was that of saxophonist-composer John Coltrane. Coltrane's 1963 composition "Alabama," followed the September bombing of a Birmingham, Alabama, church in which four Black children were killed. According to LeRoi Jones's liner notes for Coltrane's live album on which the composition appeared, producer "Bob Thiele asked Trane if the title 'had any significance to today's problems.' I suppose he meant literally. Coltrane answered, 'It represents, musically, something that I saw down there translated into music from inside me' " (Jones 1963). On his November 1963 *Coltrane Live at Birdland* recording, John Coltrane's sad, adagio tenor saxophone lines are punctuated by drummer Elvin Jones's ominous tom-tom patterns. In Coltrane's performance the brief piece became a sort of elegy for the death of the four children and for the death of dreams. Coltrane composed, performed, and recorded several Afrocentric pieces in the early 1960s, such as "Afro-Blue" and "Africa." Unlike Charles Mingus, however, Coltrane was not overtly political in his approach to composition. The homage to the ancestral homeland of his people does, nonetheless, reflect the Black pride that was central to the movement at the time.

Sun Ra (1914–1993), born Herman Sonny Blount, had been a professional musician since 1934. Although he had performed with and arranged for such notable swing-style jazz musicians as Fletcher Henderson (who himself brought an authentic African-American sound to Benny Goodman's famous band), Sun Ra made his most notable contributions with his own group, called the Arkestra. Ra was one of the first jazz musicians to experiment with electronic keyboards and was performing extended, avant-garde solos long before the free jazz movement of the early 1960s. Although part of Sun Ra's act and professional persona veered toward the absurd—for one thing he claimed that he was from another planet—he did sound a sort of back-to-Africa message through his African-styled stage dress and his use of pseudo-African vocal chants. Ra moved his base of operations from Chicago to Philadelphia before finally settling in New York City in 1961. It was there that he began capturing more attention. Black intellectuals who were part of the movement included Sun Ra as one of the prominent distinctly Afrocentric jazz musicians of the era, in spite of the quirkiness of his music and persona.

As mentioned earlier, the first student revolt on an American college campus during the counterculture era (1964) was the Berkeley Free Speech movement. The movement was precipitated by the suspension of eight University of California at Berkeley students for distributing literature about and soliciting funds for civil rights organizations on university property. As students protested for the right to speak freely about racial issues, folk revival/protest singer Joan Baez made an appearance. During the rally Baez sang Bob Dylan's "The Times They Are A-Changin'," a song that one protester described as "our generation's anthem." The student said that Baez then "walked into the building [the administration building, which the protesters had seized] leading us in 'We Shall Overcome,' left—though not before companionably sharing peanut butter sandwiches with the students" (Goines 2001, 36).

Other folk-revival musicians wrote original songs that specifically addressed some of the events of 1963 and 1964, from the June 1963 murder of civil rights activist Medgar Evers in Jackson, Mississippi, to the previously mentioned Alabama church bombing, to the July 1964 Harlem riots. Topical songwriter-singer Phil Ochs addressed all of these significant events. In "Too

Many Martyrs" Ochs deals with the murder of Evers and expresses the hope that such martyrdom for the cause of civil rights never happen again. He paints Evers as being part of a continuum of violence against Blacks in the American South. The minor-key song follows a more-or-less-classic song structure and melodic-harmonic style, allowing the story of Evers to unfold like a classic folk ballad. Ochs takes a less-straightforward approach in his Harlem riots commentary "In the Heat of the Summer." The song features an unusual rhyme scheme and provides snapshots of the riots and the reasons the rioters gave for their violence. Ochs called "Here's to the State of Mississippi" "one of my most criticized songs," and one that "happens to be my favorite" (Ochs 1965). Part of the criticism of the song, and part of the reason Ochs called it his favorite, lies in the harsh rhetorical style. In contrast to the more conservative wing of the Civil Rights movement, which emphasized the importance of appealing to moderates, Ochs pulls no punches. He takes on Mississippi courts, politicians, police, laws churches, and everyday citizens, pointing out their responsibility for the systematic and systemic mistreatment and killing of Blacks in the state. The song's chorus concludes with Ochs telling the state to become part of another country. This was not the sort of song that would win over moderates. Moderates, however, did not represent Ochs's audience. He was an event singer, never really achieving any commercial success as a recording artist (in contrast to Baez and Dylan). Ochs's audience consisted of individuals who already were part of the movement, and a song like "Here's to the State of Mississippi" served to help rally protesters by turning the intensity of the rhetoric up a notch.

White minimalist composer Steve Reich suggested the melodic quality of African-American speech patterns in his 1965 tape loop piece *It's Gonna Rain*. The phrase "It's gonna rain" was part of a street sermon by a black Pentecostal preacher of San Francisco known as Brother Walter. As the composer writes,

> In the first part of the piece the two [tape] loops are lined up in unison, gradually move completely out of phase with each other, and then slowly move back to unison. In the second part two much longer loops gradually begin to go out of phase with each other. (Reich 1987)

Reich continues to describe how the sound builds to four loops and then eight loops going out of phase to create "a kind of controlled chaos, which may be appropriate to the subject matter—the end of the world" (Reich 1987). Reich's next tape loop composition, *Come Out* (1966), uses the same types of techniques described above on a portion of a sentence spoken by one of six boys arrested for murder in the 1964 Harlem riots, Daniel Hamm. As Reich writes in describing the source of his material,

> The police were about to take the boys out to be "cleaned up" [treated for the beatings they had received at the hands of the police] and were only taking those that were visibly bleeding. Since Hamm had no actual open bleeding he proceeded to squeeze open a bruise on his leg so that he would be taken to the hospital. "I had to like open the bruise up and let some of the bruise blood come out to show them." (Reich 1987)

Reich's setting, abstract though it is, captures at least some of the feel of the scene, and like *It's Gonna Rain*, celebrates the melodic quality of Black speech. In both pieces Reich takes the sounds of streets and puts them into an abstract composition, the type of pieces for whom the traditional audience has been Whites. In the case of *Come Out,* Reich picked a highly charged incident that came out of the counterculture black struggles.

The marginalization of Blacks and the inherent racism of American society had been the subject of occasional recorded blues songs from the 1920s. The Langston Hughes–Nina Simone composition of 1967, "Backlash Blues," is a particularly interesting song in the blues genre, considering the timing of its message. The song, recorded by Simone, takes on the dominant, White power establishment for the high taxes, poor housing, and poor schools that Blacks have to endure. Simone also refers to the disproportionate number of Blacks that are serving in Vietnam. The singer suggests that the White establishment, referred to as "Mr. Backlash," is going to suffer a serious backlash from the mistreatment afforded Blacks. The implication of the lyrics is that Blacks will take drastic and possibly violent action because under their present oppression, they have nothing to lose. The song makes use of the double entendre of "backlash," implying at various points the lashings across the back that Blacks had to endure during the times of slavery, and the present-day meaning of the term. The timing of the message is important. It was during the three years leading up to 1967 that violence became more visible and more widespread in America's largely minority urban areas. The previously mentioned Harlem riots took place in 1964 and the Detroit riots occurred in summer 1967. The song's message turned out to be quite timely.

J. B. Lenoir was another blues singer-songwriter whose repertoire included topical material. In fact, Lenoir gained notoriety with his "I Got My Questionnaire," a rare Korean War–era anti-war song. His later "Eisenhower Blues" was considered politically potent enough to warrant investigation by Senator Joseph McCarthy's House Un-American Activities Committee later in the 1950s. The liner notes to the Crusade/Polydor album *J. B. Lenoir*, which pulls together several of the musician's rare singles, quote an unattributed article that claims that Lenoir was "the first blues artist who has included and incorporated the social and political situation of the contemporary negro in his work" (Liner notes to *J. B. Lenoir* 1970). Lenoir's "Vietnam Blues," probably dating from 1966 or 1967, carries a potent anti-war message; I have discussed the song briefly in the chapter on the Vietnam Conflict. In fact, it was one of the first recordings by an African-American blues musician to deal with the Vietnam Conflict. More importantly for our present discussion, however, is the civil rights message of the song.

In his definitive recording of "Vietnam Blues," J. B. Lenoir sings, accompanied by himself on guitar and an unnamed drummer. Lenoir weaves the twin issues of the war in Vietnam and discrimination together in an interesting way, anticipating the trend of a few years later, when many more Black musicians would be doing the same. The piece begins with Lenoir contrasting the political uproar the war has caused with the relative muted reaction of White America to the murder of Blacks in the Mississippi church bombing and the numerous lynchings of Blacks throughout the South. He prays that God will help his brothers fighting over in Vietnam because they may be killing *their* own brothers. In phrasing his prayer this way, Lenoir seems to be suggesting a sort of universal brotherhood and sisterhood of humankind. Lenoir closes the piece by returning to the issue of the active and tacit acceptance of racism in the United States. He suggests that those who fight for peace must fight just as hard for peace in their own house. He also calls upon President Johnson to show more concern with the plight of the disenfranchised at home.

Because of the sparse accompaniment and slow tempo of "Vietnam Blues," Lenoir's text is easily understood. The piece's style also lends itself to a rather free and expressive vocal treatment. Lenoir changes his vocal tone color and dynamics to heighten the mood. As notorious as J. B. Lenoir might have been at home, particularly after his investigation by Senator Joseph

McCarthy, "Vietnam Blues" undoubtedly had little real impact on any segment of the U.S. population. Lenoir's greatest popularity was in Europe, where he was well respected by the blues cognoscenti, and where he was seen as a defiant spokesperson for politically disenfranchised American Blacks (Pratt 1998, 181). In addition, Lenoir's style was too "old school" to be commercially successful in 1967. The sparse guitar-drums accompaniment reflected back more to the roots of blues music than to the electric blues that was more likely to make the record charts during the counterculture era. Despite the lack of widespread commercial appeal, however, "Vietnam Blues" stands as a great work of art related to the complexity of issues related to "the movement."

Interracial dating and sexual relations remained one of the primary sexual taboos in the counterculture era. Although the issue eventually would find its way into numerous American homes in topical television situation comedies like *All in the Family* (1971–1983), in 1967 the subject rarely found its way into American popular culture. Janis Ian's song "Society's Child (Baby I've Been Thinking)," was a rare exception. She had, in fact, written the song as early as 1965 when she was fourteen years old. The song could easily be taken as a typical "mom-and-dad-won't-let-me-date-so-and-so-type song"— echoes of Romeo and Juliet—had it not been for the fact that Ian's companion was Black. Once it had been established that race was the reason for the young woman's parents' rejection of her companion, race becomes the overriding issue of the song. It becomes not so much a Romeo-and-Juliet-with-a-twist song but a song that deals with the hurt and damage that racial discrimination can bring. Ian's single release of the song made it to #14 on the *Billboard* pop charts despite the controversial subject matter of the lyrics. The recording's production resembles the 1966 and 1967 work of Brian Wilson of the Beach Boys, with the incorporation of unusual musical instruments (harpsichord in the case of the Ian song), abrupt tempo shifts, and unusual tonal shifts. Ian would later be best known for her song "At Seventeen," which dealt with being an outcast for not fitting into mainstream society's teen beauty queen concept of what a seventeen-year-old girl should represent. "Society's Child (Baby I've Been Thinking)" was quite a prodigious accomplishment for a young singer-songwriter. Incidentally, the long-standing taboo of relationships between Black men and White women was taken up very effectively by Black radical activist Eldridge Cleaver in his book *Soul on Ice*. Cleaver describes an incident in 1954 in which he was not permitted to have a pinup of a White woman hung on the wall during his first of many stints in prison. He discusses the taboo in detail in the book. A reading of the passage in *Soul on Ice* makes the groundbreaking nature of Janis Ian's composition clear.

Otis Redding's composition "Respect" may seem like an unlikely counterculture song. Although the song's composer recorded it, Aretha Franklin recorded the definitive version of the song. Franklin's single release spent two weeks at #1 on the *Billboard* pop charts following its April 1967 debut. A prototype of Franklin's soul-gospel fusion style, the recording has remained a staple of television and film soundtracks, as well as oldies radio stations. As sung by Franklin, Otis Redding's lyrics can be understood on three principle levels: (1) one woman pleading for respect from one man in her life; (2) Black women demanding respect from Black men; and (3) American Blacks demanding respect from American Whites. On the surface, "Respect" sounds like a personal statement, from one individual to another. At the time of the song's presence on the singles charts, however, the very visible nature of the movement made it possible to understand the lyrics on the larger levels. Not only was it *possible* to understand the song as a plea for equal rights and treatment for women or for Blacks, anecdotal evidence suggests that some listeners *did* hear the song on one or more of the metaphorical planes. In another place, or at another time, this might not have happened, but mid-1967, despite its designation as the Summer of Love, was a time in which the issue of "respect" very much was on America's collective mind and an issue that was hotly debated.

James Brown had been one of the most prominent figures in American music for a number of years before his autumn 1968 single "Say It Loud (I'm Black and I'm Proud), Part 1." Brown was known for his energetic performances and for basically inventing soul music. His lyrics before "Say It Loud" tended not to be at all political in nature, particularly in his singles. Brown and Alfred Ellis collaborated in writing "Say It Loud," a song that complains about racial discrimination and mistreatment. Probably more importantly, the lyrics express a very real sense of racial pride. Brown expresses this pride musically in the no-nonsense heavy-duty funk style. Also significant is the background plea for more Black-owned businesses and for Blacks to become active in management roles. Although the recording fared even better on *Billboard* magazine's rhythm and blues charts, it managed to make it all the way to #10 on the pop charts, which tended to measure a record's success among a broader (and Whiter) audience. This chart success is remarkable due to the thoroughly African-American nature of both the message and Brown's funk style.

The thoroughly Black nature of James Brown's music and his ties to the Black religious music performance tradition are highlighted by noted writer LeRoi Jones. Jones wrote that

> Rhythm and Blues is part of "the national genius," of the Black man, of the Black nation. It is the direct, no monkey business expression of urban and rural (in its various stylistic variations) Black America. The hard driving shouting of James Brown identifies a place and image in America. A people and an energy, harnessed and not harnessed by America. JB is straight out, open, and speaking from the most deeply religious people on this continent. (Jones 1968, 185)

According to writer Nelson George, Brown's song about Black pride and in support of the Black Power movement (those songs date from around the time of LeRoi Jones's comments) hurt the musician's standing with Whites. George echoes Jones in his description of James Brown as one of the more notable Black musicians of the 1960s who did not assimilate into the prevailing White culture (George 1988).

The great guitarist-singer-composer Jimi Hendrix played a particularly interesting role in terms of race during his 1967–1970 popularity. Although Hendrix had solid roots in soul and rhythm and blues music as a backing musician, his initial surge of popularity as a featured star was with the interracial Jimi Hendrix Experience, which first gained notoriety in England. His drummer and bassist were both White British natives. Hendrix's early compositions were psychedelic in nature and very rock-oriented in style, putting him at odds with the tastes of Black audiences. In addition, particularly with the Experience, Hendrix's performances have been described as "minstrel" in nature. In his book *The Black Atlantic*, Paul Gilroy wrote,

> The European triumph which paved the way for Hendrix's American successes presents another interesting but rather different case [compared with Gilroy's earlier example of the Fisk Jubilee Singers] of the political aesthetics implicated in representations of racial authenticity. A seasoned, if ill-disciplined, rhythm and blues sideman, Hendrix was reinvented as the essential image of what

English audiences felt a Black American performer should be:
wild, sexual, hedonistic, and dangerous. (Gilroy 1993, 93)

Due to his decision to try "to cultivate an almost exclusively white, pop audience" through the means of his near stereotypical, minstrel show-inspired persona, and turning his back on more traditionally "Black" musical styles, Hendrix was called a "white nigger" by some Black Power movement leaders (Gilroy 1993, 93). It seems that these leaders disapproved of Hendrix's rock genre as a performance medium inappropriate for a Black man, with their implicit question being, "Why are *you* playing *their* music?" Indeed, the fact that perhaps the greatest virtuoso rock guitarist was Black, yet appealed primarily to Whites is a curiosity. Although he would not be subjected to nearly the intensity of the comments lobbed by some young radical Black political leaders at Hendrix, Prince would hear variations on the same sort of arguments in the 1980s and 1990s. Ironically, but seemingly never mentioned by radical politicos of the 1960s, was the fact that perhaps the most frequently recorded rhythm and blues lead guitarist was the White musician Steve Cropper, of Booker T. and the MGs, a band that enjoyed several substantial instrumental hits in the 1960s and served as a backup band on countless recording sessions for Black singers in Memphis.

Other commentators have dealt with the early solo Hendrix persona, of which his musical genre of choice was only part. In a sound bite included in a report on the one hundred most important American musical works of the twentieth century on National Public Radio's *All Things Considered* program, Vernon Reid is quoted as saying "He [Hendrix] was unabashedly sexual. He didn't apologize to black people for being wild, and he . . . certainly didn't ask permission from white people. He laid down a gauntlet, you know, he said 'are you prepared to be free?' " (Onkey 2002, 189). In Reid's assessment we can see the Hendrix persona as one dedicated to complete freedom of expression.

Other writers have placed Jimi Hendrix more squarely in the continuum of Black performers of the twentieth century. Biographer David Henderson wrote,

> While the young white rock 'n' rollers had often managed to copy
> and cajole the correct changes of black music, they nevertheless
> failed to present in their stage presentation "The Show." "The
> Show" was the staple of every performance, especially on the
> southern tours or at places like the Apollo. "The Show" was when
> the artists or band would do some wild, wild, way-out stuff. "The

Singer, songwriter, and guitar hero Jimi Hendrix broke musical and cultural barriers in the late 1960s. Courtesy of Photofest.

> Show" was the height of the performance, and like the saxophone
> "honkers," this display often put both the audience and the per-
> former in a transcendental state where improvisation came to the
> fore and the unexpected took everybody out. Very much akin to
> the building emotional patterns of black holiness churches, this
> crescendo, once reached, could be stretched and augmented and
> built upon all night if necessary. But for the true followers of black
> music, it was this transcendental moment everyone waited for.
> (Henderson, 77)

The Hendrix persona very well can be seen as an extension of what Henderson calls "The Show."

Whether an extension of "The Show" or a 1960s version of the stereotypes of black-faced minstrels, Jimi Hendrix, in his life and in his music, refused to let anyone tell him who he was, or what it meant to be Black. In that respect, by rejecting the violence of the Black Panthers, in forging his own way musically, and in assembling a nontraditional audience, perhaps Hendrix was ultimately more progressive than those who would require that one conform to one particular version of what it meant to be Black.

Interestingly, in the last year of his life Hendrix assembled an all Black band (Band of Gypsys) and performed and recorded material that sometimes was overtly political in nature. He made positive statements from the stage in support of the Black Power movement, as well as stinging anti-war remarks. His remarks supporting radical Black politics were especially gracious, considering the way in which he had been rejected by the movement. Greg Tate, a frequent contributor to *The Village Voice*, deals with the interesting cultural contradictions of Jimi Hendrix, including the musician's role in the Black Power movement in his recent book, *Midnight Lightning: Jimi Hendrix and the Black Experience* (Tate 2003).

Sylvester Stewart, better known as Sly Stone, was a leading proponent of "psychedelic soul" with his interracial, inter-gendered group Sly & the Family Stone. The ensemble garnered three #1 hit pop singles between 1968 and 1971, and recorded two politically charged albums, *Stand!* (1969) and *There's a Riot Goin' On* (1971). *Stand!* has been described as "the pinnacle of Sly & the Family Stone's early work, a record that represents a culmination of the group's musical vision and accomplishment" (Erlewine 2002a). *All Music Guide* critic Stephen Thomas Erlewine describes the album as "utterly stunning" in its combination of social consciousness, instrumental performance, and the craftsmanship of the compositions (Erlewine 2002a). Many listeners are most familiar with the mega-hit "Everyday People," which sat atop the *Billboard* pop charts for four weeks, and "I Want to Take You Higher," which was the centerpiece of the ensemble's performance at Woodstock. More important than those two songs from the standpoint of the movement, however, are "Stand!" and "Don't Call Me Nigger, Whitey." The two Stewart compositions demand respect for Blacks and emphasize the need for equal treatment for all people, a theme shared by the well-known song "Everyday People." "Stand!" advocates Black political and social activism. It is interesting to note that the website *All Music Guide* describes the package as "Party/ Celebratory, Summery, Exuberant, Happy, Joyous, Rousing, Boisterous, Gleeful, Passionate, Freewheeling" (All Music Guide: Stand! 2002). This suggests that perhaps some of the overtly political aspects of the recording are lost on twenty-first-century audiences.

In contrast to the optimism of 1969's *Stand!*, Sly & the Family Stone's 1971 album *There's a Riot Goin' On* is described by *All Music Guide* as "Brooding, Druggy, Detached, Tense/Anxious, Nihilistic, Paranoid, Ominous,

Weary, Difficult, Outraged" (All Music Guide: There's a Riot Goin' On 2002). The curiously titled 1970 hit single "Thank You (Fallettinme Be Mice Elf Agin)" had already hinted at this change in Stewart and company's approach. Described by writer Alice Echols as "sarcastic" (Echols 2002, 15), "Thank You" deals in part with Stewart/Stone's upbringing in the ghetto. The 1971 album finds Stewart looking more and more pessimistically at race relations and at the plight of Blacks in America. Compounding the darkness of the album was Sly's "slow descent into [heroin] addiction" (Erlewine 2002b). The music reflects the despair and militancy of the Black Power movement.

Although perhaps their recordings did not reflect an overt Black Power stance, several young Black musicians who would later rise to commercial fame were associated at least for a time with the movement. In the late 1960s, for example, the teenaged Chaka Khan was associated with not only the Chicago's Association for the Advancement of Creative Musicians but also with the Black Panther Party in Chicago. Musicians like Chaka Khan may not have produced highly politicized music later in the 1970s and 1980s, but the struggle for fair and equal rights informed their very essence. Perhaps this in part explains the cooperative and apparently democratic nature of Rufus, the group with which Khan performed throughout the 1970s. Rufus, by the way, consisted of White men, and Khan, the lone Black woman; however, songwriting credits suggest a democratic equality within the band.

By the end of the 1960s and the beginning of the 1970s even Motown Records, which had been described by LeRoi Jones with some apparent disdain as "a slick citified version of older R&B-Gospel influenced forms" (Jones 1968, 105) and as "the General Motors of rock" by historians Kenneth J. Bindas and Craig Houston (1989, 16), began to deal with society's treatment of Blacks. In some respects this was a remarkable move. Several Motown acts were at least as popular with White audiences as with Black audiences, as could be seen in singles' relative success on the pop and R&B charts. Songs like Marvin Gaye's 1971 hit "What's Going On" and Norman Whitfield and Barrett Strong's "Ball of Confusion (That's What the World Is Today)" (a 1970 hit for the Temptations) dealt with a number of society's ills, including racism. The Marvin Gaye song was a recording in which jailed Black South African leader Nelson Mandela had found solace while imprisoned on Robben Island (Gilroy 1993). While Paul Gilroy's point in including reference to Mandela and the Gaye song in his book specifically is that the flow

Motown soul singer–songwriter Marvin Gaye. His album *What's Going On* featured songs that dealt with many of the social issues of the late 1960s and early 1970s. Photography by Henry Diltz.

of Black culture can go both from Africa to America and from America to Africa, the Mandela story also serves to illustrate the importance of the song within the movement. Writer Alice Echols points to the 1971 hit single "Smiling Faces Sometimes," by the Undisputed Truth as a "watershed moment" for the Black Power movement (Echols 2002, 160). The record, which was recorded on the Motown-affiliated Gordy label, was the first overtly Black Power–oriented single to make it into the pop top 10. That it was this particular song that holds the distinction is interesting: some of the lyrics take shots at the affirmative action programs so favored by White liberals. The background message of the song is that Blacks need to take their own destinies into their own hands.

The suggestion found in some of the songs of the early 1970s that Blacks must take matters into their own hands resembles the early-to-mid-1960s political theories of Malcolm X and Eldridge Cleaver and the later Black Panther Party politics of Huey Newton and Bobby Seale. These Black leaders believed that only by separating from mainstream (read, White) American society could Blacks live in freedom. This contrasted with Martin Luther King, Jr.'s vision of a fully integrated society. The appearance of more radical approaches to racial issues in top-40 singles by Black musicians in 1970 and 1971 suggests not only a growing frustration with the lack of any discernable improvement in conditions in the United States as well as suggesting that the more general youth segment of U.S. society could accept this more radical approach.

THE FEMINIST MOVEMENT

The feminist movement started to take hold in full force in 1967 and 1968. The movement began with what were termed "consciousness-raising" meetings and the picketing of the Miss America pageant. These explorations of what it meant to be a woman in a society dominated by men led directly to several influential books from the late 1960s through the mid-1970s, including Shulamith Firestone's *The Dialectic of Sex* and Susan Brownmiller's *Against Our Will: Men, Women and Rape*. In addition, several influential magazines aimed at liberated women first hit the news stands in the early 1970s, including *Essence* and *Ms*. For further information on the books and magazines that emerged during this period and that both reported on and influenced the movement, the reader may want to see Debra Michals's article

"From 'Consciousness Expansion' to 'Consciousness Raising': Feminism and the Countercultural Politics of the Self" (Michals 2002).

The first major female contributors to counterculture music, performers who combined skills as instrumentalists, singers, and songwriters, were counted among the folk revival artists of the 1960s. Judy Collins, with her strong classical piano background backing up her distinctive singing style, and Joan Baez, as a guitarist, singer, and songwriter, made an important commercial impact and were highly visible throughout the decade. Baez, in particular, was almost omnipresent at large anti-war and civil rights demonstrations across the country. Baez and Collins performed songs written by men as often, if not more often, as songs written by themselves or other women. In many respects, they became the great communicators of the protest songs of the Bob Dylans and Pete Seegers of the movement. Later in the decade, Joni Mitchell would become recognizable for her songwriting, singing, and instrumental guitar work, and starting in 1971 Bonnie Raitt would begin reaching "blues-guitar mastery in a field previously reserved for men" (Rodnitzky 1999, 72).

Most of the music of Collins, Baez, Mitchell, and Raitt, however, was not directly tied to the women's movement in the public's consciousness. Curiously, Carole King, Gerry Goffin, and Jerry Wexler's 1967 song "(You Make Me Feel Like) A Natural Woman," which would became a #8 hit single for soul singer Aretha Franklin, could be tied to the new movement. Although not strictly a feminist song, it is notable for its honest acknowledgment of female sexual desires and satisfaction. Whether or not the song's authors intended it to do so, "Natural Woman" reflected some of the frank discussion brought forth in the consciousness-raising sessions of the day. Carole King recorded the song for her groundbreaking *Tapestry* album in 1971. The album primarily featured songs that looked at a complex array of relationship issues from a woman's perspective and was a huge commercial and critical success. In fact, *Tapestry* became the best-selling album by a female artist ever, holding that distinction for twenty-five years. Although the work may not be technically a feminist album, the wide and full range of emotions King and her collaborators expressed in the songs on *Tapestry* went well beyond those on most albums by female performers. The songs were widely perceived as being honest reflections of the variety of responses possible for modern women of the era. Perhaps as important as the lyrical content of the songs in defining *Tapestry* was Carole King's gospel-influenced piano playing, which has been called "the first widely recognized instrumental signature ever developed by a woman" (Christgau 1972).

The biggest hit song related to the women's movement was Helen Reddy and Ray Burton's composition "I Am Woman." The song originally appeared on Reddy's 1971 debut album *I Don't Know How to Love Him*. The best-known version of the song, however, was the recorded centerpiece of Reddy's 1972 album *I Am Woman*. The second version, which also topped the *Billboard* pop singles charts for one week, has been called "a heaping helping of unbridled feminism, an Amazonian declaration almost better suited to the Plasmatics' Wendy O'Williams [*sic*; the flamboyant punk singer's name was really Wendy O. Williams] in its lyrically overstated angst" (Viglione 2003). Viglione and other critics have suggested that the more muted original version of the song was perhaps the better recording. At least it was less militant sounding. "I Am Woman" (the second version) was also featured in the 1972 women's liberation film *Stand Up and Be Counted*. In assessing the impact of her song, Helen Reddy noted that the single and the album raised consciousness "among American women en masse" (Helen's Hymn 1972).

Reddy's "I Am Woman" was also connected to another aspect of the women's movement of the late 1960s and early 1970s, the burning of and not wearing of bras, which were seen as symbols of the oppression of women. When "I Am Woman" became a major hit, Reddy caused quite an uproar among television executives and censors when she expressed her desire to perform the song bra-less and with unshaven underarms. The television executive insisted that she shave but allowed her to go bra-less. The ascension of "I Am Woman" into the American consciousness coincided with the founding of *Ms.* magazine, perhaps not coincidentally.

Despite their women's movement-related hits of 1971 and 1972, Carole King and Helen Reddy would primarily focus on more mainstream material in subsequent years. As sociologist Jerome L. Rodnitzky writes: "Most feminist, musical energy has centered on producing and encouraging alternative music. Working within the system had not proved very effective. Unfortunately, whenever a Janis Joplin, Carole King, or even a Helen Reddy made it big, their focus invariably shifted to musical production rather than content and effect" (Rodnitzky 1999, 61). Although the alternative music scene to which Rodnitzky refers was just starting to develop in the first half of the 1970s, right at the end of the time period covered in this book, it is important to note the contributions of a few musicians who would find an audience for their feminist music later in the 1970s.

Holly Near made her recording debut in 1974. Her debut, *Hang in There*, primarily features the singer-songwriter's anti-war material, much of which she developed in response to what she witnessed on tours of the United States and of Southeast Asia the year before. Her subsequent work focused on a number of issues, such as women's rights, lesbian and gay rights, reproductive rights, the nuclear arms race, and the environment. Among her strongest feminist songs were "It's More Important to Me," which Rodnitzky describes as a "sensitive feminist song . . . about how competition for men drives women apart" and "Strong," which concerned the "social conditioning of women" (Rodnitzky 1999, 65). Near would eventually own her own recording company, Redwood Records, which took the music of social protest well into the post-counterculture era. Although not widely known to the general public, due to the highly political and socially charged nature of much of her work, Near was notable as a particularly strong singer both technically and expressively.

Holly Near's fellow pro-lesbian feminists Meg Christian, with her album *I Know You Know*, and Cris Williamson, with her album *The Changer and the Changed*, made similarly important stands for the rights of women starting at the end of the counterculture era. Both Christian and Williamson recorded on the female-owned label Olivia Records. It seems fitting that Near, Williamson, and Christian's most important work came at the end of the counterculture era. As historian Terry H. Anderson writes, "The 1970s became the decade of women's liberation. Compared with minorities, change was relatively quick, probably because females had more leverage with those in power—white men—and because it seemed the logical conclusion of the era" (Anderson 1995, 405).

Let us return, however, to the period just following the emergence of the music of the women's movement into public consciousness. The 1971–1972 period found some male members of the radical political movement finally expressing recognition that, in some respects, the radical politics of the late 1960s resembled a males-only social club. Women were largely shut out of leadership roles, even though many women had played key roles in the movement. Yoko Ono and John Lennon, the principal musical champions of the early 1970s radical politicos, commented extensively on the plight of women in society and within the movement.

Lennon's 1971 song "Power to the People" included a tell-tale stanza in which the singer asked male members of the movement to take a look at how they treat the women in their lives. In his choice of words, Lennon implies that these women are often left at home, presumably to do stereotypically "female" chores. Although the feminist message of the song goes by rather quickly, it does stand as something of an indictment or exposé of the "old boys" nature of the leftist political scene.

Lennon and Yoko Ono collaborated on the 1972 composition "Woman Is the Nigger of the World," a song featured on their double album–radical leftist musical manifesto, *Sometime in New York City*. Even commentators generally inclined to grant Lennon and Ono some slack with regards to some of their more off-the-wall musical exploits reacted harshly to the album. Two such writers, Roy Carr and Tony Tyler, who penned *The Beatles: An Illustrated Record*, write that the Lennon-Ono collection "stands condemned of mindless overkill, cheap rhetoric and dismaying lack of proportion. Its only real virtues—spontaneity and, in some places, first-class musicianship—did not compensate for the appallingly bad lyrics and clichéd political phraseology" (Carr and Tyler 1978, 102). Although the women's movement accounts for only part of the focus—it is an overly broad focus, if "focus" is even an applicable word in this case—this particular song was among the most notorious protest songs of the day. By using the word "nigger" as a label for half of humankind, Lennon and Ono surely make the point that the world of 1972 was undeniably patriarchal, but it also shows a gross, though unintended, insensitivity towards Blacks. Interestingly, the song, like the previously mentioned portion of "Power to the People," can be read as an indictment of the radical leftists of the late 1960s and early 1970s, most of whom were males all too happy to either exclude women or to push them into subservient roles in the movement. Insofar as "Woman Is the Nigger of the World" was issued on an album aimed squarely at the radical politicos of the day, it is interesting to find the authors placing some of the blame for the plight of women on the men of the radical left—quite a gutsy step, indeed.

John Lennon and Yoko Ono's *Sometime in New York City* also included Ono's composition "Sisters, O Sisters," a pro-feminist song that finds the singer calling her "sisters" into action to affect positive change in the world. As much as "Woman Is the Nigger of the World" teeters on the edge of offensiveness, Ono's "Sisters, O Sisters" exudes positiveness.

Although it might not ordinarily be considered a true counterculture classic, one of the great feminist songs of the 1970s was Loretta Lynn, T. D.

Bayless, and Don McHan's "The Pill." Lynn included the song on her 1975 album *Back to the Country*. Not only did the single release achieve success on the country charts, it also made it onto the pop charts. Due to the sympathetic treatment of birth control, the song was banned by Boston radio stations, which helped "The Pill" gain considerable notoriety. "The Pill" also appeared on Loretta Lynn's 1976 album *Blue-Eyed Kentucky Girl*. In the context of the latter album, which featured songs that looked at life from a uniquely female perspective, the appearance of "The Pill" suggests the extent to which reproductive freedom for women was becoming mainstream at the end of the counterculture era.

THE GAY RIGHTS MOVEMENT

A more up-front, out-of-the-closet approach to homosexuality began to appear in music in the late 1960s. In addition, several notable rock musicians, especially Mick Jagger and Janis Joplin, were making a sort of androgyny a part of their acts. Jagger's stage outfits, makeup, and dancing style suggested to his audiences that he was bisexual. Of course, this implication relied heavily on the acceptance of stereotypes. In Jagger's case, the affectations seemed just to be part of his act. Janis Joplin assumed a stage and public persona that closely resembled that of some of the prominent early African-American female blues singers: hard-living, free-loving, bisexual, and tragic. In Joplin's case, there was probably some degree of authenticity to her image.

By the early 1970s, glam-rock performers like David Bowie and the New York Dolls would fashion entire careers out of a stage persona of vague sexual orientation. Bowie, born David Jones—he had to change his name to avoid confusion with David (Davy) Jones of the Monkees—assumed the persona of Ziggy Stardust, a bisexual character of somewhat indeterminate gender, following the release of his album *Hunky Dory* in 1972. He would continue to exploit this image into the mid-1970s. In a 1972 interview, Bowie stated that he was gay, an admission that many critics suspected was simply a publicity stunt. Generally, most of Bowie's music did not explicitly suggest a bisexual orientation. A few notable songs, including "Spiders from Mars," which serves as a kind of overview of the Ziggy Stardust persona, and "John, I'm Only Dancing," however, do suggest a bisexual orientation. "John, I'm Only Dancing" finds Bowie's character apparently caught dancing with a would-be female lover by his *male* lover. Bowie's character has to sort out and deal with the complexities of bisexuality. Interestingly, Bowie's popularity grew after his "admission," suggesting that a sexual orientation outside of society's generally accepted norms need not be a detriment to a career in popular music. Other glam-rockers, like Roxy Music, the New York Dolls, and Marc Bolan with his group T. Rex, affected flamboyance as a performance and dress style. They failed to achieve the critical or commercial success of David Bowie. While these performers could be credited with helping to make outrageously flamboyant and androgynous clothing and makeup more acceptable, such dress suggests a stereotypical caricature of "gayness" and did not deal in any serious way with gay issues.

The case of famed songwriter-singer-pianist Elton John is curious, especially considering the extent to which David Bowie made a career out of a perceived gay persona. John had long been rumored to be gay, but finally admitted that he was bisexual in a 1976 interview. John would later admit that he was gay and that his claim of bisexuality was really something of a cop-out; he had been afraid to disclose the complete truth. Elton John's fortunes went into a dramatic decline following the 1976 disclosure. It would take him several years to regain his popularity. For example, between 1973 and 1976 John had six #1 pop singles on the *Billboard* charts, and a total of thirteen in the top 10. In the next nine years, he would make the top 10 only five times and would not have another #1 single until 1985. Eventually he would become a strong spokesperson for AIDS awareness in the 1980s and 1990s and would become a leading composer for musical films. A few of the early Elton John–Bernie Taupin collaborations vaguely suggested a gay view of life. Certainly, the well-known hit "Daniel" *could* be interpreted as a male–male love song. The singer's use of the word "brother" in referring to the character of Daniel could be metaphoric rather than literal. In any case, the 1973 song, which reached #2 on the *Billboard* pop singles chart, expresses a tender male-male bond, either of brotherly love or veiled romantic love.

The real start of an authentic gay male–oriented music developed during the first half of the 1970s with the emergence of disco music. Robert McRuer, in his article "Gay Gatherings," emphasizes the importance of disco music and the disco scene throughout the 1970s in the emergence of an openly gay counterculture. According to the author, the popularity of Black female singers like Grace Jones, Donna Summer, and Gloria Gaynor among male homosexuals reflected a transference of "Black" as minority status to "gay" as minority status (McRuer 2002). Other writers would notice the close ties between Blacks and gays due to their minority status within mainstream

American society. Braunstein 1999 writes, "For the first half of the 1970s, disco was an extended conversation between black musicians and gay dancers" (Braunstein 1999, 55). As early as the late 1960s commentators were describing the growing gay scene as being essentially blind to social or economic class. Anti-war activist Paul Goodman was quoted as saying in 1969 that, "Queer life . . . can be profoundly democratizing, throwing together every class and group more than heterosexuality does" (Heinemann 2001, 191). Certainly disco would continue this blurring of class and economic lines within the gay community. Some commentators of the early 1970s, particularly Karla Jay and Allen Young in their book *Out of the Closets: Voices of Gay Liberation,* would even go so far as to directly link the emergence of gay culture with the rise of disco in a cause-and-effect relationship (Jay and Young 1972).

In the case of songs written from a lesbian point of view, much of the music was more introspective than disco. The leading singer-songwriters who supported the rights of lesbians were also closely aligned with the women's movement. As mentioned in the discussion of the women's movement above, members of the women's movement generally welcomed the participation of lesbians. Singer-songwriters like Holly Near, Meg Christian, and Cris Williamson, all dealt with both movements. Their music reflected the old folk revival of the late 1950s and early 1960s and also bore some resemblance to the work of the newly emerging introspective singer-songwriters of the early 1970s, musicians like Carly Simon, James Taylor, and Carole King. Instead of the party atmosphere of disco, Near, Christian, and Williamson dealt sensitively and thoughtfully with serious issues like the acceptance of a lesbian lifestyle in "straight" American society, problems with relationships, the general gender-based inequities in society, and others, with acoustically based musical settings. Much of the work of these songwriters, however, is outside the historical scope to which this book is adhering, with much of their best-known music coming after 1975.

THE AMERICAN INDIAN MOVEMENT

While music related to the American Indian Movement (AIM) was not as visible as anti-war music or counterculture music supporting other causes, music did play a role. Several songwriters dealt sympathetically with the Native American takeover of Alcatraz Island in 1969–1970; at least one prominent non–Native American musician of the era took on the persona of a shaman; some Native American musicians, who had formerly pursued European-based art music performance, turned to the music of their own heritage; songs that dealt with the plight of America's native peoples made the *Billboard* charts in the early 1970s; and more trivially, rock musicians and fans aped Native American clothing fashions from 1967 on. While some of these Native-garbed musicians were living at least part of their ethnic/racial heritage—Jimi Hendrix frequently wore headbands and other Native American–styled articles of clothing and was of mixed African-American and Native-American heritage—many were doing so because it was fashionable and because it was symbolic of the tribal nature of the counterculture/hippie lifestyle. By the early 1970s, hippies living off the land considered themselves to be kindred spirits with the Native Americans.

The history of Alcatraz, an island in San Francisco Bay and the long-time site of a notorious federal prison, is fascinating and certainly deserving of further study. The island was considered sacred to Native Americans of the region. The U.S. government had abandoned the island in the early 1960s when it proved no longer to be a practical prison site. In 1969, members of the Sioux tribe cited an old treaty that gave them the right to occupy unused federal land. They proceeded to occupy the island in November. Negotiations to end the occupation continued throughout 1970. The occupation of Alcatraz Island became part of the larger push for equal rights and restitution by Native Americans and spawned several books that dealt with Native issues, such as Edgar S. Cahn's *Our Brother's Keeper: The Indian in White America* and Vine Deloria, Jr.'s *Custer Died for Your Sins: An Indian Manifesto.* As historian Terry H. Anderson writes, "Red Power spread like wildfire throughout the first half of 1970" (Anderson 1995, 335). This was the historical context that spawned several Native American rights-related songs.

Leon Russell dealt sympathetically with the loss of Native lands and the near extermination of Native Americans in his 1971 song "Alcatraz." Although Russell probably made his biggest musical contributions as a studio musician and songwriter, and although his recorded performances as a singer led to only two singles reaching the top 40, he was extremely visible in 1971. Russell was one of the principal musicians who contributed to George Harrison's Concert for Bangla Desh (which was one of the great experiments in putting 1960s-style idealism to good practical use, and which set the stage for future charitable rock concerts), and he appeared on numerous recordings by other major stars of the era. Russell, a gravelly voiced singer and keyboardist, enjoyed some success with his albums in the early 1970s. "Alcatraz" was featured as an album cut on one of those releases, *Leon Russell and the Shelter People.*

The best-known and most frequently heard song about the Native Americans' struggle against oppression and for the preservation of their cultural identity, however, was John D. Loudermilk's "Indian Reservation (The Lament of the Cherokee Reservation Indian)." Ironically, the song had first been a British hit for Dan Fardon. The U.S. hit version was recorded by the Raiders (formerly known as Paul Revere and the Raiders) and made its *Billboard* pop chart debut on April 10, 1971. The single reached #1 on the charts and was on the charts for twenty-two weeks, nearly two months longer than any of the group's other twenty-three chart singles. In fact, "Indian Reservation" was the Raiders' sole #1 single. Powered by Mark Lindsay's vocals, Paul Revere's electronic organ, and a steady, pseudo–Native American–styled tom-tom beat, the song makes extensive use of the minor pentatonic scale, found in much Native American music. Loudermilk's lyrics speak of the disarming of the Native Americans, the forced use of English and the attempted extermination of the Cherokee language, the attempts to forcibly assimilate the Cherokees into European-American–based U.S. society through the banning of Native clothing and hair styles, and the stealing of Native American lands by the U.S. government. Possibly because it was so much a song and recording of its time, this #1 hit single is largely forgotten today. As music critic Bruce Eder writes, "Somewhat ironically, history has rendered 'Indian Reservation' as the least significant of the group's [the Raiders'] hits. It comes off as a piece of early-'70s, heart-on-the-sleeve topical ersatz" (Eder 2002a). In fact, the overt pop nature of the song with its use of stereotypical Native sounds could be labeled (at best) derivative or (at worst) exploitive. Despite this, the sheer popularity of "Indian Reservation" brought at least some of the issues with which the AIM was concerned to a greater, and Whiter, segment of the U.S. population.

As previously mentioned in reference to music of the anti-war movement, Holly Near made reference to the plight of earlier generations of Native Americans in her 1973 song "No More Genocide." Near included the song on her album *Hang in There,* which focused on the Vietnam Conflict. In rhetorically linking the slaughter of Vietnamese with the slaughter of Native Americans, she joined the protest singers of the early part of the counterculture era; several of the *Broadside* songs of the early 1960s had done the same sort of thing. Holly Near, however, was writing and recording at a time in which the AIM was well established and the plight of indigenous peoples was garnering much more public attention. In fact, it was in February 1973 that approximately 300 members of the AIM occupied Wounded Knee, South Dakota, taking eleven hostages in the process. Although in retrospect the hostage-taking episode and the internal squabbling among the protesters doomed the protest and represented one of the last gasps of the movement, the Wounded Knee occupation at least continued to keep the AIM and plight of native peoples in the media spotlight. This strengthens Holly Near's song in relationship to the similar songs of the early days of the counterculture era. It should also be noted that the acclaimed 1932 book *Black Elk Speaks* (Neihardt 1972) was republished in 1972, right in the middle of the Native American rights movement. Black Elk (1863–1950) had been an important, and one of the last figures, in the so-called "Messianic movement" among the late nineteenth-century and early twentieth-century Native Americans.

One of the more intriguing outcomes of the growth in Native American consciousness of the late 1960s and early 1970s was the growth in interest in authentic Native American music. In particular music for the Native American flute took off and today enjoys fairly widespread popularity. One of the most popular flutists of the past thirty years has been R. Carlos Nakai. Nakai had studied classical trumpet at Northern Arizona University but turned from this European instrument to the Native American flute in 1973 at age twenty-seven. He has been widely quoted as saying and writing that it was his feeling of being called to preserve and advance his own Native American heritage that led to this dramatic musical shift (Nakai and De Mars 1996). Nakai has been largely responsible for the popularity of Native American flute music, both on its own and in the context of "New Age" music of the 1980s and 1990s.

THE HISPANIC CAUSE

The plight of American Hispanics was dealt with by some of the early counterculture *Broadside* protest songwriters. For example, Phil Ochs's well-known song "I Ain't Marching Anymore" mentions the fact the United States basically stole California from Mexico. This song was first published in *Broadside* in early 1965 and is detailed in the discussion of anti-war music elsewhere in this book. The serious struggle for equal treatment and empowerment for Hispanics roughly coincided with the emergence of the radical Black Power movement in the late 1960s. For example, a Chicago-area revolutionary Hispanic group, the Young Lords, gathered significant publicity as they worked for "adequate food, decent housing, relevant education, police brutality cessation and employment for their people" (Fields 1969). The entire nation, however, took notice when the famous labor leader Cesar Chavez called for the boycott of California grapes to protest the conditions under which Chicano farm laborers worked in the state's agricultural industry, again starting in the late 1960s.

The movement for Hispanic empowerment was not played out musically to the same extent as the Black Power movement had been brought to U.S. airwaves. The sound of Hispanic musical styles and a few prominent Hispanic musicians did, however, come into prominence as the political movements to improve the plight of Hispanics as a minority group became increasingly active. The clearest example is Carlos Santana and his rock band, Santana. Although the band had been performing in the San Francisco area from 1966, it was the group's appearances at the Monterey Pop Festival and (especially) at Woodstock that propelled their brand of Latin-based music into the forefront of American popular consciousness. Santana's first chart single, "Jingo," did not reach the top 40 when released in 1969, but two 1970 singles, "Evil Ways" and "Black Magic Woman," made it into the Billboard top 10. Although "Oye Como Va" and "Everybody's Everything" enjoyed sales success in 1971, Santana largely faded, especially with Carlos Santana's solo work, which began in 1972. The main venues for Latin music connected with the movement were protests themselves; however, the ascension of the basically apolitical Santana in 1969–1971 was important in bringing some aspects of Hispanic popular culture to the American mainstream.

CONCLUSION

While social movements of the counterculture that focused on the plights of women and minorities used songs from the folk tradition ("We Shall Overcome," for example), songwriters contributed many new works. Some of these compositions may have been derivative and perhaps today are viewed as doing little more than cashing in on the fashionableness that the counterculture had achieved by the early 1970s. Most, however, came from authentic-sounding voices (James Brown's "Say It Loud" and Sly Stone's

"Don't Call Me Nigger, Whitey" are probably the two best examples). Re-gardless of the motivation behind any of these songs, their presence on the record charts and on the radio airwaves served to bring the plight of the oppressed to the attention of the wider American public.

5

Music and Radical Politics

Because of the complexity of defining "the movement," it is difficult to say where aspects of the counterculture ends the next begins. In the present chapter, we shall be looking at the relationship between music and radical politics in the form of organized political entities—the White Panther Party and the Youth International Party, to cite two examples—as well as in the form of the more general call to revolution. Although violence certainly became part of the movement on both sides, there was considerable debate over whether the revolution many radicals sought would be won on the streets or in the homes. Bruce Harris alludes to this in his liner notes to *Weird Scenes inside the Gold Mine*, a 1972 compilation of songs by the Doors. In reference to the deceased singer and principal songwriter of the band, Jim Morrison, Harris writes,

> And America got scared, because it wasn't just show biz anymore. Because this guy really meant it, and because he was too smart. It wasn't just another rant for revolution. We didn't have the guns, we had the numbers, and it was only when all else failed that blood became our last resort. This revolution would not take place in the streets where it could be seen and stopped, but in every house, in every room, where it would never be found until the sides had already changed. (Harris 1972)

We shall see both kinds of revolutionary music—street and home—in our study.

Although the musician would quickly eschew overt political lyrics in his songs, Bob Dylan was closely followed by some of the radical politicos of the 1960s into the early 1970s. Charles B. Hersch (1998) cites several examples of persons affiliated with the Students for a Democratic Society (SDS) who saw themselves as being aligned with the early protest songs of Dylan. Hersch writes that

> Dylan's "folk" music embodies the early New Left's civic republi-
> canism, with its faith in truth and reason and its vision of a vir-
> tuous community of authentic souls. These early songs seek to
> unmask evil by portraying it truthfully and teach authenticity, the
> rejection of social roles in favor of the honest presentation of a
> core self. His later, electric songs reject the ideas of a core self and
> truth, and indeed all ordering hierarchies, embracing the counter-
> culture's devotion to unmediated experience, play, and spontane-
> ity. (Hersch 1998, 128)

As described by Hersch, the Dylan songs that were most closely related to the New Left of the famous Port Huron Statement period were the songs of the albums *The Freewheelin' Bob Dylan* and *The Times They Are A-Changin'*. In fact, the title song of the latter album became something like *the* anthem of the entire radical political movement. Those in the movement agreed with Dylan that the times certainly were changing, and saw themselves as the ones to carry out these grand societal and political changes.

In virtually every work he published, whether liner notes, articles, or books, John Sinclair made the point that "rock music *is* revolution." Sinclair, who in addition to being a poet, disc jockey, record producer, and manager of the MC5, co-founded the radical White Panther Party. He made the point repeatedly that while the counterculture era may not have witnessed a huge number of songs that openly touted evolution, the entire gestalt of the rock music experience, which included high volume, drugs, sexual freedom, re-bellion against authority, and so forth, symbolized the revolution that radical politicos sought. In other words, Sinclair expressed the belief that, to quote the misquote attributed to Canadian mass media expert Marshall McLuhan, "the medium is the message." McLuhan actually said, "The medium is the massage" (McLuhan and Fiore 1967).

The MC5, the rock band that John Sinclair managed, symbolized the politically revolutionary nature of rock probably better than any other group. As Sinclair's earlier quote suggests, the MC5 did this largely without specializing in New Left sloganeering or lecturing; it was the entire MC5 experience that *was* the revolution come to life. Central to the Detroit group's appeal was the live show. Sinclair wrote of these performances that,

> as the performer puts out more[,] the energy level of the audience
> is raised and they give back more energy to the performers, who
> are moved onto a higher energy level which is transmitted to the
> audience and sent back, etc., until everything is totally frenzied.
> This process makes changes in the people's bodies that are mo-
> lecular and cellular and which transform them irrevocably just as
> LSD or any other strong high-energy agents do. (Sinclair 1969, 11)

The MC5's live shows featured deafening feedback, heavy distortion, the simple chord structures and screamed lyrics later associated with punk rock in the mid- to late-1970s, (what conservatives would consider) desecration of the U.S. flag, profanity, and long, free jazz–inspired improvisations.

The MC5's tie-ins with the radical left were solid. As mentioned previously, band manager John Sinclair was one of the cofounders of the White Panther Party. As music critic Jason Ankeny writes, "As the official house band of the White Panthers, they became musical conduits for the party's political rhetoric, taking the stage draped in American flags and calling for a revolution" (Ankeny 2002). The MC5's performance style prompted numerous confrontations with police and with club owners in the greater Detroit area. Their most notorious song, "Kick Out the Jams," was usually preceded by singer Rob Tyner's profane and incendiary shouted introduction, "Kick out the jams, motherfucker!" As MC5 scholar Steve Waksman writes, " 'KICK OUT THE JAMS, MOTHERFUCKER' as a shout would not have raised the audience to such a fever pitch if not for what followed: 'Kick Out the Jams,' the song, which was itself a sort of exhortation . . . a musical statement full of both fury and joy" (Waksman 1998, 72). Yes, the live performance truly was "the thing" for this rock group. In reference to the decision to make the MC5's debut album a live recording, guitarist Wayne Kramer said that, "The live show was the central experience. That was who we were. We wanted to present that" (Guterman 2000, 8). Incidentally, the MC5's greatest impact in the Detroit area coincided with the summer 1967 riots and the height of John Sinclair and the White Panthers' politicking.

Let us take a brief look at some of the musical characteristics that defined the MC5 in two of its best-known songs. The band's most commercial song, "I Can Only Give You Everything," resembles both the punk rock of the late 1970s and the riff-oriented style of the 1964–1965 Rolling Stones in its use of a guitar-based riff, harmonic usage, and general tone color. In fact the song is a near-perfect link between the roots/punk music of the early 1960s and the late 1970s. "Kick out the Jams," easily the group's most notorious and most important song, exhibits the same characteristics. Again, it is built around a simple riff. In this case, a five-note guitar figure that uses but two pitches, tonic and the flatted third scale degree. The fast tempo of "Kick out the Jams" and its unrelenting energy anticipates both the Ramones and the Sex Pistols, although the song's place in the politics of the late 1960s clearly set the stage for the latter 1970s punk band.

It is important to note that while groups like the MC5 sang about and lived a lifestyle revolving around drug use and free sex, the political tactics of the White Panthers suggest that these aspects of the counterculture were not meant to be an end unto themselves, as might have been the case with the hippies. In the case of the MC5, violence, free sex, and drugs were seen as the means to a complete revolutionary overthrow of the U.S. government. *All Music Guide* critic Jason Ankeny probably sums it up best when he writes, "Under the guidance of svengali John Sinclair (the infamous founder of the radical White Panther Party), MC5 celebrated the holy trinity of sex, drugs, and rock & roll, their incendiary live sets offering a defiantly bacchanalian counterpoint to the peace-and-love reveries of their hippie contemporaries" (Ankeny 2002).

The political style and tactics of the White Panthers and the MC5 were not entirely successful. Not only did the United States not succumb to revolution brought on by sex, drugs, and rock and roll, but the tactics of these revolutionaries alienated many members of the political left wing. The MC5, their fans, and Sinclair's followers viewed themselves as "white Negroes" (Waksman 1998). Indeed, the name of Sinclair's political party was based on that of the radical Black Panther Party. Those associated with the White Panther Party saw themselves as outcasts from American society, much like Blacks felt themselves to be marginalized and much-maligned outcasts from a society that had once legally enslaved them. Both the Black Panthers and the White Panthers were largely male-dominated movements. The MC5 itself, and the larger movement presented an extremely aggressive masculine, macho persona. The radical political arm of the movement, especially as represented by the MC5 and the various Panthers tended to turn left-wing politics into a nearly exclusively male club, much to the ultimate detriment of the movement. Incidentally, by the 1970s, John Lennon and Yoko Ono would take on this aspect of the movement, pointing out its hypocrisy on their *Sometime in New York City* album.

Unlike many of the musical ensembles of the 1960s, the MC5 directly influenced music of the second half of the 1970s. The musical characteristics of "Kick Out the Jams" and other MC5 recordings and live performances, combined with the group's radical political rhetoric is clearly a direct antecedent of 1970s British punk rock. Although many commentators have traced manager Malcolm McLaren's establishment of punk's most notorious band, the Sex Pistols, to what he heard in the mid-1970s performances of New York City bands like the Ramones, the entire Sex Pistols gestalt: distortion; an aggressive shouting-singing style; overtly anti-government, foul-mouthed leftist politics as a basis for the lyrics; violence; and a simple riff-based harmonic motion, comes much closer to the MC5 than probably any other earlier rock group.

The Fugs did not generate the same degree of sonic fury or the same degree of musical influence on the 1970s as the MC5. The Fugs were part of the New York radical street theatre scene that spawned figures like Abbie Hoffman and Jerry Rubin. Although musically different from the MC5, the Fugs' shocking brand of street theatre "had much in common with the MC5's shocking stage antics," according to writer Jeff A. Hale (2002, 140). And the Fugs fit right in with the sometimes strange political happenings that Hoffman and Rubin cooked up. Jerry Rubin recalled that at the infamous Hoffman–Rubin attempt to levitate the Pentagon in 1967, "There were Ben Spock and Norman Mailer leading, and thousands of people in a very festive environment, and there were the Fugs playing outrageous music, and the hippies. It was just a great big beautiful be-in demonstration, you know" (Morrison and Morrison 1987, 286). The one specific song by the Fugs that perhaps best typifies their political and musical style is "Kill for Peace," which I have previously dealt with in the chapter on music and the anti-war movement.

Huey Newton, one of the central figures of the Black Power movement, influenced the more general radical politics of the counterculture era. Newton urged his followers to practice "revolution in small groups" (Newton 1967) and emphasized the numerical superiority those who wanted change possessed over those in uniform, be they police or military. Other radical politicos made the same point. "Five to One," by the Doors, makes the same point, claiming that while the police might have the guns, "we've got the numbers." This musical call to revolution was featured as the final track on the group's best-selling *Waiting for the Sun* in the year of revolution, 1968. Musically the track is potent, easily the heaviest song on the album. "Five to One," however, is something of an anomaly: most of the output of the Doors is not *overtly* political. As alluded to in the quote from Bruce Harris at the beginning of this chapter, the Doors were about the revolution, but in terms of a more general and not specifically political change of lifestyle. By this time, even some of the avowed leaders of radical politics were beginning to question whether the revolution would be won on the streets through political means or through a massive and harder-to-see general lifestyle change. Radical political leader Jerry Rubin, for example is quoted as saying, "When the day of the big Be-In arrived, I went and I made a political speech, and it went over to a resounding ho-hum from the audience. I became very influenced by this. I thought maybe the real battle of America is not politics, it's lifestyle" (Morrison and Morrison 1987, 283).

While several prominent members of the old left wing dismissed the tactics of the new radical left, disagreeing particularly on the relationships between drugs and politics, at least a few members of the earlier folk revival/ protest movement aligned themselves with the New Left. The most prominent of these musicians was Malvina Reynolds. Writer Doug Rossinow points to the importance of Reynolds, who happened to be one of the oldest of the folk revival musicians still active in the 1960s, embracing the New Left. According to Rossinow, Reynolds "played to the young radicals, telling them that they were better than their predecessors" (Rossinow 2002, 105). Reynolds saw the leftists of earlier generations as having been rather inhuman in their approach to politics in comparison with the radicals of the late 1960s.

The most popular of all 1960s groups, the Beatles, made their own statement on revolution. Although the song is credited to both John Lennon and Paul McCartney, "Revolution No. 1" was probably exclusively the work of Lennon. The Beatles included the song on their 1968 album *The Beatles*, commonly known as "The White Album." The song is directed at someone who is calling for the violent overthrow of society. Lennon cannot decide if he is for the destruction or against it. When the song was re-recorded, at a much faster tempo and with heavier, more electric instrumentation for release as the B-side of the "Hey Jude" single, Lennon slightly changed the lyrics, indicating that he should be counted out of any violent revolution.

Ironically, the faster version of "Revolution" practically exudes revolution in its musical setting. Noted rock critic Greil Marcus discussed this irony in his influential book *Rock and Roll Will Stand* (1969). Marcus appears to feel that the musical setting, with its fast tempo, distorted electric guitars, and Lennon's near shouting of the melody, overwhelms the literal reading of the text. Although Jerome L. Rodnitzky does not specifically mention "Revolution," he confirms Marcus's take on the song when he writes that, beginning with the pyschedelia of 1966 and 1967, message songs were replaced by mood songs (Rodnitzky 1971b). In short, the musical style and performance practice of the musicians became the message. Robert G. Pielke, writing in his book on the relationship of rock music and American culture, states that

> as one facet of both the immanence and transcendence, authentic art will negate the established order, focusing on its fundamental values and the way they may be institutionalized. Of course, the negation must also involve a critical perspective on the historically conditioned embodiment of the revolution itself. The negation of art is total, all-encompassing. By far the best example of this is the ambiguous "Revolution" by The Beatles. (Pielke 1986, 18)

The fast version of "Revolution" certainly received maximum exposure, as "Hey Jude" was a massive seller, and the B-side itself appeared on the pop charts.

One of the great ironies of the association of music with revolutionary politics during the counterculture era is that perhaps the most famous example, the entire essence, the entire being of the MC5, made little nationwide impact, at least in terms of record sales. Several more commercially oriented performers aligned themselves with the movement, and to a much greater extent than the Beatles did in one isolated song. Interestingly, most commercially successful artists who aligned themselves with revolutionary politics have received much less attention than groups like the Fugs or the MC5 from sociologists who have studied the counterculture. One of the more successful American recording acts of the 1970s and the 1980s, Chicago, began life as the Big Thing in 1967. They subsequently changed their name to the Chicago Transit Authority, finally settling on Chicago in 1969. In addition to the top-40 pop hits "Does Anybody Really Know What Time It Is?" and "Questions 67 and 68," the jazz-rock ensemble's first album, the four-sided *Chicago Transit Authority*, contained a sort of musical "suite" of revolution in the form of the side-four cuts "Prologue, August 29, 1968,"

"Someday (August 29, 1968)," and "Liberation." "Prologue," which leads directly into the song "Someday," is a recording of Black militants exhorting the crowd of demonstrators at the Democratic National Convention, with the famous chant "The whole world is watching."

Chicago II, a product of 1970, primarily featured top-40–type pop music, but also included the politically motivated four-movement suite *It Better End Soon*. In many respects the suite of thematically linked songs is not much more than a plea for an end to the violence of war and the violence of the police and demonstrators. The song takes on greater significance, however, due to the fact that it is the only selection on the two-record set to have its lyrics appear in print on the inside of the fold-out album package. The lyrics are followed by a statement from band members Robert Lamm, Terry Kath, Walter Parazaider, James Pankow, Lee Loughnane, Daniel Seraphine, and Peter Cetera, as well as record producer James William Guercio saying, "With this album we dedicate ourselves, our futures and our energies to the people of the revolution. . . . And the revolution in all of its forms" (Liner notes to *Chicago II* 1970).

By the time of 1972's *Chicago V*, the political material, which consisted of the songs "State of the Union," "While the City Sleeps," and "Dialogue," dealt primarily with the theme of personal inner conflict and conflict within the movement. Robert Lamm, keyboardist and singer, wrote all three songs. "State of the Union" deals with the songwriter's inner conflict between the need for violent revolution, and the desire for nonviolent, perhaps more gradual societal change. "Dialogue" deals with the same conflict between radicalism and liberalism, but because of Chicago's use of various voices in presenting the ideas, reflects the lack of direction of the late stages of the movement. "While the City Sleeps" finds Lamm exposing the violent back-room plotting of the establishment; however, he balances this with an expression of hope that the world will soon be changing. Of course, like its predecessors, *Chicago V* balanced this political material with songs of obviously greater general audience appeal. In fact, when released as a single, "Saturday in the Park" became the band's highest charting single to date, reaching #3 on the *Billboard* pop charts.

Chicago V represented the end of overt reference to "the revolution" for the popular jazz-rock ensemble. Perhaps indicative of the approaching end of the counterculture era, 1974's *Chicago VIII* included only one even vaguely political song, "Harry Truman." Hardly revolutionary in nature, the song expressed a longing for the plain-speaking style of the former president and was as gentle a reaction to the Watergate scandal and the excesses of the Nixon administration as could be. Throughout the period of their politicking, however, Chicago managed not to appear as a particularly serious threat to the establishment. The radical political material formed a relatively small part of their output and they certainly didn't overtly take on the establishment like the MC5. Interestingly, though, because the band's material was overwhelmingly pop in nature, both musically and lyrically, the top-40–style textures of this rock band with brass and woodwinds earned them a wide appeal. This wide appeal translated into album sales that allowed what radical political messages were contained in Chicago songs to find their way into many American homes.

Although Bob Dylan had been one of the more prominent musicians composing and performing political material in the early years of the movement, he had rejected politics by the mid-1960s. The ghost of the political Dylan reemerged in 1969; however, the radical faction of the Students for a Democratic Society took up the moniker "the Weathermen," a name taken from a line in Dylan's earlier "Subterranean Homesick Blues." If nothing else, this suggests the esteem in which the New Left still held Dylan, despite the fact that most of his late 1960s material no longer carried the overt political messages of earlier songs like "Masters of War," nor the symbolist impressionistic lyrics of "Subterranean Homesick Blues." Within the context of "Subterranean Homesick Blues," the Weathermen's choice of name suggests that they felt that they had their finger on the pulse of the underground and were at the forefront of seeing in which direction the movement was moving.

John Lennon and Yoko Ono released their single "Power to the People" in March 1971. The song, with its support of street protests, represented a change in approach in particular for Lennon, whose sole previous politically oriented 45-rpm single, "Give Peace a Chance," of two years earlier, was a gentle request for peace. Musically and lyrically, "Power to the People" was harder edged, featuring a thick, rock instrumental texture and heavy use of studio echo on the ex-Beatle's voice. The song, like several of the songs of the late summer 1972 album *Sometime in New York City*, directs the radical politicos of the day to take a look at how they treat those around them—specifically, how the male members of the movement are treating the women in their lives—suggesting a recognition of the double standard of which the radical left was being accused at the time. The photograph of Lennon and Ono that graced the picture sleeve of the single showed the two in Japanese riot helmets and Lennon holding his up-raised fist in the "rabble rousing," to quote Roy Carr and Tony Tyler, authors of *The Beatles: An Illustrated Record* (Carr and Tyler 1978, 94), salute of those days of increasingly violent street protests. Ono, incidentally, and in sharp contrast, makes the two-fingered peace sign. "Power to the People" suggests that Lennon had recanted his earlier statement of the 1968 song "Revolution" that he should be counted out of a coming violent revolution. Reaction to "Power to the People" among those who were active in the movement was mixed. One of the most telling statements condemning the song came from counterculture writer Hunter S. Thompson in his book *Fear and Loathing in Las Vegas*. Thompson describes the Lennon song as being "ten years too late," and quotes his attorney as saying "That poor fool should have stayed where he was. . . . Punks like that just get in the way when they try to be serious" (Thompson 1971, 21).

Speaking of John Lennon and Yoko Ono's *Sometime in New York City* album, the 1972 recording stands as one of the best-known single musical documents of the era's radical political scene. The highly politically motivated nature of the entire album is suggested by the statement buried among the song lyrics printed in the package that reads, "Don't think they didn't know about Hitler" (Lennon and Ono 1972). Although the statement is rather oblique, one possible meaning is the theory that government officials outside of Germany during the reign of the Third Reich knew about the murders of millions of Jews and others, but kept the information from their citizens as they worked to appease Adolf Hitler. The implication of this statement in relationship to the situations Lennon and Ono deal with on *Sometime in New York City* is that perhaps the many apparently unconnected acts of political oppression going on in the 1960s and 1970s were probably more closely related than the public realized and under some sort of clandestine government control.

Let us take a look at some of the songs of *Sometime in New York City*, keeping in mind that the subject of the British occupation of Northern Ireland comes up in several songs and is outside the scope of this book.

The Lennon-Ono collaboration "Angela" concerns the radical Communist Black leader Angela Davis who was accused of conspiracy in an extremely highly publicized failed escape of Black prisoners that left a judge and three others dead in 1970. (Details on Davis, her political philosophies, and the events that led to her eventual acquittal of conspiracy charges in 1971 are detailed in the A–Z of Music and the Counterculture Era chapter of this book.) "Angela" is one of the few songs on *Sometime in New York City* that finds Lennon and Ono singing in unison. It should be noted that the Angela

Davis case, from her work with the prisoners through her arrest and acquittal made headlines across the country; however, it was even more of a *cause célèbre* among the radical politicos of New York City. Lennon and Ono's song characterizes Davis as a victim of official political repression on account of her gender, her race, and her leftist political views.

Interestingly, the repression of women by those *inside* the counterculture left wing was taken up by Lennon and Ono in their "Woman Is the Nigger of the World." While I have discussed the controversial song earlier with regard to the women's movement, it is worth mentioning several aspects of the song here. A longtime problem with the left was its tendency to be something of an "old boys club." Even back in the 1930s Communist and Socialist movements in the United States, women were quite active, but often had to play subservient roles. In some respects comedian, actor, and filmmaker Woody Allen was right on the mark in his portrayal of a radical underground movement of the future in his movie *Sleeper* (1974). In the film, the leader of "the underground" is a macho, charismatic, almost Messianic figure who seems to keep everyone, especially the female members of the movement, completely in check and in lockstep. Fueled by the saxophone-driven instrumental work of the New York band Elephant's Memory, "Woman Is the Nigger of the World" finds Lennon as a singer passionately taking on sexism in general, but also hitting the double standard of sexism with the progressive and radical movements squarely in the head. Although critical reaction to this song in particular was generally scathing, one must give Lennon and Ono credit for taking on problems *within* the movement in a song *of* the movement.

Sometime in New York City's "New York City" is an upbeat, rock and roll number that documents some of the colorful characters of the radical chic in New York City in the 1971–1972 period. Perhaps naturally, Lennon includes reference to movement leader Jerry Rubin. He also, however, includes reference to various people of the street, including the street musician David Peel, someone not widely known outside of New York. Peel, probably most famous (or infamous) for his song "The Pope Smokes Dope," along with other pro-marijuana ditties, made several recordings that did not do much from a commercial standpoint. No, the way that people had heard of Peel during this period of time was to have heard him on the streets of New York. I have discussed Peel in more detail in relationship to his many pro-drug songs in the discussion of music and recreational drugs elsewhere in this book. Lennon deals with these figures, nationally recognized and only locally well-known, with good humor, but he makes an important political point, too. Commenting on the suppression of freedom and perhaps on his own well-publicized immigration problems—Lennon was refused a green card for several years due to a marijuana conviction in his native England—he holds up the Statue of Liberty as a New York icon that invites all to the shores of the United States, where they are guaranteed freedom. With respect to Lennon's immigration problems, subsequently it has been established that the primary reason for his difficulty in obtaining the green card was because of his involvement in the anti-war movement and in the New York radical political scene, the very stuff of *Sometime in New York City*!

The album track "Attica State" deals with the prison uprising at Attica State Prison in western New York State. The song also laments the plight of prisoners everywhere, taking the stand that many of the prisoners are where they are due largely to discrimination on account of race, social class, and political stands. Yoko Ono's song "We're All Water" is one of the less frequently mentioned songs in reviews of *Sometime in New York City*. It is an interesting song, with a somewhat sing-song melodic line, in which Ono points out the broader connectedness of humanity by juxtaposing such well-known figures as the Pope and Charles Manson, President Richard Nixon and Chinese Communist Party Chairman Mao, American Black activist Eldridge Cleaver and the Queen of England, and so on. The sing-song nature of the music with which she sets the thought-provoking and controversial juxtapositions provides for a high level of bitter irony. Because of its focus on and support of the more radical aspects of U.S. and U.K. politics, *Sometime in New York City* alienated many audience members. The authors of *The Beatles: An Illustrated Record*, Roy Carr and Tony Tyler, write that Lennon and Ono's characterization of the entire population of England as knowing agents of genocide against the Irish damaged John Lennon's reputation for the rest of his career in his homeland. Some might suggest that the songs that characterized the United States as a repressive, genocidal, racist, female-enslaving, war-loving society did similar damage to his standing in the United States. While some of, or even most of, the accusations Lennon and Ono made in the album may have been true, *Sometime in New York City* is one-minded as a political manifesto.

Notorious as it was, *Sometime in New York City* also represented something of a "last hurrah" for high-profile music in support of the radical politics of the counterculture era. The radical political scene itself was transforming between 1972 and 1975: Huey Newton fled the United States in 1974, Jerry

Rubin renounced violence and radical politics, and Bobby Seale renounced the violent overthrow of the White political establishment and turned to local community improvement projects. As the 1970s progressed and moved into the 1980s, the trend in politically motivated music was for songwriters to address specific issues (nuclear proliferation, nuclear power, women's rights, basic human rights, gay rights, etc.) in a progressive, liberal, and generally inclusive way—in sharp contrast to the sometimes cliquish, and often confrontational manner of the MC5, the Fugs, and Lennon and Ono's *Sometime in New York City.*

6

Music and Other Social and Lifestyle Issues

The counterculture era did not just focus on political activism. Many members of the movement rejected the values of mainstream, White, middle-class, suburban America to the extent that they consciously moved into various alternative lifestyles. Rejection of mainstream values could be seen in the hippie lifestyle, the Back to the Land movement, the use of recreational (and especially psychedelic) drugs, among other lifestyle choices that intentionally ran counter to the norm. Much, but certainly not all, of the music that glorified these lifestyle choices reflected the high amplification levels, sonic distortion, simple harmonic schemes, and driving rhythms that rebellious youth craved, and that their parents abhorred.

RECREATIONAL DRUG USE

Allusions to various mind-altering drugs can be found before the counter-culture era, as it is defined for the purposes of this book, for example: early jazz artists, such as Louis Armstrong and Bunk Johnson made no secret of their use of marijuana, and included references to the drug in their songs as early as the 1920s, and Cole Porter's famous song "I Get a Kick Out of You," makes reference to cocaine in the uncensored version of the song. Musicians made numerous references to recreational drugs throughout the counterculture era. Although drug usage was not a prerequisite for participation in "the movement," it was widespread and was seen as a way of rebelling against "straight" society, gaining a near-religious insight into the meaning of life, and a way of breaking down resistance to revolutionary change.

Very early in the counterculture era author Ken Kesey's so-called Merry Pranksters were among the first LSD experimenters. Author Barney Hoskyns, who documented the development of the counterculture hippie drug scene in San Francisco's Haight-Ashbury district, describes Kesey and the Merry Pranksters "wiring up equipment and speakers in the house and in the redwoods surrounding it so they could groove to Rahsaan Roland Kirk records while chopping wood" as they embarked on their acid trips (Hoskyns 2001, 108). Kirk, a woodwind player, used the full resources of decade upon decade of jazz tradition. His main accomplishment was in creating a driving musical intensity, sometimes through his technique of playing multiple instruments simultaneously, or by circular breathing so that the audience would never be aware of his stopping to take a breath, and sometimes just by the careful construction of his improvised solos. Just when the listener thought that Kirk had reached the peak, the musician would raise the excitement level even higher. This technique ties in very closely with many of the descriptions of the LSD experience. Virtually all of Timothy Leary's writings on LSD (including several collected in Leary 1968) describe the sensory overload created by the drug in a way that could easily describe the musical intensity of Rahsaan Roland Kirk. Incidentally, Kirk was born in Columbus, Ohio, in 1936 and died in Bloomington, Indiana, in 1977. He became blind at age two and was considered by many critics to be one of the most exciting, blues-based saxophonists of the 1960s.

While the reader might be surprised to learn that a jazz instrumentalist like Rahsaan Roland Kirk was a strong early influence on the recreational drug takers of the counterculture, it might not be too surprising to know that Eastern religion and philosophy were also associated with the Haight-Ashbury scene. That is, unless one knew of the strict rules against mind-altering drugs articulated by Meher Baba, Maharishi Mahesh Yogi, and other Indian spiritual leaders of the time (see further discussion below, under "The Counterculture Religious Experience").

Incidentally, radical political leaders of the early counterculture era differed widely in their opinions about drug use. In his famous book *Soul on Ice*, Eldridge Cleaver wrote that the long hair, interest in and support of African-American music, use of recreational drugs, and free and mystical attitudes of the young White radicals of the mid-1960s toward sex "are all tools of their rebellion" (Cleaver 1968, 75). Indeed, LSD guru Timothy Leary suggested that the use of drugs would decondition youth, allowing them to be deprogrammed and reprogrammed (apparently for the better good of society). Likewise, well-known radical politico Jerry Rubin saw a political meaning in the criminalization of the possession and the use of marijuana. Rubin wrote, "Grass shows us that our lives, not our consciousness, are at stake. As pot-heads we came face to face with the real world of cops, jails, courts, trials, undercover narcs, paranoia and the war with our parents." He went on to say that marijuana use, because it is illegal, "teaches us disrespect for the law" (Rubin 1970, 100).

Leftists who had grown up following the cue of the 1940s and 1950s radical leaders, however, disagreed. Leftist folksinger-songwriter Phil Ochs, as well as leader of the Students for a Democratic Society, Tom Hayden, spoke and wrote about the political problems associated with drugs—primarily that drug users were so busy getting stoned that they were not out fighting the revolution. The Phil Ochs song "Outside of a Small Circle of Friends" uses biting humor to deal with apathy in the United States of the mid-1960s. In one stanza Ochs points a finger at marijuana as one of the causes for the lack of social and political activism among some young people.

As the world of recreational drug use began receiving more attention, songs referencing drugs started to appear. Interestingly, one of the first to achieve wide appeal was the anti-drug song "Kicks," taken to #4 on the *Billboard* pop singles charts in spring 1965 by Paul Revere and the Raiders. The basic premise of the song is that use of drugs will cause addiction and that "softer" drugs can lead to the use of "harder" drugs.

The Byrds were perhaps the first group to record and release obviously psychedelic drug-inspired material. Their recordings "Eight Miles High" and "5D (Fifth Dimension)" both appeared in 1966. Band members Jim McGuinn, David Crosby, and Gene Clark composed "Eight Miles High," a song that features McGuinn playing his twelve-string electric guitar not in a traditional major or minor key, but in a mode. While modal, so-called raga rock (so named for the scales used in the music of India) would become increasingly commonplace, "Eight Miles High" was quite unusual sounding at the time. Add to the unusual melodic guitar material lyrics that convincingly describe an LSD trip, and "Eight Miles High" created quite a bit of controversy. It was one of the first records of the 1960s to have been largely banned from radio airplay. Despite this official suppression, "Eight Miles High" reached #14 on the *Billboard* pop charts. Don McLean immortalized this song in his huge 1971–1972 hit "American Pie." Although it only reached #44 on the singles charts, McGuinn's "5D (Fifth Dimension)" continued the Byrds' tripping theme. Perhaps not as musically interesting as "Eight Miles High," "5D" nonetheless vividly describes the out-of-body feeling of a person experiencing LSD.

A songwriter whose lyrics often have been subject to a variety of interpretations, Bob Dylan included the song "Rainy Day Women #12 & 35" on his 1966 album *Blonde on Blonde*. The recording features a drunken-sounding New Orleans–style brass band. Incidentally, the Rolling Stones would create a similar soundscape in "Something Happened to Me Yesterday" later in 1966. "Rainy Day Women #12 & 35" can be interpreted on at least two distinct levels. On one hand, Dylan could be saying that the nature of life dictates that everyone must "get stoned," in the sense of being physically or emotionally attacked. On the other hand he could be saying that one must "get stoned" on drugs in order to deal with the harsh realities of society. Listeners of the time understood the singer-songwriter on both levels. Some critics have called *Blonde on Blonde* (a double album) Dylan's best collection of songs, and some claim that the set contains the best realizations of Dylan's songs. "Rainy Day Women #12 & 35" with its sly double entendre stands as one of the best songs on *Blonde on Blonde*.

Composed by Tandyn Almer in 1965, "Along Comes Mary" was recorded by the Association in 1966. The single, which was the group's first top-100 record, reached #7 on the *Billboard* pop charts after a June 1966 chart debut. On the surface, the song could be about a woman named Mary; however, the song was widely interpreted as referring to marijuana. The lyrics speak of "Mary" coming along and affecting positive change in the singer's life and in the lives of the other "kids" around him. Mary opens up the singer's eyes and suggests that many bring "her" into their lives as they search for greater truths. All of these references certainly make sense in terms of the great near-religious insight many of those taking psychedelic drugs, such as marijuana, peyote, and LSD, claimed to achieve while tripping. Musically, the song packs a fast-paced wallop, with the text setting rapid, resembling a musical parallel to fast-frame film techniques.

Since the early days of Ken Kesey's acid tests were accompanied by the music of such avant-garde jazz luminaries as Rahsaan Roland Kirk, who at times used some of the techniques of free-jazz musicians such as Ornette Coleman and Don Cherry, combined with his unusual abilities to play several wind instruments simultaneously and to do circular breathing, perhaps it was natural that rock musicians would extend some of those same techniques in developing a new style influenced by psychedelic drug use. Guitarist-composer Frank Zappa and his band, the Mothers of Invention, did just that. Zappa's 1966 and 1967 live performances featured what he termed the "freak out," basically long, loud, frequently atonal group improvisations. The sensory overload of these musical sections corresponded to the sensory overload described by many who experienced LSD trips. Ironically, Zappa (who totally abstained from both alcohol and drugs) often parodied, and even outright mocked the drugged-out hippies of the era. Like the 1961 and 1962 German audiences in Hamburg's notorious *Reeperbaun* who were openly mocked by the Beatles, those on the receiving end of Zappa's invectives were also some of his staunchest fans.

There was a most curious tie between the use of psychedelic drugs, LSD in particular, and Eastern music, religion, and philosophy. Bruce Hoffman, who taught English at Rockland Community College in New York for many years, told authors Joan and Robert K. Morrison about his first LSD experience in an interview for the Morrison's book on the counterculture. Hoffman told the interviewers that his "guide" had "arranged for records of Ravi Shankar, the marvelous sitar player, and Napoleons from the pastry shop and candles and all the paraphenalia [sic] that went into a 'good trip' " (Morrison and Morrison 1987, 213). Hoffman went on to tell the authors that he grew disenchanted when he witnessed the abuse of drugs, including heroin, among those who at one time had been careful to adhere to Dr. Timothy Leary's rather strict rules about taking LSD. He gave up drugs and turned to the religion and philosophy of Meher Baba, who was also guitarist Pete Townshend's guru. The curiosity here is the connection between Indian music and LSD. Adherents of the various branches of Hinduism generally have taken a very firm stand against drugs. For example, the Beatles had to give up drugs when they studied with the Maharishi Mahesh Yogi. In fact, many young people would eventually turn to the Maharishi's brand of Transcendental Meditation as an alternative to psychedelics. And Meher Baba was an outspoken critic of the use of drugs to attain spiritual enlightenment. Somehow, though, the outward trappings of India and Indian philosophy became associated with psychedelics, for a time at least.

The Grateful Dead played a particularly important role in the early San Francisco Bay–area acid experimentations of 1965 and 1966. While Ken Kesey was a leading LSD proponent, he was not a manufacturer of the drug.

Augustus Owsley Stanley III, better known simply as Owsley, was a University of California at Berkeley student who opened what would be the most famous LSD factory in 1965 (the drug remained legal until 1966). As author Kenneth J. Heineman puts it, "Owsley soon established a national distribution network for his product. He also underwrote a Bay Area rock-and-roll group that sought to propagate the gospel of acid—The Grateful Dead" (Heineman 2001, 182). Despite their having been closely associated with Ken Kesey and the Merry Pranksters' experimentations with LSD and with Owsley in the early and mid-1960s, the Grateful Dead did not make a career out of songs with drug-related lyrics. Several of the band's songs made reference to drugs, but in a curiously matter-of-fact way. "Casey Jones" tells the story of the famous railroad engineer of the early twentieth century, but leaves open the possibility that his use of cocaine—not that there was any historical evidence to suggest that he used the drug—may have been partly responsible for the train wreck that ended his life. In the song, Casey Jones becomes a metaphor for a 1960s user of the drug. Likewise, "Truckin' " makes reference to drugs in a manner not glorifying them, rather, songwriters Jerry Garcia, Phil Lesh, Bob Weir, and Robert Hunter lament what "reds" and cocaine have done to Sweet Jane, presumably a well-known Deadhead. Clearly the Grateful Dead drew a clear distinction between psychedelics and other frequently abused drugs of the counterculture era.

Many in the political left wing of the first half of the 1960s were less than pleased with the use of recreational drugs by young people. Despite the widely held belief that all leftists encouraged drug use to assist in brainwashing young people—a view published in numerous books and articles by right-wing authors—as mentioned early, many politicos and musicians associated with the aims of the so-called Old Left felt that drug use was creating an entire generation of young people who would be lost to activism: they were simply too stoned to participate in politics or protest. Phil Ochs suggested as much in his song "Outside of a Small Circle of Friends." While the song deals with apathy in American society in general terms, one stanza deals specifically with a friend who was imprisoned for thirty years for possession of marijuana. The singer, in a sarcastic tone, states that the prisoner's friends would like to help him, but that they are too stoned. Interestingly, executives at Ochs's record company completely missed the point of the stanza and refused to release the song—which certainly had commercial potential—as a single, believing that the lyrics promoted marijuana use. By the second half of the decade, some of the more radical factions of the political left, specifically John Sinclair's White Panther Party (See discussion in Chapter 5, "Music and Radical Politics") advocated the use of drugs to bring down the establishment. Contrary to the Ochs-style leftists, Sinclair and his followers believed that drugs would turn young people away from the established order. In Sinclair's own words, "There are three essential human activities of the greatest importance to all persons, and that people are . . . healthy in proportion to their involvement in these activities: rock and roll, dope, and fucking in the streets" (Heinemann 2001, 191).

Combining imagery taken from Lewis Carroll's *Alice in Wonderland* and overt references to psychedelic drugs, Grace Slick's composition "White Rabbit" had been part of the Great Society's repertoire during summer 1966. When Slick became the lead singer of the Jefferson Airplane in October 1966, the song followed. The Airplane recorded the song in November 1966, issuing it on their *Surrealistic Pillow* album. The White Rabbit of the song's title is, of course, a character in the Lewis Carroll story. At the same time, however, White Rabbit was also the nickname given to the LSD manufacturer Owsley. "White Rabbit," like the contemporary Rolling Stones song "Mother's Little Helper," makes a clear distinction between the kinds of drugs advocated by suburban straight society and psychedelics, dismissing the former and advocating the latter. The Jefferson Airplane's *Surrealistic Pillow* also contained the Jorma Kaukonen–Marty Balin composition "She Has Funny Cars," another song whose impressionistic lyrics were inspired by psychedelics.

By 1966 record albums were becoming increasingly important in the music industry in general, but especially among the counterculture. The Jefferson Airplane's *Surrealistic Pillow* collection, for example, was an entire package of songs that was listened to intently by fans, not just for a few favorite songs, but as a whole work of art. During the 1950s and the early 1960s, albums had largely consisted of some hit singles, plus their "B-sides" and often what could best be described as filler. While *Surrealistic Pillow* was not necessarily a concept album—concept albums revolved around a theme that was taken up by all or nearly all of the individual songs—the work was taken by young people as an integrated whole. Adding to this effect was the increasing importance of the cover art, song lyrics, and liner notes that were printed on some album covers. The entire gestalt of an album like *Surrealistic Pillow*, consisting of music, packaging, the group photograph, and so on, enhanced the general pro-hippie, pro-experimentation, counterculture "message" the Airplane was projecting. Around this same time FM radio came

more and more into prominence among members of the youth counterculture. Free of many of the top 40–related and time-limit restrictions of AM
radio (and capable of a much better audio quality than AM radio), FM became an important source for album cuts, songs not even released on 45-
rpm singles. FM disc jockeys at counterculture rock stations could even
program an entire album, which also helped to reinforce the view of albums
as whole pieces of art, sort of like the multimovement song cycles of classical
music.

After a December 10, 1966 debut, "I Had Too Much to Dream (Last
Night)" by the Electric Prunes reached #11 on the *Billboard* pop singles
charts. The song with its revved-up psychedelic style and lyrical allusions to
a night filled with psychedelic visions could never be understood as referring
to a simple dream-filled night. Clearly, the implication of songwriters Nance
Mantz and Annette Tucker is that some sort of unnamed chemical agent
brought on these dreams. Indeed, the instrumental overload and nightmar-
ish images of the text point to effects Timothy Leary details in his collection
of essays on the effects of and the political ramifications of LSD, *The Politics
of Ecstasy* (1968).

Speaking of Dr. Timothy Leary, the Beatles' *Revolver* album contained the
song "Tomorrow Never Knows," principally written by John Lennon, that
included lyrics drawn from Leary's translation of the *Tibetan Book of the
Dead*. The song features a never-changing, drone bass note (specifically, the
pitch "C"), sitar-like sounds, electronic manipulation of Lennon's singing
voice, and numerous studio effects, including speeded up material and backwards recording. The entire effect is said to reflect the LSD trip. Even though
it was not a concept album (not having been built around a common theme
or lyrical or musical material that links songs to other songs), the entire
Revolver album was viewed by critics and musicians alike as a package filled
with strong songs—the kind of album that reflected the new emphasis on
the album as a unified work of art. *Revolver* contained obvious drug references ("Tomorrow Never Knows" and "She Said, She Said"), lyrical pop music ("Here, There, and Everywhere" and "Good Day Sunshine"), political
commentary ("Taxman"), and even what could be taken as either a drug-
related song or an innocent children's song ("Yellow Submarine"). ("Yellow
submarine" was a slang term of the time for a type of pill.) Brian Wilson of
the Beach Boys writes in several places in his autobiography of the esteem
in which he and other musicians held *Revolver* and its broad range of high-
quality songs (Wilson with Gold 1991). Wilson also indicates that he wrote

and recorded the concept album *Pet Sounds* largely as a way of trying to compete with the Beatles' new emphasis on albums reflected by *Revolver*.

Although a British band, the Rolling Stones made a tremendous impact in the United States during the counterculture period. The song "Something Happened to Me Yesterday," co-written by Rolling Stones Mick Jagger and Keith Richards, appeared on the late 1966, early 1967 album *Between the Buttons* (an album that many critics suggest was a response to the Beatles' *Revolver*). The song uses a musical vocabulary suggesting the British music hall style and traditional jazz, with Jagger singing with a bit of country "twang" in his voice, something not found that frequently in the counterculture pop music best known in the United States. In fact, the use of the British music hall–traditional jazz style in a counterculture song was highly ironic, considering that this style was used in some of the most inane pop/rock songs of the 1965–1968 era. Jagger and Richards make what might be termed "wink, wink, nudge, nudge," sly references to recreational drug usage. Those "in the know" would have been able to easily put together the hints to know that the "something" that happened to the singer-protagonist yesterday was a drug trip. In one of the more subtle "clues" a spoken voice, asks quietly, "What kind of joint is this anyway," with the key word being "joint." In context, it seems likely that the "joint" in question is not a bar or nightclub, but rather a marijuana cigarette. According to *All Music Guide* critic Matthew Greenwald, "Something Happened to Me Yesterday" is "one of the most accurate songs about LSD," focusing on "what happens after the trip and how it relates to the subjects dealing with society" (Greenwald 2002b). Still, the song resembles Bob Dylan's "Rainy Day Women #12 & 35" a bit too much, both in general musical style and in the sly use of double entendre. Many critics have commented upon the Rolling Stones' uncanny knack of almost parodying the latest album release of the Beatles throughout the second half of the 1960s (the *Sgt. Pepper's Lonely Hearts Club Band* vs. *Their Satanic Majesties Request* comparison is the most frequently mentioned example); perhaps they had Dylan's earlier song in mind when they wrote and recorded "Something Happened to Me Yesterday."

"Let's Go Get Stoned," a composition by Jo Armstead, Nickolas Ashford, and Valerie Simpson, was first recorded by rhythm and blues singers Chuck Jackson and Maxine Brown in 1966, but not issued until 1967. Ray Charles issued the song as a mid-1966 single, reaching #31 on the *Billboard* pop charts. British singer Joe Cocker also featured the song on his famous Mad Dogs and Englishmen tour of 1970.

A group mentioned in other sections of this book, the Doors have their own drug-related claim to fame. The song "Break on Through (To the Other Side)," which leads off their self-titled debut album was edited for the album. The word "high" had to be deleted from the final mix of the song in order for Elektra to release it. The use of the word in the context of the song could only have meant a drug-induced high. A later compact disc remix by the 1967 album's original engineer, Bruce Botnick, inserts the word back where it belonged. Obviously the ensuing decades had softened concerns in the entertainment industry about appearing to endorse drug use.

Robby Krieger, guitarist of the Doors, had his best-known composition, "Light My Fire," also included on the band's first album. Although the word "higher" was included on both the album and the 45-rpm single version of the song, the context is considerably more vague than had been the case with "Break on Through (To the Other Side)." To call "Light My Fire" a hit would be something of an understatement. The single, which had to have the extensive electric guitar and organ improvisations edited considerably due to the length of the original recording, held the #1 spot on the *Billboard* pop charts for three weeks. "Light My Fire," the first chart single for the Doors, was *the* smash hit of the summer of 1967. Naturally, the success of the record led to much radio airplay and many television appearances. One of the most popular of the television variety programs was Ed Sullivan's show. Back in the 1950s Sullivan featured Elvis Presley on his program, in early 1964 Sullivan had introduced American television audiences to the Beatles, and in 1967, he was still including new rock acts on his show. When the Doors were booked to perform "Light My Fire," television executives refused to allow Jim Morrison to sing the word "higher." After changing the text for the dress rehearsal, the group performed the song as originally written on the live broadcast. They were never invited back to perform on the Sullivan program.

Arguably one of the most important albums of the entire rock era, the Beatles' summer 1967 release *Sgt. Pepper's Lonely Hearts Club Band*, was scoured by fans for drug references. Most obviously, the front cover of the album featured a flourishing bed of marijuana plants. Lyrically, the most talked about apparently drug-related song on the album turned out to be "Lucy in the Sky with Diamonds." Although many people to this day suspect that the title of the song is an anagram for LSD, the song's principal writer, John Lennon, claimed to his dying day that a picture drawn by his son Julian inspired the song's title. According to the elder Lennon, Julian brought home a picture he had drawn in school one day; the younger Lennon had titled the picture "Lucy in the Sky with Diamonds" in the manner of numerous famous paintings. Although Lennon produced the picture for the media and claimed that he had no idea that the key words of the title spelled L.S.D., the song's highly impressionistic, colorful lyrics combined with the slightly otherworldly musical setting certainly suggest the hallucinogenic drug experience.

"Being for the Benefit of Mr. Kite!" joined "Lucy in the Sky with Diamonds" as one of *Sgt. Pepper's* supposedly drug-related songs. Like "Lucy in the Sky with Diamonds," it features highly impressionistic lyrics. So impressionistic, in fact, that many people assumed that Lennon (who wrote most, if not all of the song) must have been describing visions he had had under the influence of LSD or some other psychedelic drug. To nearly everyone's surprise, except Lennon, the song's lyrics were taken almost word for word from on old circus poster Lennon had obtained. The swirling organ sounds and other sound effects, some created by changing tape speed and some created by playing the original instrumental tracks backwards, support Lennon's vocal track (which itself sounds like it was treated using an electronic flanger) in a way that suggests not a nineteenth-century circus advertisement, but the drug-related interpretation of the song. Lennon was misinterpreted once again in the song "A Day in the Life." This song was banned in Great Britain because of a reference to the numerous "holes" that could be found in Blackburn, Lancashire. Authorities took the word to mean needle marks in the arms of drug addicts. Lennon claimed that he was quoting from a newspaper report he had read about the number of potholes in the roads of the town. Curiously, Paul McCartney, who contributed the middle section of the song, found his reference to having "a smoke" virtually ignored by the censors. This, despite the fact that McCartney's having a smoke is followed immediately by the beginning of a "dream." Based on McCartney's widely known, long-time use of marijuana, one might easily conclude that he was making a sly reference to the drug. If he was, he got away with it, while Lennon in his apparent lyrical innocence, did not!

The Youngbloods recorded the George Constable Remaily song "Euphoria" in 1967 for their *Earth Music* album. While the song is one of only thirteen titles registered by the songwriter with the licensing agency BMI, it has gained considerable notoriety. "Euphoria" has also appeared on more recent compact disc compilations of drug-related music. Remaily's lyrics describe the floating sensations of a drug-induced trip. Musically, the Youngbloods' recording resembles the Rolling Stones' ragtime, traditional jazz, musical hall–influenced "Something Happened to Me Yesterday." This style, which was popular among jug-band/folk musicians like the Youngbloods and the Lovin' Spoonful, seemed to be especially attractive for marijuana-related songs. The frequently political band Country Joe & the Fish included the group-composed song "Marijuana" in numerous live performances. The song, which *All Music Guide* critic Bruce Eder describes as a "counterculture singalong" (Eder 2002b), includes references to the ragtime/traditional jazz in some of the cadential formulas. "Marijuana" is decidedly minimalistic in its musical and lyrical content and reflects the decidedly less-than-serious approach many songwriters and singers take in dealing with the use of recreational drugs.

The recreational drug scene was in part tied to the rise of an alternative press around the United States in 1967. Rock music played a prominent role in this alternative press. Concert promoter Bill Graham founded his magazine *Oracle* in 1967. The most important and the most successful alternative magazine to be founded in 1967, however, was *Rolling Stone*, which remains a prominent rock-related magazine into the twenty-first century. Both *Oracle* and *Rolling Stone* focused on current rock music, and particularly that with musically heavier tendencies.

While some radical political leaders and some counterculture musicians considered the use of drugs to be a political act, other musicians took a more light-hearted approach to the 1960s drug culture. In particular, the use of marijuana was the subject of several humorous songs in the late 1960s and early 1970s. The title of Dr. Hook and the Medicine Show's "I Got Stoned and I Missed It" pretty much sums up the humorous irony of getting so stoned as not to enjoy being in an intoxicated state. Probably the most famous drug-related song in terms of humor was "Don't Bogart that Joint," recorded by such groups as Little Feat and Fraternity of Man. The Fraternity of Man's version of the song, listed as "Don't Bogart Me (aka Don't Bogart That Joint)," was included in the counterculture film *Easy Rider* and the subsequent soundtrack album. In the song the singer asks a friend not to bogart (or hog) a joint (or marijuana cigarette), and to pass it to the singer. The Fraternity of Man's recording of the song is interesting due to its slow country style, complete with pedal steel guitar. While the use of the country style in a pro-marijuana song might seem to be curious, if not oxymoronic (the anti-drug sentiments of Merle Haggard's "Okie from Muskogee" were more typical of country music), it certainly fits in with the renewal of interest in country music associated with the Back to the Land movement. Due to its inclusion in the soundtrack of *Easy Rider*, "Don't Bogart Me" or "Don't Bogart that Joint," (both titles were used somewhat interchangeably, with the "Don't Bogart Me" versions of the title probably concocted to avoid censorship) gained a great deal of exposure and notoriety. Of special note is the long pregnant pause as the singer asks his friend to roll another joint—waiting to exhale perhaps!

One artist whose entire output combines a definite tongue-in-cheek humor with a veiled background seriousness, David Peel has been active as a singer-guitarist-songwriter since the 1960s. Unlike most of the musicians mentioned in this book, Peel has truly been a musician of the people, working as a street musician and political activist in New York City for decades. In fact, as of the early twenty-first century he was still "found singing these songs in New York's Tomkins [*sic*] Square Park" (Kurutz 2002). A strong supporter of marijuana and against marijuana laws, Peel wrote and regularly performed songs such as "Have a Marijuana," "Show Me the Way to Get Stoned," "Here Comes a Cop," and "The Pope Smokes Dope," pro-marijuana songs with a healthy dose of humor. Peel recorded two albums for Elektra, *Have a Marijuana* (1968) and *American Revolution* (1970) that made considerable noise in counterculture circles. John Lennon met Peel in St. Mark's Square in New York shortly after the ex-Beatle moved to the United States (Peel 1984). John Lennon thought enough of Peel to have the street musician record an album, *The Pope Smokes Dope*, for Apple Records in 1972. In fact, it was through Lennon that Peel achieved most of his notoriety outside of New York City. Lennon's *Sometime in New York City* album of 1972 included the song "New York City," in which Lennon recounts his experiences in the radical chic world of Jerry Rubin and Abbie Hoffman. Lennon also refers to David Peel's "The Pope Smokes Dope" in the song. Jaded individuals might consider Lennon's mention of an obscure musician who just happened to have recorded for Lennon's record label to be an example of callous commercialism. Although loaded with humor, Peel's recorded performances tended to be out of tune renderings of marginal material, sadly lending some support to the views of the jaded.

Probably one of the best-known drug-related songs of the entire counterculture era, the 1967 Jimi Hendrix composition "Purple Haze" has achieved classic status. As a single, the song only reached #65 on the *Billboard* pop charts. It was featured on the optimistically titled *Smash Hits* album. The song, however, received much more radio airplay than its somewhat-meager chart "success" would ordinarily warrant. Indeed, a number of listings of the most significant American compositions of the twentieth century compiled around the start of the new millennium included "Purple Haze" alongside works like Aaron Copland's *Fanfare for the Common Man* and George Gershwin's *Rhapsody in Blue* (National Public Radio 2004). Hendrix describes the state of unreality caused by LSD, and not just through his lyrics. The instrumental tracks and the recording's mix suggest the disorientation, the out-of-one's-head-and-body nature of the psychedelic trip. Electric guitar tracks and distorted voices (Hendrix overdubbed) pan from channel to channel and mysterious, otherworldly spoken voices treated with echo complete the mix. The song refers to heavy metal (which was not even an "official" style yet), electric blues, and even a touch of raga rock. This heavy rock approach represented the best of American-style acid rock. Incidentally, "Purple Haze" was the name for a particularly potent form of LSD making the rounds at the time.

The Jimi Hendrix Experience featured "Purple Haze" on its groundbreaking debut album *Are You Experienced?* in 1967. That album, along with the Beatles' *Sgt. Pepper's Lonely Hearts Club Band* and the Doors' self-titled debut album, was among the several collections that helped to elevate the album above the level of a collection of hit songs plus filler material. *Are You Experienced?* also included "Manic Depression," "Hey Joe," "Fire," "Foxey Lady," and "The Wind Cries Mary," all songs that were important album cuts that received much airplay on progressive FM stations and continue to be included in film and television soundtracks into the twenty-first century. While the other songs on the album are not as well remembered today, *Are You Experienced?* has continued to be viewed as one of the most stunning rock albums not only of 1967, but of the entire counterculture era. And, although the drug-inspired imagery on the album can most clearly be heard in "Purple Haze," *Are You Experienced?* is filled with the screeching lead guitar, echo, phase shifting, and other studio effects, as well as impressionistic lyrics that reflected the psychedelic experience of LSD.

By late 1967, even the Monkees released a psychedelic recording: Michael Nesmith's song "Daily Nightly" was issued on the group's November 1967 album *Pisces, Aquarius, Capricorn & Jones Ltd.* The song features highly impressionistic lyrics and one of the first performances of the new Moog synthesizer in a pop recording. Although the song does not specifically mention mind-altering drugs, the rich array of disconnected, distorted images contained in it were clearly linked to the psychedelic experience, a fact made clear by the otherworldly treatment of lead singer Micky Dolenz's voice, as well as the weird space-age synthesizer licks played by Dolenz. A January 1968 episode of the group's television program featured the song bringing psychedelia into homes across America and to a significantly younger audience than much of the material descriptive of drug trips usually reached. It is also worth noting that at a June 1967 concert in London, Monkees Michael Nesmith and Micky Dolenz wore black armbands to show support for Rolling Stones Mick Jagger and Keith Richards, who had been arrested on drug charges days before.

Although not necessarily a strongly pro-drug song, the Moody Blues' "Legend of a Mind" celebrated the exploits of Dr. Timothy Leary, the former Harvard University psychology researcher and teacher who became America's principal advocate for the use of LSD in controlled situations in order to expand the taker's mind. Written by flutist-percussionist-singer Ray Thomas (who sings the lead vocal on the Moody Blues' recording of the song), the song appeared on the group's 1968 album *In Search of the Lost Chord*. Interestingly, Thomas is not particularly specific about Leary's LSD-related activities of the early and mid-1960s; he focuses more on Leary's late 1960s theories about space travel and extrasensory perception. At least that is the more literal reading of the song's text. Metaphorically, of course, the trip on the astral plane that forms the focus of the Thomas song could represent a drug-induced trip. Interestingly, Thomas deliberately mixes two meanings of the word "plane," that of a flying vehicle and that of a level. The song features mixolydian-mode melodic material. This musical scale, a major scale with a lowered seventh scale degree, is nearly identical to one of the commonly used raga, or scale-melodic patterns of Hindustani music. As I have already mentioned, Hindustani, or Indian, music had a curious tie with the use of psychedelic drugs, marijuana and LSD in particular.

After developing a strong live following on the U.S. west coast, Steppenwolf signed a contract with Dunhill Records. Within a year the group would record songs related to several aspects of the counterculture, including the hippie lifestyle, draft resistance, the biker subculture, and, naturally, drugs. Their 1968 debut album, *Steppenwolf,* contained several potent counterculture hits, including "The Pusher." This song was composed by folk musician Hoyt Axton, the son of Mae Axton, composer of the Elvis Presley hit "Heartbreak Hotel." Reportedly, Steppenwolf's lead singer John Kay heard Axton performing the song on the folk circuit and decided that "The Pusher" would benefit from the heavier rock sound his band could bring to it. The song's lyrics pronounce the damnation of the Almighty on pushers of hard addictive drugs. This was probably a result of the increased use of heroin in the late 1960s. Various sociologists have attempted to explain the move from hallucinogens and psychedelics like marijuana and LSD to addictive drugs like heroin among people in 1968 and 1969. A common theory is that the harsh realities of the Vietnam Conflict and civil unrest in the United States probably played a role. The growing disenchantment with the war among military personnel themselves could also be seen in the ever-increasing use of hard drugs, including heroin, among those serving in Indochina in the late 1960s (Neufeld 1988, 212). In any case, Axton's song favorably compares the marijuana and pill dealer to the pusher. In this sense the song is pro-drug, provided that the drugs are psychedelics. Curiously, though, *All Music Guide* reviewer Bruce Eder calls "The Pusher" "an anti-drug song turned into a six-minute *tour de force* by the band" (Eder 2002c). Steppenwolf does put together a fine performance. The otherworldly lead electric guitar portrays the lost life of the heroin addict. John Kay's vocal convincingly exhibits the anger of the lyrics. "The Pusher" reemerged in the 1969 film *Easy Rider*, a counterculture classic.

Steppenwolf's second album, the appropriately titled *Steppenwolf the Second*, featured "Magic Carpet Ride," a 1968 composition by John Kay and R. Moreve. The song was also issued as a single and reached #3 on the *Billboard* pop singles charts after an October 5, 1968 chart debut. The recording with its near-freakout instrumental work (including the use of distortion and feedback) and lyrics recounting visions somewhat outside of the realm of reality strongly suggest a trip on psychedelics. The album also included John Kay's composition "Don't Step on the Grass, Sam," which has been described as a "marijuana anthem" (Eder 2002d). The song, which begins with a rather long fade-in, suggesting an ongoing instrumental jam, finds lead singer Kay presenting and parodying the official establishment party line about marijuana: that it will lead to the ruin of the country and will lead users in the direction of hard, addictive drugs. Kay and company conclude that [Uncle] Sam has lost the fight, and that young people do not believe the lies that they have been told about marijuana. The song ends with a *musique concrète* recording of a drug bust with the users presumably flushing their stash down the toilet.

Although the LSD craze had somewhat played itself out by late 1968, the Status Quo, a British group, scored its only U.S. hit with "Pictures of Matchstick Men," a song undoubtedly inspired by the drug. Also featured on their album *Picturesque Matchstickable Messages from the Status Quo*, the single version of the song reached #12 on the *Billboard* pop charts. The lyrics deal with an impressionistic collage of visions and distorted colors, common results of LSD experiences. Wah-wah pedal, flangers, and other studio effects added to the instruments and voices add significantly to the impressionistic, psychedelic effect. Although Status Quo is something of an obscurity in the United States, "Pictures of Matchstick Men" is available on several compilation compact discs.

Another 1968 piece of psychedelia, Donovan's #5 pop hit "Hurdy Gurdy Man" features impressionistic music about what seems to be a mysterious street musician who plays the hurdy-gurdy. In this case, the hurdy-gurdy, originally a simple sort of pre-programmed organ, represents or is represented by a wild, psychedelic electric guitar. On Donovan's hit recording of the song the guitar soloist is future Led Zeppelin member Jimmy Page (Leitch 1999; Unterberger 2003b), although some sources (Sasfy 1988) give Jeff Beck (who was not even involved in the recording session) or Allan Holdsworth (who did play on the recording, but did not perform the psychedelic solo breaks) as the guitarist. Interestingly, Donovan apparently originally intended the song for Jimi Hendrix, but the guitar virtuoso was unavailable to record the song. While the lyrics do not promote psychedelic drugs—they deal more with visions that one would experience doing Transcendental Meditation under the guidance of a guru—the distorted treatment of voice and guitar, as well as the dreamlike lyrics combine to produce a record capable of enhancing a drug-induced trip, or suggesting the perceptions associated with psychedelics to the sober listener. Incidentally, Tommy James and the Shondells' 1968 #1 hit "Crimson and Clover" achieves a similar musical effect using very similar recording techniques. In his liner notes to the compact disc reissue of *Donovan's Greatest Hits*, Donovan writes, "the lyric announced that meditation had arrived in pop culture" (Leitch 1999), pointing out the curious tie between the sound and style of drug-induced psychedelia and drug-replacing Eastern philosophy and religion.

Quite possibly the most covered rock song of the late 1960s and early 1970s by amateur rock bands, Creedence Clearwater Revival's "Proud Mary" spent three weeks at #2 in the *Billboard* pop charts in early 1969. The John Fogerty composition expresses a rejection of "straight" society's emphasis on steady, well-paying jobs and supports a near-communal life on the river. The "Proud Mary" which keeps burning throughout the song was widely understood as marijuana. A similar use of the feminine name Mary to represent the drug had been used previously in the Association's hit "Along Comes Mary."

Arlo Guthrie's "Coming into Los Angeles," a 1969 song, appeared on the singer-songwriter's album *Running Down the Road*, but gained considerably more fame due to its performance by the composer at Woodstock, and its inclusion on the subsequent film and album from the festival. Guthrie tells the tale of flying into the Los Angeles airport with a couple of kilos of marijuana. He implores the immigration agent not to search his bags, lest the drugs be found. The famous Woodstock performance rocks along, and clocks in at just over two minutes, capturing the reality of late-1960s drug smuggling well in a short, tuneful composition filled with a mixture of seriousness and humor.

A song that perhaps captures the harrowing nature of the pain experienced by the drug addict better than any other, John Lennon's "Cold Turkey," made its debut at a September 1969 live performance in Toronto. The performance was captured on The Plastic Ono Band's *Live Peace in Toronto 1969* album. Interestingly, upon their return the England after the concert, John Lennon and Yoko Ono were arrested for possession of cannabis. By October 1969, "Cold Turkey" had been recorded in the studio and issued as a single. The recording reached #30 in the United States and #13 in the United Kingdom. The studio version of the song features Eric Clapton on lead guitar and Lennon on vocals. Clapton's heroin addiction has been well documented, and several writers have suggested that Lennon was experimenting with heroin at various points in 1968 and 1969. Each of the principals in "Cold Turkey," (singer-rhythm guitarist and lead guitarist) therefore, had a first-hand knowledge of the addictive drug and the pain of quitting it cold turkey. The intensity of Lennon's and Clapton's guitar playing and the way in which the electric guitars are boosted in the recording's mix, combine with Lennon's screams of terror and moans of pain to paint an ugly picture of the realities of addiction and cure. That Beatle John Lennon painted that picture came as a great surprise to many fans of the most popular rock band of the counterculture era. Fans knew of the Beatles' use of marijuana and LSD, but few probably suspected that any members of the band had experience with heroin. "Cold Turkey" is undeniably potent. Unfortunately, John Lennon cheapened the impact of the song, as well as giving ammunition to those who questioned the sincerity of his peace messages, when he returned his MBE (Member of the Order of the British Empire) award to the Queen of England "in protest against Britain's involvement in Biafra and Vietnam—and against 'Cold Turkey' slipping down the charts" (Carr and Tyler 1978, 85).

Randy Newman's 1970 song "Mama Told Me (Not to Come)" has been described as a "fear-of-partying song" (Newsom 2002) and turned out to be a huge hit for the pop/rock group Three Dog Night. Although included on the group's album *It Ain't Easy*, the song probably had its greatest impact through Three Dog Night's single. The single held the #1 position on the *Billboard* pop charts for two weeks. According to critic Matthew Greenwald, the song "says more about the rock & roll underworld of the time than any other song. Loaded with black humor, this is Randy Newman at his sarcastic best" (Greenwald 2002a). Although not nearly as well known as Three Dog Night's recording, Randy Newman issued his song on his 1970 album *Twelve Songs*.

By the time of the Rolling Stones' 1971 song "Sister Morphine," the reality of the results of abuse of hard drugs was widely known, particularly in the music industry. In this song, the singer, Mick Jagger, pleads with Sister Morphine and Cousin Cocaine to bring him relief from his pain. The singer expresses the hope that this time of doing the drug might be the last, and the harsh realization that the experience might be his last, should it end his life. Jagger uses no overt affectations to try to sell the song, allowing the text to tell the story. Well, not quite the text alone. . . . The musical setting, in particular the lead guitar fills, suggests the pain and the alienation of the protagonist of the song. "Sister Morphine" perhaps conveys the hopelessness of the junkie's plight as well as any other song of the era. The song was featured on the Rolling Stones' *Sticky Fingers* album.

Some of the more obviously drug-related songs of the counterculture era were reissued on the 1998 compact discs *Feel the Buzz: No Pain*, *Feel the Buzz: Spacin'*, and *Feel the Buzz: Hit Time*. The songs and performers on these compilations include: "Psychotic Reaction" (Count Five); "The Pusher" (Steppenwolf); "Casey Jones" (the Grateful Dead); "One Toke over the Line" (Brewer and Shipley); "Seeds and Stems Again Blues" (Commander Cody & His Lost Planet Airmen); "Dealer" (Deep Purple); "Truckin'" (Grateful Dead); "Stoned" (Orleans); "She Has Funny Cars" (the Jefferson Airplane); "Amphetamine Annie" (Canned Heat); "I Got Stoned and I Missed It" (Doctor Hook); "I Had Too Much to Dream (Last Night)" (the Electric Prunes); "Don't Step on the Grass, Sam" (Steppenwolf); "Marijuana" (Country Joe & the Fish); "Panama Red" (New Riders of the Purple Sage); "Don't Bogart that Joint" (Little Feat); and "White Rabbit" (the Jefferson Airplane). Other songs in the collections glorify alcohol.

THE HIPPIE LIFESTYLE

The hippie lifestyle of peace, turning on, tuning out, dropping out, sexual freedom, long hair, loud rock music, and communal living found its way into many songs of the counterculture era. I will deal with several of these that advocate or reflect this lifestyle to varying degrees. Some of the songs simply dismiss the commercialism and consumerism and materialism of the era's suburban lifestyle, while other songs advocate wholesale rejection of "straight" society's social norms.

Rejection of the 1950s and 1960s American suburban lifestyle did not come just from young rock musicians. Folksinger-songwriter Malvina Reynolds penned the song "Little Boxes" early in the counterculture era. Pete Seeger recorded the song live at a June 1963 concert at New York's Carnegie Hall. Seeger's record label, Columbia, released the recording as a single. Although the record reached only #70 on the *Billboard* pop charts, it incredibly represents Seeger's only solo top 100 pop single in a well-known career that spanned over six decades. Seeger included the song on his 1965 Folkways album *"Little Boxes" and Other Broadsides*. Songwriter Reynolds describes the utter sameness of life in suburbia, from the work-a-day jobs, to the cookie-cutter houses, to the stereotypical roles played by the 1950s American middle class. Perhaps it was not quite a hippie song, but "Little Boxes" and its rejection of traditional work and materialism, were closely related to the values of the later hippies.

Certainly not your typical example of the hippie lifestyle, the Monkees, that made-for-television group, appealed to young people and sounded several counterculture themes. The rejection of traditional suburban values could be seen in the frequently spotted, and vaguely communistic, "Money Is the Root of All Evil" poster hung in their television apartment. One of the Monkees' biggest hit singles, and a prominent album cut, was Gerry Goffin and Carole King's "Pleasant Valley Sunday." The song also mocks suburban middle-class values, and can be heard as a sort of "Little Boxes" for 1967. In their television roles, in fact, the Monkees seemed to be living in something of a communal setting. As struggling rock musicians, the characters certainly could not live out the middle-class lifestyle they sometimes mocked.

It is worth mentioning that Goffin and King, certainly not typical counter-culture songwriters—they came out of the New York City Brill Building, corporate songwriting scene—provided the Monkees with two other pieces that at least could be taken as being drug related. In the book *Groove Tube: Sixties Television and the Youth Rebellion*, writer Aniko Bodroghkozy described Goffin and King's "Take a Giant Step" as "a somewhat trippy invitation" (Bodroghkozy 2001, 72). Indeed, the lyrics invite the listener to step outside of his or her mind. Although the nature of this stepping is not detailed in the song, it could be taken as an endorsement of psychedelics. Goffin and King's "The Porpoise Song," featured prominently in the Monkees' film *Head*, which has achieved something approaching cult status, features a melodic, orchestrational, and lyrical style clearly aligned with the British-style acid rock of Beatles songs such as "I Am the Walrus" and "Strawberry Fields Forever." The spontaneous romps and nonlinear production techniques of the television program had great kid appeal, but also paralleled the sensory overload of the psychedelic drug experience. In fact, even LSD guru Timothy Leary discussed the psychedelic nature of the television program in his book *The Politics of Ecstasy* (1968).

The second season of *The Monkees* featured an appearance by counterculture musician extraordinaire Frank Zappa. Bodroghkozy writes, "The presence of Zappa, the very epitome of counterculture hip, seemed calculated to bestow on the Monkees a certain amount of perverse hip authenticity" (Bodroghkozy 2001, 74). Zappa also appeared briefly in the group's 1968 film *Head*, telling Monkee Davy Jones that the youth of America needs the Monkees to show them the way. Although Zappa's remarks can certainly be taken in a sarcastic light—the great irony of the scene is that Zappa's true meaning is left somewhat vague—there was an element of truth in the suggestion that this television "band" played an important middleman role in bringing the hippie lifestyle, and the counterculture in general, to the youth of America. Furthermore, the good-natured version of the counterculture the television program's producers and writers brought to the small screen every week for two seasons was palatable even to some adults. As mentioned earlier, Zappa openly mocked hippies, and (what he saw as) overly commercial musicians, like the Beatles, as well as older, conservative Americans. He pointed out hypocrisy wherever he saw it, often offending the political right and the political left.

There was also a curious tie between hippies and some of the older avant-garde and pop visual artists in the mid- and late 1960s. New York's East

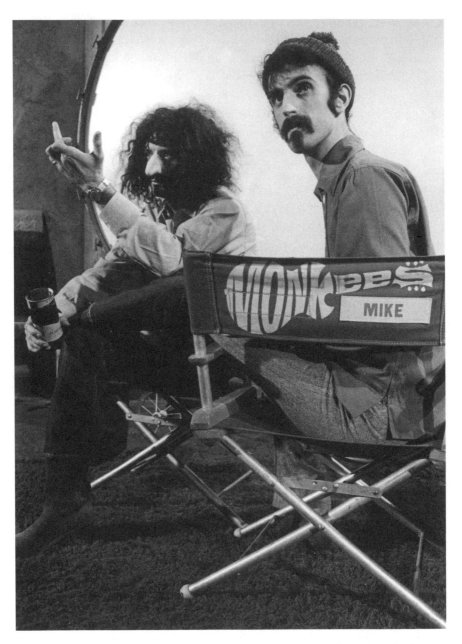

Monkee Michael Nesmith and counterculture composer-guitarist Frank Zappa trade identities on the set of *The Monkees* television program. Photography by Henry Diltz.

Village, a hotbed of activity for both camps, found artists like Claes Olden-burg, Andy Warhol, and Robert Rauschenberg staging multimedia happen-ings at galleries while rock bands did the same at the famous Fillmore East. It is also interesting to note that Warhol was associated for a time with the Velvet Underground and the "total environment" (multimedia) show "The Exploding Plastic Inevitable" (Mele 2000, 163). The Velvet Underground itself featured dark moody songs by singer-guitarist Lou Reed. Reed's songs, like "Heroin," "I'm Waiting for the Man," and "Venus in Furs," dealt frankly with life on the street, the violence of big city life, drug abuse and addiction, and sexual ambiguity, fetishes, and perversions. The instrumental work of Reed and classically trained bass, keyboard, and viola player John Cale made reference to rock and the classical experimental avant-garde styles. Although the Velvet Underground achieved little commercial success as a result of their critically acclaimed albums (*The Velvet Underground & Nico* [1967], *White Light/White Heat* [1967], and *The Velvet Underground* [1969]), the group developed an intensely loyal cult following among disenfranchised, White, urban youth. The group's audience was a relatively small, fringe sub-set of the counterculture based largely in New York City—young people who felt themselves to be outcasts from society at large and outcasts from even the prevailing youth counterculture. After the Velvet Underground dis-banded in 1973, they became increasingly more appreciated and more gen-erally popular. This difficult-to-categorize band was an important influence on 1970s and 1980s American punk rock singer-songwriter Patti Smith and well-known British singer-songwriter David Bowie.

By 1967 long hair had become established as one of the more obvious outward symbols of the counterculture hippie lifestyle. Jimi Hendrix's song "If Six Was Nine," which was included on the album *Axis: Bold as Love*, is one of the first songs, if not the first song, to refer to long hair, and the associated stylistic accoutrements of the hippies as a "freak flag." Hendrix's song, which features much panning from channel to channel in a sort of drug-inspired "freak out" electric guitar solo, clearly counterpoints the hippie lifestyle with that of conservative corporate America. The "flag" of long hair at once symbolizes defiance against "straight" society and serves as a symbol of its wearer being part of the "in" crowd to likeminded "freaks." David Crosby's "Almost Cut My Hair," recorded in 1970 by his band Crosby, Stills, Nash & Young for their #1 charting *Déjà Vu* album, even more clearly paints long hair as a symbol of the hippies' rejection of society's norms. Interest-ingly, some prominent rock critics credit Crosby with popularizing the "freak

As a member of the Byrds and Crosby, Stills, Nash & Young, David Crosby wrote and recorded several counterculture classics. Photography by Henry Diltz.

flag" metaphor, despite the fact that it had been part of the lexicon of counterculture rock songs for several years. Lindsay Planer, for example writes, "The song is also notable for first popularizing the phrase 'let[ting] my freak flag fly'—which took on new meaning in the late '80s after Crosby served a year in a Texas prison" (Planer 2003). Planer also credits David Crosby with giving "perhaps the most impassioned lead vocal of his career" on the song (Planer 2003). Set in a moderately slow, but musically heavy, way, and featuring two separate lead electric guitar parts, in "Almost Cut My Hair" Crosby deals with the paranoia he feels about police persecution, but ultimately concludes that cutting his hair would symbolize his giving into the norms of society. Clearly the lines between short-haired conservative America and long-haired counterculture America were very sharply drawn, especially at the time of the song's recording: the January 9, 1970 recording session significantly came right between perhaps the most successful experiment in the hippie lifestyle, the Woodstock festival, and what many saw as the pivotal "them versus us" battle of the counterculture era, the May 4, 1970 shootings at Kent State University.

Speaking of Woodstock, the Crosby, Stills, Nash & Young album *Déjà Vu* also featured Joni Mitchell's song "Woodstock." The song briefly chronicled the famous rock festival and pointed out the positive aspects of the event: thousands upon thousands of young people coming together in peace, living communally with each other and at one with the land—although the massive clean up required after the festival calls into question the environmental benignancy of having a half million people crowded onto a relatively small land mass without adequate sanitary facilities—in short, the song is an anthem of the success of the hippie lifestyle. The lyrics go so far as to imply that the festival approached the way life must have been in the biblical Garden of Eden. Curiously, Mitchell herself never had the kind of commercial success with "Woodstock" that others did; the Assembled Multitude took their single release of the song to #79 on the *Billboard* pop charts, Matthews' Southern Comfort took their version to #23, and the Crosby, Stills, Nash & Young version reached #11. Also highly ironic was the fact that in the *Déjà Vu* recording sessions that produced this paean to communal cooperation, CSN&Y was barely functioning as a band.

Certainly one of the most famous examples of the communal hippie lifestyle was that of the Deadheads, followers of one of San Francisco's most famous bands, the Grateful Dead. According to Robert Sardiello, who researched the unusually close ties between the Grateful Dead and their fans (Sardiello 1994, 1998, and 2000), the sense of unity between musicians and the Deadheads makes for a concert experience that "closely resembles a religious festival" (Sardiello 1994, 115). In fact, Sardiello goes on to detail the extent to which the Deadheads' following of their band became a near religion. It shaped their daily lives to an extent unseen elsewhere during the counterculture era. Interestingly, although many aspects of the counterculture faded away in the mid-1970s, the Deadhead phenomenon extended well beyond the counterculture era as we have defined it in this book. In some respects, the phenomenon may well represent the most obvious vestige of the counterculture to live into the 1980s and 1990s. This near-spiritual tie between the musicians and their audience was seen by Grateful Dead guitarist-singer Jerry Garcia as being representative of the most important legacy of the counterculture era, not the political or social movements, but a movement toward a greater spirituality (Sardiello 1994, 122). Sardiello saw the persistence of the Deadheads, well beyond the generally accepted time constraints of the counterculture era and the relatively wide range of ages among their members, as indicating that the phenomenon went beyond a mere extension of the hippie movement (Sardiello 1994, 131). Be that as it

Although she never made it to the festival, Joni Mitchell documented the August 1969 Woodstock Music and Art Fair in her song "Woodstock," a hit for Crosby, Stills, Nash & Young.
Photography by Henry Diltz.

may, the Deadhead phenomenon probably would not have been possible had
it not first been part of the hippie counterculture movement.

The freedom and the dropping out from "straight" society of the hippies
was captured especially well in the song "Born to Be Wild." Composed by
ex-Steppenwolf member Mars Bonfire, the song was recorded by Steppenwolf and issued on their first album. Dunhill Records also issued the song
as a single in summer 1968. The record spent three weeks at #2 on the
Billboard pop charts. When actors and film writers Peter Fonda and Dennis
Hopper put together their counterculture classic *Easy Rider*, the song found
its way into movie theatres. According to Dennis Hopper,

> We shot it [the movie] in five-and-a-half weeks and I came back
> with all this footage—about 40 hours of film that we were unable

to view on location. Because we couldn't see any dailies, I edited the film over a year; and during that period of time, I put music to it that I heard on the radio coming to work everyday. So basically, that's how I put the score together. "Born to Be Wild" was probably one of the first things I heard along with the "The Pusher." (Ragogna 2000)

The subsequent soundtrack album for *Easy Rider* generated further exposure for the Steppenwolf song; the album reached the top 10 in the autumn of 1969.

Janis Joplin, a White blues shouter, probably did as much as Jimi Hendrix in blurring the racial lines of music in the 1960s. She was not really a hippie, exactly, but did represent almost a complete rejection of societal norms in her own music and life. Her style of delivery can be traced back to the great Bessie Smith, and Joplin's heavy drinking, hard loving, and vague sexual orientation also hearken back to some of the other early female blues singers of the 1920s. Curiously, Janis Joplin's recorded output does not deal much with counterculture issues. Rather, her entire openly sexually promiscuous, drug-taking, heavy drinking persona and cross-racial psychedelic blues style exemplified a true and complete living outside the musical and lifestyle norms of 1960s society. She was the ultimate outcast who made it very big and died tragically young.

In many respects the high point of the hippie lifestyle and philosophy was seen at the Woodstock Music and Art Fair. The festival, easily the most famous concert event of the 1960s, was held August 15–18, 1969, on Max Yasgur's farm in White Lake, Town of Bethel, Sullivan County, New York. The festival attracted some 400,000, and featured performances by Richie Havens, Jimi Hendrix, the Who, Country Joe & the Fish, Janis Joplin, Santana, Sly and the Family Stone, and the Grateful Dead, among others. The demographics of the festival's attendees are detailed in Weiner and Stillman 1979. Basically, the crowd was 55% male, 45% female; 95% White, 1.5% Black, 1% Hispanic, 1% other race, 2% no answer; 3% upper class, 30% upper middle class, 43% middle class, 18% lower middle class, 5% lower class; 30% were from the northeast, 21% were from the south, 24% from the central United States, 25% from the west or southwest; 43% were born in 1950–1952, 40% were born in 1946–1949, and 17% were born in 1940–1945; 43% were single, 30% were married, 14% were cohabitating, 13% were divorced; and 1% had attended high school, 5% graduated high school, 31%

had some college experience, 27% were college graduates, 35% had done post-graduate college work. In short, they were young, White, and more generally well-educated than the population of the United States at large. In many respects, the successes of the hippie lifestyle were seen at the Woodstock festival. Due to a variety of external factors, including the size of the crowd, the weather, festival attendees had to put into action the idealistic, socialistic catch phrases that they had uttered for several years. They had to work and cooperate with each other and, for several days at least, live off the land. Interestingly, this communal experience was facilitated by members of the Hog Farm, one of the earliest hippie communes, and their colorful leader Wavy Gravy, an ex-stand-up comic who was born Hugh Romney.

Musically, too, the Woodstock Music and Art Fair embodied the spirit of the hippie lifestyle. Writer and Woodstock attendee Lauren Onkey saw Jimi Hendrix's second performance on the final day of the festival as representing something of an affirmation of all of the positive aspects of both the festival and the hippie lifestyle. Onkey writers, "The image of Hendrix playing the national anthem has become symbolic of the counterculture. He looked as funkily elegant as always, sporting an Afro banded by a red silken scarf, and Indian-fringed suede jacket, blue velvet bell-bottom pants, beads, and silver earrings in both ears" (Onkey 2002, 190). She continues by describing the crowd's reaction and the deep symbolism of Hendrix's performance. "The crowd was struck dumb by this bravura deconstruction of our national hymn, which managed to simultaneously evoke chauvinistic pride for and unbridled rage against the American way of life. Hendrix's 'Star-Spangled Banner' signified a proud and revolutionary voice at the end of this successful, cooperative festival" (Onkey 2002, 190).

Charles Manson's so-called "Love and Terror Cult" represented the dark side of the hippie lifestyle. I will not detail the activities of Manson and his followers in reference to the brutal August 1969 Tate and LaBianca murders, as they have been widely documented elsewhere. It is worth pointing out, however, the ironic timing of these murders: August 1969's Woodstock festival represents the high point of hippiedom, while the same month's Tate–LaBianca murders represent its low point. And, although I will not deal extensively with the murders and the subsequent bizarre court trials, I do wish to discuss some of the fascinating musical ties to Manson and his group's activities.

The most famous tie-in between music and Manson was probably that which involved Beach Boy drummer Dennis Wilson. The Beach Boys, in

Blues-rock singer Janis Joplin performs at the Woodstock Music and Art Fair, August 1969. Photography by Henry Diltz.

fact, recorded the Manson composition "Cease to Exist," retitled as "Never Learn Not to Love." The song was released on the not-so-successful album *20/20*. Brian Wilson writes in his biography *Wouldn't It Be Nice* that his brother Dennis was responsible for the group recording the Manson song. Dennis Wilson had initially been quite taken with the cult leader, and with the sexual opportunities Manson's female followers promised. Wilson actually allowed the "Family" to live in his house for a period of time. Wilson tried to distance himself from Manson between the August 1969 murders and the subsequent arrest of Manson and several of his followers. As brother Brian Wilson writes,

> One afternoon, Manson showed up at his house brandishing a pistol. Dennis was on tour and Manson left a message. Removing a bullet, he handed it to one of Dennis's friends and said, "When you see Dennis, tell him this is for him." In November 1969, Manson and a group of his disciples were arrested for the Tate–LaBianca murders. Apparently, Manson attempted to reach Dennis from the police station, calling his home. When Dennis's friend wouldn't accept the charges Manson screamed, "You're going to be fucking sorry!" Upon hearing the news, Dennis freaked and spent days piecing together all of his eerie run-ins with Manson. (Wilson 1991, 184)

Adding to Dennis Wilson's "freaking" was the speculation at the time of the arrests that actress Sharon Tate's house was chosen because the previous resident, record producer Terry Melcher, had rejected Manson's demo recordings. Indeed, every producer with whom Manson had contact would eventually receive death threats.

Before the Beach Boys recorded "Never Learn Not to Love," Manson had made the previously mentioned demo recordings. The fact that he was a singer-songwriter-guitarist had been one of the drawing points he used in recruiting followers. The demo recordings include songs that feature Manson performing alone on voice and acoustic guitar, as well as songs that incorporate members of the "Family" singing and playing a diverse group of instruments including electric guitars, percussion, and French horn. Interestingly, in spite of the conviction of Manson and several members of his group for the murders, these recordings were available for several years after 1987 on a 33⅓-rpm vinyl album from Aware One Recordings. The "company," now apparently known as Awareness Recordings, is currently operating out of a New Jersey post office box and has reissued the Manson demos on compact disc. These pre-murder recordings make for interesting study, both in terms of getting into Manson's philosophies and as examples of certain key aspects of the hippie lifestyle.

In Charles Manson's "Look at Your Game Girl" finds the singer tells a girl to avoid playing games in life; she should be free and honest. The lyrics get at the rejection of pretense that characterized the youth rebellion of the counterculture era. "Ego" laments the limitations of the ego, again advocating rejection of "straight" society's fixation on material things and social advancement. Although somewhat blunt, the lyrics of these two songs do not differ substantively from the lyrics of a plethora of other anti-establishment songs of the second half of the 1960s.

Manson's "People Say I'm No Good," "Home Is Where You're Happy," "Big Iron Door," and "Garbage Dump" also de-emphasize the ego and go even further in portraying the composer as a societal outsider, making specific references to the time he had already spent in prison. The lyrics of these songs suggest that Manson and his followers see themselves as being even outside of society to a greater extent than the hippies of the era. None of the Manson demos hint at the violence that was to come, but songs like "People Say I'm No Good" and "Garbage Dump" are eerily complete in their rejection of mainstream, White, middle-class society's norms. The *leitmotif* of de-emphasis of individual egos was also central to Manson's ability to put together a group of people willing to follow their leader's every explicit or implicit command. The songs that Manson recorded feature musical influences ranging from raga rock to a blues-ish Bo Diddley style to folk revival textures and melodic shapes reminiscent of Phil Ochs to a near-Grateful Dead style.

The Beatles also figured prominently in the Manson philosophy. Manson proclaimed the English group as great prophets and took some of the songs on the album *The Beatles*, more commonly known as "the White Album," as foretelling a great race war between Whites and Blacks. The songs "Helter Skelter" and "Blackbird" in particular, were supposed to have contained messages related to the upcoming race war. "Helter Skelter" supposedly told of the chaos the race war would cause, while "Blackbird" was supposedly an exhortation to members of the Black race to rise up against the predominantly White establishment. Of course, Paul McCartney, who was principally responsible for composing the two songs, had no such thing in mind (Miles 1997, 487–90). This would be neither the first nor the last time when Beatles lyrics would be misinterpreted; it was, however, the deadliest.

Charles Manson's communal "Family" proclaimed the hippie philosophy of peace, love, and understanding; however, they ended up completely violating this philosophy. The vast majority of communal groups of the counterculture era, however, fully embraced the philosophy and organized so that peace, love, freedom, equality, and communal sharing of resources could be fully implemented. Unlike most members of the counterculture, who remained part of mainstream society even though their values differed greatly from those of the mainstream, the organizers of hippie communes chose to set up their own societies. Naturally, music played a role in these communes. For example, in her book *Scrapbook of a Taos Hippie*, Iris Keltz tells of days spent at a well-known hippie commune in Taos, New Mexico in the late 1960s and early 1970s. Although the specifics of music's role in the commune are somewhat vague, the author makes several references to music, suggesting that music was always around. In a caption to one of the photos in her book Keltz writes, "Taos had musicians from folk guitarists to psychedelic bands to Middle Eastern to classical and everything in between" (Keltz 2000, 196). The two photographs of communal ensembles included in the book are of acoustic country bands, including banjo, guitar, dulcimer, and harmonica. In many respects the communes can be understood as a subset of the Back to the Land movement (See further discussion below, under "Back to the Land Movement"): the communes tended to emphasize good stewardship of natural resources and organic farming methods. Those who went back to the land, like the Taos hippies, tended to go back to earlier roots music. This usually meant country music and even earlier Anglo-American and Celtic-American folk song and folk dance music.

The tight links between music and the hippie lifestyle began to unravel in full public view at the end of 1969 and into 1970. The Rolling Stones' disastrous concert at California's Altamont Speedway in December 1969 was the scene of numerous drug overdoses and "bad trips." Members of the Hell's Angels motorcycle gang, who had been hired to work security, stabbed one concertgoer to death. Although the Rolling Stones had planned for Altamont to be their west coast version of Woodstock, the violence and intense drug-related problems associated with the concert ultimately made it stand in sharp contrast to the peace, love, understanding, and general cooperation of the Woodstock Music and Art Fair of a scant few months before. The

1970 Isle of Wight festival in Britain saw young people booing folk and rock musicians who had formerly been the heroes of the worldwide youth movement of the 1960s. These musicians, many of whom were millionaires, were seen as being disconnected from the audience. A very few performers were able to continue to connect completely with the hippies. It is probably not too surprising that the hippie lifestyle began to morph into something slightly different.

THE BACK TO THE LAND MOVEMENT

Today, organic foods have become if not commonplace, at least not unusual, even in mainstream supermarkets. That has not always been the case. The initial interest in organic foods came directly out of the counterculture era's Back to the Land movement. Curiously, there were strong ties between this movement and Ken Kesey's Merry Pranksters. In fact, historian David Farber credits Stewart Brand, one of Kesey's original LSD experimenters, with coordinating "an effort that produced *The Whole Earth Catalog*, a compendium of practical and theoretical information for people who wanted to set up rural communes or otherwise take part in the back-to-the-land movement" (Farber 2002, 36).

Part of the interest in forming self-sufficient, environmentally friendly communes seems to have come out of the horrors of the violent anti-war protests and the general breakdown of society in 1968. Marty Jezer, writing in his article "From City Protesters to Country Communes," points to the unexpected violence at the 1968 Democratic National Convention as providing him with the revelation that living in a commune apart from mainstream society was the only option (Jezer 2001).

The Back to the Land movement can be closely tied to the spirit of environmentalism that started to emerge early in the counterculture era and that came to a fruition with the first Earth Day in 1970. Even before the communalism of the Back to the Land movement, however, songwriters had been expressing concern with the environment. Most notably, Malvina Reynolds, probably most famous for her indictment of suburbia "Little Boxes," wrote the very poignant song "What Have They Done to the Rain." Joan Baez recorded the song in 1962 on her *Joan Baez in Concert, Part 1* album. "What Have They Done to the Rain" became a modest hit (#29 on the *Billboard* pop singles charts) for the Searchers, a British band, in 1965. The song points to things and people that have disappeared, presumably because of the poisoning of the environment. Reynolds suggests the connectedness of all of nature and of humans to nature. Although the versions of the song by Joan Baez and the Searchers are far better known, the reader might be interested to know that Malvina Reynolds's own original version recently was reissued by Smithsonian/Folkways on the five-CD set, *The Best of Broadside, 1962–1988.*

While the environmental movement eventually would become more mainstream than some aspects of the counterculture, it had its radical ties early on. Jack Weinberg, who was one of the leaders of the Berkeley Free Speech movement, became project director for the Environmental Defense Fund (Morrison and Morrison 1987, 225). Interestingly, Weinberg is the individual credited with first uttering the famous counterculture slogan, "Don't trust anyone over thirty." By the late 1960s, the environmental and Back to the Land movements would become the most generationally integrated parts of "the movement."

The Back to the Land communes featured a return to rural living, farming, and a resurgence in interest in traditional folk and country music. I mention aspects of this in my discussion of the hippie lifestyle elsewhere in this book. Even apart from the communes, there were close ties between the interest in returning to the land and renewed interest in American roots music. Joan Baez's performance of old Carter Family songs was one noteworthy outcome of this renewed interest in old, traditional country music. In fact, Baez was instrumental in introducing Mother Maybelle Carter to a new generation of listeners when she invited Carter to perform at concerts in the late 1960s. This Baez-Carter connection was especially interesting, given the apparent political gulf between the two. Baez had been intimately involved with the anti-war movement since the start of the 1960s, while Maybelle Carter's recorded commentary on the Vietnam Conflict was the 1966 Charles Dennis/Tom T. Hall song "I Told Them What You're Fighting For." The song was an answer to Hall's earlier "What We're Fighting For," a country hit for Dave Dudley. Carter plays the role of the mother of a soldier fighting in Vietnam and assures her son by letter that she will let the anti-war demonstrators know that the U.S. troops in Southeast Asia are fighting for the noble cause of American freedom. Late 1960s Back to the Land–type audiences seemed to have forgiven Carter's support for the war and Carter herself expressed pleasure at having been rediscovered by young people. Maybelle Carter's daughter Helen said, "At all these festivals the audiences were mostly young people, half-stoned out of their heads. As we made our way through the crowds, we could hear them saying, 'Look, look, it's Mother Maybelle!' and they'd make a path for her" (Zwonitzer with Hirshberg 2002, 370). The young people showed Carter a great deal of respect and genuine admiration. In addition to renewed careers for performers like Maybelle Carter and Doc Watson, some newer acts, most notably the Incredible String Band (who combined traditional Scottish and Anglo-American folk influences with Hindustani-inspired modal improvisation), The Byrds (during the period Gram Parsons was in the group), and New Riders of the Purple Sage, incorporated new takes on folk, country, and roots styles in their performances.

As the communal, living-off-the-land spirit of the Woodstock festival brought the Back to the Land movement (or at least a small, visible part of it) to the attention of the nation, so did a Woodstock performance capture the spirit of the new concern with living with the natural environment. Alan Wilson's composition "Going up the Country" had been a top-20 hit for his band, Canned Heat, debuting on the pop charts in late 1968. The song took on special significance when Canned Heat performed it at Max Yasgur's farm at Woodstock. Canned Heat boasted perhaps one of the more unusual-sounding rock styles of the era, due to singer Bob "Bear" Hite's falsetto style. Hite's unique vocal style was actually modeled on an early African-American rural blues style. The song deals with the fact that the singer is going to move away from the city and the hassles of modern life and go up to the country. By using the specific directional word "up" in reference to rural (and probably communal) life, Wilson elevates a lifestyle of simple communality with nature above the lifestyle usually elevated by "straight" American society. Wilson's lyrics contain a clear pro-environmental focus as well. He refers to the sweetness of the water out in the country, an obvious allusion to its purity. Interestingly, one of the stanzas concerning the protagonist's travels away from city life mentions that he might even leave the United States. While the text does not in any way suggest the draft resisters who left the United States of America for Canada, it does suggest that one's ultimate allegiance must be to one's self and the environment and not to nation, itself something of a counterculture suggestion.

Although several prominent pop musicians, notably the Byrds during the brief time Gram Parsons was in the band, Michael Nesmith, Rick Nelson, and the Flying Burrito Brothers (another Gram Parsons–led band), had been combining country and rock during the 1967–1969 period, probably the biggest boost to acceptance of the new country-rock style was provided by Bob Dylan. Dylan's *Nashville Skyline* album (1969) included a duet with Johnny Cash on "Girl from the North Country," a slight rewriting of an old, traditional English ballad, and the #7 hit single "Lay Lady Lay." According to a staff biographer at MTV.com,

> *Nashville Skyline* was an extraordinarily influential record. It brought a new hipness to the hopelessly out-of-fashion Nashville . . . and it heralded a new genre of music—country rock—and a new movement that coincided with, or perhaps helped to spawn, the Woodstock Festival of the same summer. A return to simplicity and a love that was in truth only a distant relation of that psyche-delically celebrated by the hippies in San Francisco a couple of years earlier, to whom Dylan paid no heed whatsoever. (MTV. com 2003)

In other words, Dylan's *Nashville Skyline* represents a move toward simple values, like those of the Back to the Land movement. The album (as well as the work of Nesmith and the Byrds) also shows that the pedal steel guitars of country music and performers/audience members with exclusively right-wing political views did not *have to* go together. This, too, was one of the great revelations of the tie between the Back to the Land movement and the newfound interest in country music.

In addition to Dylan's *Nashville Skyline*, probably one of the most obvious symbols of the new acceptance of country music by younger people was Graham Nash's song "Teach Your Children Well," which Crosby, Stills, Nash & Young featured on their #1 hit album of 1970, *Déjà Vu*. The group also released the song as a single, reaching #16 on the *Billboard* pop charts. The song is not as obvious in its celebration of the counterculture as some of the songs on the album, notably "Woodstock" and "Almost Cut My Hair." In fact, "Teach Your Children Well" supports a generational connection (be-tween members of the counterculture and their children) that seems in some ways to contradict the "find your own way" or "do your own thing" mentality of the 1960s. In addition to contributions by the rest of Nash's band mates, "Teach Your Children Well" features a prominent pedal steel guitar played by none other than Jerry Garcia of the Grateful Dead.

One of the great meetings of old-time folk and country music and rock was the Nitty Gritty Dirt Band's 1972 album *Will the Circle Be Unbroken*. The Dirt Band members, young musicians fluent in blues, rock, and country

One of the leading folk revival/protest singer–songwriters of the early counterculture era, Bob Dylan later embraced both rock and roll and country music. Photography by Henry Diltz.

styles, recorded the album with older guest artists such as Maybelle Carter, Doc Watson, Roy Acuff, and Earl Scruggs. In addition to his appearance on *Will the Circle Be Unbroken*, blind guitarist, singer, and banjoist Doc Watson was another favorite of the Back to the Land–related folk music festivals of the late 1960s and early 1970s. In fact, based largely on the new exposure he received from his performance on the Nitty Gritty Dirt Band album and at these festivals, Watson became more popular in the 1970s than he had been in the 1940s and 1950s during the height of his career as a roots-based musician.

The Grateful Dead represent both a tie to Ken Kesey's Merry Pranksters and the newfound fascination with country and traditional folk music of the communal Back to the Land types of the late 1960s and 1970s. The band had been the house band for the Merry Pranksters' acid tests. Unlike many psychedelic bands of the era, the Grateful Dead fully embraced many of the instrumental stylings of country music by the late 1960s. For example, as previously mentioned, Dead guitarist Jerry Garcia contributed the prominent pedal steel guitar part to Crosby, Stills, Nash & Young's 1970 hit song "Teach Your Children," and Garcia's guitar playing on several Grateful Dead songs, perhaps most notably "Cosmic Charlie," strongly hints at country blues. Of course, the communal, living-off-the-land (at least temporarily) nature of the band's fervent followers is famous. The Deadheads would continue to follow the band well after the counterculture era had "officially" ended and carried at least part of the spirit of the era into the 1980s and 1990s.

Motown singer-songwriter Marvin Gaye also made a valuable contribution to the environmental part of the movement in the form of his song "Mercy Mercy Me (The Ecology)." The song was one of many socially conscious works on Gaye's 1971 concept album *What's Going On*. "Mercy Mercy Me" was also issued as a single and reached #4 on the *Billboard* pop charts and #1 on the rhythm and blues charts. In the song Gaye deals with environmental degradation and society's failure to take on the issue.

There were certainly other, less obvious ties between the Back to the Land/environmental/communal movements and music. A 1972 issue of *Natural Life Styles* magazine that I own (vol. 2, no. 1) contains articles on natural child birth, communes of Japan, recipes for organic/vegetarian dishes, an anti–food additive article, advertisements aimed at followers of psychic Edgar Cayce, a brief article on the different types of yoga, suggestions for taking effective political action to ensure healthier organic food, and even a brief article on how to make a guitar sound like a sitar. While music does not hold a special position in this magazine, the presence of the guitar-modification article alongside everything else presumably of interest to the Back to the Land adherents to which the magazine was aimed, shows that music was just a normal, everyday part of communal life.

THE COUNTERCULTURE RELIGIOUS EXPERIENCE

As young people of the counterculture era tried to find meaning in life, many turned to religion. Mainstream Judeo-Christian traditions, however, were not where they looked for their spiritual awakenings. The counterculture era saw young people turning to non-mainstream Christianity, Hinduism, the Unification Church, Transcendental Meditation, various gurus, the occult, Scientology, Native American traditions, and others. Kent 2001 includes extensive study of the appeal of many of these within the counterculture. According to Kent and others, many of the young people who turned to these religious movements did so out of the sense of meaninglessness they felt with the violence of the anti-war movement. The riots of 1968 and, most especially, the Kent State University shootings of 1970 caused the disillusioned to seek peace from a higher power. The growing realization of the destructive potential of drug abuse, which came with a dramatic increase in the use of hard drugs such as heroin in 1968–1970, also fed into the growth of counterculture religious movements. Politics might fail, drugs might fail, so many turned to the spiritual realm. And why the turning away from mainstream Christian denominations? In part, the answer may lie in the conservative stance taken by the various Protestant denominations in response to the Vietnam Conflict. Although the Pope had taken a strong stance against war, some U.S. Roman Catholic leaders either officially or tacitly sanctioned the war effort. Of course, these contradictions were not ignored by the counterculture. As discussed earlier, they form the entire rhetorical argument behind a song like "Sky Pilot." Other songwriters took war-sanctioning religious leaders to task. For example, Tom Paxton's song "The Cardinal" takes on Cardinal Spellman, and Shurli Grant's "Are You Bombing with Me, Jesus?" points out the hypocrisy that ran throughout much of mainline Christianity of the time. Generally, religious messages have not been delivered in very much of the pop music of the twentieth century, the occasional Christmas song or Christian-oriented hymn notwithstanding. The counterculture era, however, found new music espousing several of the non-mainstream

religions and philosophies. Some of the songs would make significant impact on the pop charts.

I have mentioned the somewhat tenuous ties between the beatniks of the
1950s and the hippies of the 1960s elsewhere. In the area of religion, too,
there was some slight connection between the young people of the two eras
who tended to operate somewhat outside of traditional society. In particular,
several of the Beat poets, Allen Ginsberg and Jack Kerouac among them,
had expressed a fascination (if not a strong connection in the case of Ginsberg) with Eastern philosophy and religion. Zen Buddhism and Hinduism
would emerge in the mid-1960s as important counterculture religions.

A growing interest in things Indian, if not in things specifically Hindu,
could be seen in some rock music as early as 1965. In fact, it was on the
set of the 1965 Beatles film *Help*, that George Harrison first encountered
the sitar. Harrison's interest in this stringed Indian instrument would eventually lead him to study music with the famed Indian musician Ravi Shankar
and would also lead to Harrison's devotion to Hinduism through the Hare
Krishna movement. The Beatles met with Maharishi Mahesh Yogi in 1967,
with Paul McCartney and Ringo Starr eventually spending approximately six
weeks, and Harrison and John Lennon spending nearly three months with
the holy man in the winter and spring of 1968. Although Lennon would
write off the Maharishi as a charlatan in his song "Sexy Sadie," which was
included on the group's so-called "White Album" (released in November
1968), George Harrison remained devoted to the Krishna Consciousness
movement, eventually following several different gurus. He and Paul Mc-
Cartney produced recordings for several Hindu-related musical ensembles.
Harrison's religious thoughts showed up in many of the songs he composed
following the 1970 breakup of the Beatles. Although numerous critics would
complain that Harrison tended to preach a message that his audience was
not prepared to hear, let alone follow in any strict way, he remained true to
his beliefs as a songwriter. Probably the most important connection between
Harrison's religion and music, however, was his massive Concert for Bangla
Desh. This August 1, 1971 superstar event featured Harrison, Ravi Shankar,
Billy Preston, Leon Russell, Bob Dylan, Badfinger, Ringo Starr, and a host
of other important rock figures. Although it took many years and much legal
wrangling to get funds from the concert and the subsequent album to the
United Nations' relief fund for the Bangla Desh refugees, Harrison's event
became a prototype for other charitable rock concerts of the next three decades.

Incidentally, there were two other Beatles-related incidents with religious implications that made headlines around the world in the 1960s. In 1966, John Lennon was interviewed for London's *Evening Standard*. In the interview he discussed, among other things, his feelings that organized religion, and traditional Christianity in particular, were in serious danger of becoming completely irrelevant for young people. American fundamentalist Christians took Lennon's comment that "the Beatles are more popular than Jesus now" out of context, inferring that Lennon felt that the Beatles were more important than Jesus of Nazareth. Beatles records were burned in several U.S. cities and were boycotted for a short time, and the band members, who would shortly perform a concert tour of the United States, feared for their safety when they appeared in the Bible Belt. Lennon was forced to appear in a press conference and explain that he only meant to bemoan the lack of spirituality in mainstream religion of the day.

The second Beatles-related counterculture religious reference may seem to be somewhat obscure, but it does make for interesting consideration of just how important pop stars of the day were to their audiences. In October 1969 a rumor floated around the United States that Paul McCartney was dead. What apparently started out as a joke in a university newspaper swept the country. Beatles records were scoured for clues that supposedly could be found indicating the musician's demise. Andru J. Reeve has authored a very good history and sociological study of the short-lived "Paul is dead" phenomenon, *Turn Me On, Dead Man: The Complete Story of the Paul McCartney Death Hoax* (1994). Reeve and others attribute part of the reason behind the extremely quick way in which this rumor spread and the way in which huge numbers of Beatles fans sought hidden meanings in song lyrics, by playing songs backwards, and through study of "clues" found in photographs on album covers, to a near religion that had developed around the group.

The Hare Krishna movement and Transcendental Meditation found other devotees among popular musicians in the mid-1960s. Among the more outspoken devotees was Michael Love of the Beach Boys. Other rock musicians found other Indian gurus to lead them on their spiritual journeys, with Pete Townshend, guitarist-composer extraordinaire of the Who, becoming a follower of Meher Baba.

Even the outward symbols of the Hindu religion became widespread enough in 1967 that they were also used somewhat superficially, to create a "hip" visual effect. Perhaps the best example of the use of faux-Hindu symbology for the sake of art is the cover of the Jimi Hendrix Experience's *Axis:*

Bold as Love album. The Indian style of the album's gatefold cover has nothing to do with the music. That Krishna Consciousness and Transcendental Meditation were becoming more widespread and noticed by the general public in the late 1960s is evidenced by the famous "Hare Krishna Mantra" chanted in the 1968 musical *Hair*.

The chanting of the Hare Krishna mantra at anti-war rallies became increasingly commonplace by the late 1960s. Beat poet Allen Ginsberg often led chanting at the anti-war events he attended. This use of music in political protest was especially interesting since many of the Hindu and Krishna Consciousness leaders, as well as many of the other leaders of counterculture religions were decidedly conservative in their political philosophies.

To some, however, Jesus of Nazareth was seen as the ultimate counterculture, hippie-type figure of all time. Well before the emergence of hippiedom, of course, painters had depicted the Christ with long hair and a beard. Many young people who would become known as "Jesus Freaks" noted that the resemblance, however, went well beyond visual appearances. They noted that Jesus, like hippies, rejected materialism (the sincerity of the hippies in doing so would be hotly questioned in such anti-counterculture songs as "The Ballad of Two Brothers"), lived a communal lifestyle, preached love as opposed to hatred and war, and in doing these things was rejected by the political establishment of his day.

Several Jesus-centered movements arose right around 1970 and coincided with several Jesus-related songs making the charts. The first of these was Lawrence Reynolds's pop-country recording of "Jesus Is a Soul Man," which hit #28 on the *Billboard* pop charts in the autumn of 1969. Gospel composer Arthur Reynolds's "Jesus Is Just Alright," the last chart single for the Byrds, was issued as a single in early 1970. The recording made it only to #97 on the *Billboard* pop charts, but was also featured on the band's album *Ballad of Easy Rider*. The Doobie Brothers covered "Jesus Is Just Alright" in late 1972 and took the song to #35 on the charts, also including it on their album *Toulouse Street*. At the same time as the Doobie Brothers found their recording on the charts, Kris Kristofferson took his composition "Jesus Was a Capricorn" to #91 on the pop charts.

But we must go back to the period between the two previously mentioned recordings of "Jesus Is Just Alright" for the best-known example of Jesus-as-counterculture-hero in music, the rock opera *Jesus Christ Superstar*. Written by composer Andrew Lloyd Webber and lyricist Tim Rice, this groundbreaking musical first appeared in album form. Of the album, music critic William Ruhlmann writes that it "succeeds in all ways" (Ruhlmann 2002). Ruhlmann and other critics credit Lloyd Webber and Rice with penning the first true rock opera, and with breaking the established show business precedent of not dealing with religious subjects in potentially controversial ways. The show later had a highly successful run in London and on Broadway. Due to the use of contemporary popular music in the show, *Jesus Christ Superstar* made a significant impact on pop charts, in jukebox play, and on the radio airwaves. The opera's title song reached #74 in early 1970 for Murray Head. When the record was reissued in January 1971, it went to #14, and remained in the *Billboard* Hot 100 for twenty-four weeks. Another song from the show, "I Don't Know How to Love Him," reached #13 on the *Billboard* pop charts for Helen Reddy and #28 for Yvonne Elliman, both in early 1971.

The counterculture significance of *Jesus Christ Superstar* lies in the way in which Jesus is portrayed as an almost hippie-like, communal holy man at odds with the "straight" society of his day and in the rock music of the score. Perhaps it is really the combination of the historical Jesus and his rejection by society with the driving music of the score that helped Jesus to be seen as a very real hero figure to the disenfranchised youth of the early 1970s. Interestingly, the Jesus-as-counterculture-hero motif had earlier been hinted at in the musical *Hair*. In fact, the song "Hair" mentions Jesus's appearance and contrasts *his* mother's reaction to his hair with the reaction of the mother of the character singing the song in the show.

Some of the popular counterculture musicians of the era also had a curious sort of religious aura surrounding them. Most notable was Jim Morrison, singer and one of the songwriters of the Doors. Morrison, in his presentation and in his lyrics, often played the role of a shaman in a pseudo–Native American-inspired manner. He made frequent references to Native Americans and to animals that some Native Americans, and others, thought to have special religious significance, lizards in particular. In fact, the singer characterized himself as the Lizard King. Morrison's persona became well known to the extent that he was often characterized as a sort of "dark shaman" by press and music fans alike. The shaman-like aspects of Morrison's "act," primarily a near-fixation on death and sex, are detailed to great effect by Jerry Hopkins and Daniel Sugerman in their book *No One Here Gets Out Alive* (Hopkins and Sugerman 1980). The Doors' 1968 album *Waiting for the Sun* makes for especially valuable study for those interested in Jim Morrison's dark shaman persona, as the liner notes include the text of his poem

"The Celebration of the Lizard," only part of which is set to music on the album. Pseudo-religious images abound not only in "The Celebration of the Lizard," but in many other Morrison poems as well.

SEXUAL FREEDOM

John Sinclair, leader of the radical White Panthers and manager of the pro-totypical punk rock band the MC5, was quoted as saying, "There are three essential human activities of the greatest importance to all persons, and that people are . . . healthy in proportion to their involvement in these activities: rock and roll, dope, and fucking in the streets" (Heinemann 2001, 191). Although the context for Sinclair's statement was highly politically charged in nature, sexual freedom certainly was one undeniable component of the counterculture era. It would be difficult to list every reference to premarital sex or sexual experimentation in songs of the counterculture era, because, for one thing, there were so many at least partially veiled references. The fact that taboo sexual practices were "coming out of the closet" during the 1960s is probably best illustrated by the song "Sodomy," from the musical *Hair*.

Although there were many, many references to free love and casual sex in songs of the counterculture era, let us take a look at just a few which represent a variety of styles. First, let us consider an undeniably "pop" song, Gerry Goffin and Carole King's "Star Collector," recorded by the Monkees in 1967. This was one of the first pop songs to deal with the life of groupies: female hangers-on who would willingly provide sex to male rock stars. Sung by David Jones, who was *the* major teen idol of the year, the song describes a groupie who can easily be used and then discarded. Although the reader will see several references to the Monkees as counterculture figures through-out this book, "Star Collector" stands as a most unusual song, insomuch as it admits to the groupie phenomenon and suggests the near disdain in which the character singing the song holds the groupie, that is, after he has allowed her to provide him satisfaction. It would be years before the subject of sex with groupies would be tackled with the same degree of head-on bluntness, when the Rolling Stones recorded their controversial song "Star Star."

The Rolling Stones' song "Let's Spend the Night Together" makes for interesting study, especially since at the time of this writing it is being used by a major hotel chain in its television advertising campaign. The song appeared as both the B-side of the #1 hit 1967 single "Ruby Tuesday" and on the album *Between the Buttons*. Incidentally, the song itself made it to #55 on the singles charts even though customarily B-sides did not generate much sales interest. Written by Mick Jagger and Keith Richards, and sung by Jagger, the song is about a young man practically begging and pleading with a young woman to spend the night with him so that they each might find sexual satisfaction. Clearly, the couple is not married. This kind of invitation to premarital sex aroused considerable controversy among the older generation, as one might imagine. In fact, the Rolling Stones were asked to change the words of the song when they were to perform it on the *Ed Sullivan Show*. They did so, changing the title line to "Let's Spend Some Time Together." Curiously, Jagger's nearly lewd mugging each time he sings the line was probably an even more vivid portrayal of the young man's intentions than the words themselves!

The Kinks' "Lola" was one of the great pop songs of the counterculture era that questioned gender roles, questioned sexual orientation, and dealt with the issue of transvestitism. In the song, lead singer and composer Ray Davies seems to have met the girl of his dreams, only to discover in a case of mistaken identity that she is actually a he. He then has to decide if he will stay with his newfound love, despite the fact that "she" is not exactly what or who she seems to be. The Kinks' 1970 recording of "Lola" made it into the *Billboard* pop top 10 in the United States and is still heard on oldies stations into the twenty-first century. Aside from its commercial appeal, part of the significance of "Lola" is that the song seems to infer that the moral standards of society with regards to sex can be, and possibly should be, shrugged off based solely on what a particular individual wants to do.

Two songs that were banned from radio airplay in many markets and had sales banned in some markets were Yoko Ono's "Open Your Box" and "Touch Me." "Touch Me," which should not be confused with the Doors' song of the same title, was issued as the B-side of John Lennon and the Plastic Ono Band's "Power to the People" in the United States, while "Open Your Box" backed up the same Lennon song in overseas release. These songs were widely interpreted as endorsing casual sex for the sake of pleasure. It is interesting to note that some 1971 and even pre-1971 songs by male artists were probably just as sexually suggestive; however, they were not banned. (The Beatles' own 1969 song "Come Together," which includes moans of apparent sexual ecstasy during the fadeout, was taken by many listeners as a sly reference to simultaneous orgasm—the song enjoyed extensive airplay and the single release reached #1 on the Billboard pop charts.) It seemed that part of the furor over Ono's material was because she was a woman. Official society during the 1960s and 1970s frowned more strongly on women overtly expressing sexual desire in music than on men's expressions of the same. Later in the decade, some of the overtly sexual recordings of the disco divas (Donna Summer's "Love to Love You Baby," for example) would also cause outrage among parents.

A musician whose very way of life touched many aspects of the counter-culture, Jim Morrison, also deserves mention here. I have already mentioned Morrison's near fixation with death and sex in his lyrics. Some of his songs, "The End" most notably, contain references to taboo subjects ("The End" deals very explicitly with the kill-the-father, rape-the-mother story of Oedipus put into a 1967 context). He made headlines across the nation when he was accused of exposing himself in public—at a concert, no less. Although Morrison was convicted of the crime, many who were present, including Doors keyboardist Ray Manzarek, maintain that Morrison was not guilty. In his biography *Light My Fire: My Life with the Doors*, Manzarek (1998) describes his band mate making suggestive statements and asking suggestive questions of the audience, building their anticipation to the point where some audience members thought Morrison exposed his penis. Such was the sexual-shamanic power of this rock musician over his audience.

I have dealt with the connections between disco and the emergence of the gay pride movement earlier in this book. Certainly disco contained plenty of overt reference to sex and the ecstasy of orgasm, whether male or female, and whether homosexual or heterosexual. For example, Donna Summer emerged with the 1974 album *Lady of the Night* (a suggestive enough title) and the 1975 song "Love to Love You Baby" which featured graphic moans of sexual satisfaction, for nearly seventeen minutes, no less. Likewise, several disco performers, like the Village People and Sylvester, were openly gay and celebrated their sexual orientation and free and open sexual activity.

7

An A–Z of Music and the Counterculture Era

Altamont

On December 6, 1969, the Rolling Stones performed a free concert at California's Altamont Speedway. This concert was meant to conclude their tour of North America and looked to be a northern California–Rolling Stones version of the Woodstock festival of only a few months before. Unfortunately, the Hell's Angels motorcycle gang was hired to work security and ended up killing one concertgoer and injuring others. The concert was the site of numerous drug overdoses and "bad trips." If Woodstock represented the height of the hippie lifestyle in action, then Altamont can be said to represent the low point.

American Indian Movement

Unlike many of the constituent parts of the 1960–1975 counterculture, the American Indian Movement (AIM) truly was an organization. The group staged demonstrations, including the 1973 occupation of Wounded Knee, South Dakota, in which some 300 members of the AIM took eleven hostages. The organization also worked within the U.S. legal system for Native American rights and for restitution for the wrongs that had been done for years to indigenous peoples.

Are You Experienced?

After working as a studio guitarist and touring with several soul and R&B acts in the early 1960s, Jimi Hendrix set off for England. Chas Chandler, former bass guitarist with the Animals, "discovered" Hendrix in London and organized a band for the American guitarist. The Jimi Hendrix Experience's 1967 album *Are You Experienced?* introduced the trio (Hendrix on guitar and vocals; Noel Redding on bass, electric guitar, and background vocals; and Mitch Mitchell on drums and background vocals) to America. The album took counterculture America by storm and is described by rock critic Richie Unterberger as, "One of the most stunning debuts in rock history, and one of the definitive albums of the psychedelic era" (Unterberger 2003a). Listeners were greatly impressed by the guitar virtuosity of Hendrix, the otherworldly studio effects, impressionistic drug-oriented lyrics, and the unique musical style of Hendrix's compositions and arrangements, a style that combined rock, blues, soul, and pop in a way that sounded unlike that of any other musician of the era. The most notable tracks on *Are You Experienced?* are "Purple Haze," "Hey Joe," "Manic Depression," "Fire," "The Wind Cries Mary," and "Foxey Lady," all songs that enjoyed a strong presence on progressive FM radio stations during the late 1960s and songs that still find themselves in television and movie soundtracks, as well as on oldies radio stations today. The album has been reissued on compact disc in a collection that includes the ten songs on the original U.S. release, plus seven other songs (including "Are You Experienced?" and "Red House") that were included only on the original United Kingdom release of the album.

Baba, Meher

Born Merwan Sheriar Irani on February 25, 1894, in Poona, India, Meher Baba (as he became known to his followers) was one of the great Indian spiritual leaders of the twentieth century. He was the spiritual advisor to Mahatma Gandhi in the 1930s and became the spiritual advisor to several Western musicians in the 1960s. The most famous of these was guitarist Pete Townshend of the Who. Meher Baba created some controversy among members of the counterculture when he vocally opposed the use of LSD and other drugs that young people were using at the time in their quest for spirituality. He died in 1969.

Baez, Joan

Born January 9, 1941, in Staten Island, New York, Joan Baez became one of the most visible musical figures of the folk revival. Baez appeared frequently at anti-war rallies throughout the counterculture era, usually singing old folk songs and the songs of her contemporaries like Phil Ochs and (mostly) Bob Dylan. While other musicians may have composed the greatest anthems of the anti-war movement, Baez was highly influential in getting the music out to a wider public and in rallying like-minded protesters. Baez also encouraged older traditional country and folk musicians like Maybelle Carter and Doc Watson to perform at concerts aimed at young people. In doing so, she was in part responsible for some of the newfound popularity of these forms with new audiences, many closely aligned with the Back to the Land movement.

Beatles, The

Arguably the greatest recording act of the 1960s, the Beatles (John Lennon, rhythm guitar and vocals; Paul McCartney, bass guitar and vocals; George Harrison, lead guitar and vocals; and Ringo Starr, drums and occasional vocals) figured prominently in the lives of many members of the counterculture. Although the vast majority of their songs, most of which were composed by Lennon and McCartney, were not overtly political in nature, the group, with their long hair, flippant humor, and highly amplified music was seen as a serious threat to traditional conservative American values.

Bowie, David

Born David Jones on January 8, 1947, David Bowie became a major pop music fixture beginning in 1969. He changed his name to Bowie in 1966 so as to avoid confusion with the popular David (Davy) Jones of the Monkees. Bowie created a stage persona and composing style that combined high technology and space-age themes, sexual ambiguity (and an avowed bisexual orientation), and a fascination with the societal outsider. Although some writers have questioned the authenticity of Bowie's avowed bisexuality, supposing it to be merely one of the singer-songwriter-guitarist-saxophonist's many "masks," calculated to sell records, Bowie can be credited with taking bisexuality out of the closet, as it were, in the early 1970s. At least one of his better-known songs, "John, I'm Only Dancing," deals with the complexity of maintaining an active bisexual lifestyle.

Broadside

Back in the time of the great British playwright and poet William Shakespeare, political statements printed on large pieces of paper were known as broadsides. During the counterculture era, leftist political songs, largely of the folk revival style, were distributed around the United States by the magazine *Broadside*. The magazine's title and its purpose were tribute to the old English broadside tradition. Leading protest singer–songwriters of the early 1960s, including Bob Dylan, Pete Seeger, Phil Ochs, Joan Baez, Malvina

Reynolds, Tom Paxton, and numerous others had their song texts and sheet music versions of their songs published in this highly influential magazine.

Byrds, The

Formed in 1964, the Byrds originally consisted of David Crosby, Gene Clark, Chris Hillman, Mike Clarke, and Jim (aka Roger) McGuinn. Their early folk-rock style was defined by vocal harmonies similar to those of the Beatles, generally fuelled by McGuinn's twelve-string electric guitar. Their recording of Pete Seeger's "Turn! Turn! Turn! (To Everything There Is a Season)" was a #1 pop hit single and brought the music of Seeger to a much wider audience. Their songs "Eight Miles High" and "5D (Fifth Dimension)" both contain psychedelic drug references. Another of their songs, "Draft Morning," deals with the feelings of a young man on the morning he is to report to his local draft board for service in Vietnam. The Byrds, and most notably McGuinn, were involved in the soundtrack for the counterculture film classic *Easy Rider*.

Carter Family, The

Back in the late 1920s, Alvin Pleasant Carter, his wife Sarah, and his sister-in-law Maybelle Carter were among the first and biggest stars of country music. Maybelle's guitar style was highly influential on later country music and some of the songs composed by Alvin continued to be recorded by other artists into the 1970s and beyond. After the original group broke up, Maybelle continued on with her daughters. One of the daughters, June Carter, later became a popular country artist and married fellow country singer Johnny Cash. Maybelle herself saw a resurgence of her career in the late 1960s when, spurred on by the Back to the Land movement, young people renewed an interest in traditional folk-related country styles. Interestingly, Maybelle, the darling of the communal hippies of the late 1960s, recorded a song in support of the United States' involvement in the Vietnam Conflict, "I Told Them What You're Fighting For."

Cleaver, Eldridge

Born in Wabbaseka, Arkansas in 1935, Leroy Eldridge Cleaver became an important figure in radical Black politics in the mid-1960s. Cleaver spent much of the period 1954–1966 in prison for various crimes, including rape. Although he wrote for *Ramparts* magazine from 1966, he is best known for his 1968 book *Soul on Ice*. This manifesto of the Black Panthers has been widely reprinted and remains one of the best documents of one man's experience growing up Black in America in the 1940s and 1950s and ending his life as part of the prison system. Cleaver fled the United States after some members of the Black Panthers were involved in a shoot-out with Oakland, California police. He later broke with the Black Panthers and eventually returned to the United States in 1975. Cleaver died in 1998.

Coleman, Ornette

Born in Fort Worth, Texas in 1930, Coleman was a leading avant-garde jazz saxophonist of the 1960s. His influential albums *The Shape of Jazz to Come* (1959) and *Free Jazz* (1960) have been hailed as musical symbols of the growing Black consciousness of the counterculture era. Coleman's free approach to jazz, in intonation, form, and melody, can be tied to the age-old African-American struggle for freedom in American society at large. Interestingly, Ken Kesey and his entourage, the Merry Pranksters, who were early experimenters with the drug LSD, were fans of Ornette Coleman's improvisatory music.

Concept Album

Until 1966, 45-rpm single records ruled the record industry, especially in pop music. Albums often were not much more than a collection of single hits, plus their "B-sides," plus what was sometimes little more than filler material. In 1966 and 1967, some rock musicians shifted their focus toward albums as wholly integrated works of art. Common themes might be found in several or even all the songs on an album and musical motifs or melodic phrases might tie one song to another. Smooth transitions from song to song might obscure the borders of the individual songs in order to make the entire album stand as a work of art. In addition, a album's cover art might further enhance the message or mood that tied the package together. The Beach Boys' *Pet Sounds* (almost entirely the work of Brian Wilson with Los Angeles studio musicians), Pink Floyd's *Piper at the Gates of Dawn*, and the Beatles' *Sgt. Pepper's Lonely Hearts Club Band* are three of the earliest concept albums of the counterculture era and all date from this 1966–1967 period. It is interesting to note that the rock opera *Jesus Christ Superstar* actually started out as a concept album; only later did it become a full theatrical work. Concept albums became important means by which musicians of the counterculture era could deliver a unified political, lifestyle, or other message to their audience.

Country Joe & the Fish

Joe McDonald, born in El Monte, California, January 1, 1942, led one of the most important political bands of the second half of the 1960s. McDonald's

"I-Feel-Like-I'm-Fixin'-to-Die Rag" remained a potent anti-war song from 1965 through the Woodstock era. The song, and many other songs by McDonald and company, featured biting, dark humor.

Creedence Clearwater Revival

Consisting of singer-songwriter-lead guitarist John C. Fogerty, rhythm guitarist Tom Fogerty, bass guitarist Stu Cook, and drummer Doug Clifford, Creedence Clearwater Revival possibly was the most commercially successful rock band in the world between early 1969 and mid-1971. Their straight-ahead, blues, Louisiana swamp, and soul-influenced rock and roll included several important counterculture songs, such as the anti-war songs "Run through the Jungle," "Who'll Stop the Rain," and "Fortunate Son." Their best-known recording, "Proud Mary," was understood as a rejection of "straight" society's emphasis on high-paying jobs and in support of the freedom of the hippie lifestyle and recreational use of marijuana.

Crosby, Stills, Nash & Young

Originally formed as Crosby, Stills & Nash in 1968, CSN&Y was one of the first true super groups. Each member of the group was an established rock star: David Crosby had been a member of the Byrds, Stephen Stills and Neil Young had been with Buffalo Springfield, and Graham Nash had been a member of the Hollies. The group recorded several counterculture classics, including Joni Mitchell's composition "Woodstock," Crosby's "Almost Cut My Hair," and Young's "Ohio."

Davis, Angela

Born January 26, 1944 in Birmingham, Alabama, Angela Davis became one of the most famous symbols of the Black struggle for equal rights in the early 1970s. Davis's parents had educated her as a young girl about the struggle of American Blacks in the segregated south. Because of her acceptance into an innovative program that enabled southern Black high school students to attend school in the north, she attended Elizabeth Irwin High School in Brooklyn, living with a host White family for a time. During this period Davis became increasingly interested in socialism and communism. After studies at Brandeis University and in Europe, Davis became involved with the Student Non-Violent Coordinating Committee and the Black Panther Party in the late 1960s. After travel to Cuba to study communism firsthand, Davis, by then working on her Ph.D., became Assistant Professor of Philosophy at the University of California, Los Angeles (UCLA). With the nationally publicized denial of the renewal of her appointment at UCLA in

1970, Davis began helping who she saw as victims of the racist American political system in earnest. During the trial of George Jackson, a prisoner who had apparently been wrongly convicted earlier, an uprising took place, leaving four people dead in the courtroom. Davis was accused of plotting the failed escape attempt of Jackson and the other Soledad Prison inmates. She went underground in New York City's Greenwich Village. She was apprehended and tried. An all-White jury found her innocent on the conspiracy charges. Since that time she has been on the faculty of several universities, has authored essays and books, and ran for Vice President of the United States twice on the Communist Party ticket. During the time of Davis's disappearance, arrest, and trial in 1970 and 1971, hers was a *cause célèbre* among radical leftist politicos, including John Lennon and Yoko Ono, who in their song "Angela" expressed the viewpoint that Davis's tribulations were based entirely on racism and official government suppression of leftist ideas.

Deadheads

The fans and followers of the Grateful Dead. An entire subculture emerged in the 1960s of fans who would follow the band from gig to gig, sometimes literally around the world. Many of the Deadheads knew each other, and they lived in a communal atmosphere with its own unique social hierarchy. The near-religious nature of this phenomenon has been intensely studied by sociologists. *Deadhead Social Science* (Adams and Sardiello 2000), presents several fascinating articles about this subculture of the counterculture.

Déjà Vu

This 1970 album by Crosby, Stills, Nash & Young was one of the most anticipated album releases up to that time. The group spent hundreds of hours in the studio, even though studio tricks and special effects are noticeably absent on *Déjà Vu*. The album included several important counterculture-related contributions, including a hit recording of Joni Mitchell's "Woodstock," David Crosby's song of paranoia and generational strife "Almost Cut My Hair," and Graham Nash's country-influenced "Teach Your Children."

Doors, The

This Los Angeles–based rock band consisted of singer Jim Morrison, keyboardist Ray Manzarek, guitarist Robbie Krieger, and drummer John Densmore. Although their biggest hit, "Light My Fire," was written by Krieger, the Doors are usually most closely associated with the songs of Jim Morrison, which combined poetic images revolving around sex and death with a theatrical performance approach. Morrison became a counterculture icon and in his writings and performances played the role of a counterculture shaman. The Doors made their national debut on the record charts in 1967. Although the group made several recordings after Morrison's death in 1971, it became sadly clear that the general public was more interested in the theatrical nature of the deceased singer's lifestyle and performance style and less in the fine jazz and Latin-influenced music of the group. Although several of their albums sold more copies, the Doors' self-titled debut album (which contained the hit songs "Break on Through" and "Light My Fire") created quite a stir when the package was issued in 1967. In a year in which the 33⅓-rpm album became a more important means of expression to some rock bands than the 45-rpm single, *The Doors* held its own against important albums like *Sgt. Pepper's Lonely Hearts Club Band* (the Beatles) and *Are You Experienced?* (the Jimi Hendrix Experience).

Dylan, Bob

Born Robert Zimmerman in Duluth, Minnesota on May 24, 1941, the singer, guitarist, and composer took his pseudonym from the poet Dylan Thomas. Dylan was an important part of the early 1960s folk revival, composing and performing such songs as "Blowin' in the Wind" and "Masters of War." His use of a backing rock band at the 1965 Newport Folk Festival initially caused outrage among the folk revival traditionalists, but provided impetus to the emerging folk-rock style. Dylan's impressionistic lyrics were allegedly tied to the use of marijuana, a drug he allegedly introduced to the Beatles. Dylan has been widely regarded as one of the greatest poets in the history of American popular music. Dylan stopped writing protest songs in 1964, although he would return to the genre in the 1970s. During the late 1960s and the remainder of the counterculture era he would explore styles ranging from highly personal, impressionistic songs, to songs with obtuse Biblical references ("All Along the Watchtower" is the best known), to Nashville-style country music and just about everything in between. All, however, were marked by Dylan's highly creative lyrics. Dylan's recordings are on the Columbia label and his anti-war material from 1962–1963 and the more impressionistic material from 1964–1966 and beyond are widely available in compact disc reissues.

Easy Rider

A 1969 film starring Dennis Hopper, Peter Fonda, and Jack Nicholson that brought together many aspects of the 1960s counterculture, including rock music, free love, long hair, anti-war sentiments, communal living, and hallucinogenic drug usage. Interestingly, the film largely was financed through money that writers and producers Bob Rafelson and Bert Schneider made with their successful television series *The Monkees*. The soundtrack, which was largely assembled by Dennis Hopper, utilized songs that were receiving radio airplay at the time, including Steppenwolf's "Born to Be Wild" and "The Pusher," the Byrds' "Wasn't Born to Follow," the Jimi Hendrix Experience's "If Six Was Nine," and Fraternity of Man's pro-marijuana classic "Don't Bogart Me (aka Don't Bogart that Joint)." Roger McGuinn of the Byrds also contributed several songs to the soundtrack.

Electric Prunes, The

Although they were not a household name back in the 1960s, the Electric Prunes, a rock band from Seattle, recorded the drug-oriented classic "I Had Too Much to Dream (Last Night)" in 1966. The band also appeared in the soundtrack of the counterculture film *Easy Rider*, with their innovative rock setting of the "Kyrie Eleison" text from the Roman Catholic Mass.

Elephant's Memory

A New York City rock band with a hard-edged sound driven by the saxophone of group leader Stan Bronstein. Elephant's Memory's biggest claim to fame was that they became former-Beatle John Lennon's backing band for a time in the early 1970s. Elephant's Memory appears on Lennon and Yoko Ono's musical manifesto for radical street politics, the album *Sometime in New York City*.

Fonda, Jane

Born December 21, 1937, Jane Fonda may be best known in the late twentieth century and early twenty-first century as the star and producer of exercise videos. Fonda is the daughter of actor Henry Fonda and the sister of actor Peter Fonda. Jane Fonda made her film debut in 1960 and became the first major American actress to appear nude in a foreign movie when she did so in *La Ronde* (1964). Fonda's greatest tie to the counterculture, however, was the anti-war work she did in the late 1960s and until the end of the Vietnam Conflict. She traveled to North Vietnam at the height of the war, earning the nickname "Hanoi Jane." Political activist Tom Hayden, whom Fonda would later marry, actor Donald Sutherland, and singer-songwriter Holly Near also accompanied Fonda on her anti-war tours in the 1970s. Although she was despised by nearly every veteran of the Vietnam Conflict, due to her infamous trip to Hanoi, her film career took off in the

1970s. Fonda continues to work as a political activist, most recently working on Native American rights projects.

Fonda, Peter

Born February 23, 1939, actor Peter Fonda is the son of actor Henry Fonda and the brother of political activist and actor Jane Fonda. Fonda's main tie to the counterculture is an important artistic one: he co-wrote, co-produced, and co-starred in the film *Easy Rider*. Fonda received an Academy Award nomination for Best Original Screenplay for the film. He continues to be active as an actor, writer, and producer, and recently published a tell-all autobiography, *Don't Tell Dad*.

Fugs, The

A thoroughly political rock band, the Fugs were closely aligned with leftist street theatre in New York City. The band's lyrics were designed to shock audiences; their "Kill for Peace" is an excellent example. Even the name of the group was meant to shock the sensibilities of straight-laced American society: it is a slight variation on the notorious "f-word."

Grateful Dead, The

Originally known as the Warlocks, this ensemble was the house band for Ken Kesey and the Merry Pranksters' acid parties in 1966. Led by guitarist-vocalist Jerry Garcia, the band had a somewhat fluid membership over the years. They were an important part of the San Francisco music scene in the mid-1960s and were a popular concert draw; however, the band never met with commercial success on the singles charts. The Grateful Dead was influenced by many musical styles and developed a sound that reflected this eclecticism. The extensive concertizing of the band became almost legendary and a large group of fans, known as Deadheads, followed them around the country, turning each Grateful Dead concert into a near-communal festival. The continuing influence of this band and the strength of the following in the twenty-first century is evidenced by a report that a concert held August 3–4, 2002 in East Troy, Wisconsin, drew 70,000 Fans (Waddell 2002).

Hair

Music by Galt MacDermot, lyrics and book by Gerome Ragni and James Rado. While some critics fail to acknowledge *Hair* as the first rock opera, due primarily to the loose connections of the "plot," as well as the purported inauthenticity of the "rock" music of the score, the show, which developed throughout 1967 and 1968, was groundbreaking. *Hair* brought the long hair, sexual freedom, popular music styles, and glorification of mind-altering drugs of the "Summer of Love" to Broadway. The show spawned several hit singles for a wide variety of artists, some associated with staged productions of *Hair*, and some of whom recognized the commercial potential of these topical songs.

Hayden, Tom

Political activist and politician Tom Hayden was born December 11, 1939. Although he was a member of the California State House and State Senate in the 1980s and 1990s, Hayden might best be remembered nationally as an anti-war activist in the 1960s and an anti-nuclear activist in the 1970s. Hayden is credited with drafting the famous Port Huron Statement in 1962, a political statement that guided the New Left throughout the decade. He was a co-founder of the Students for a Democratic Society, an organization that organized anti-war and pro-free-speech rallies. In the late 1960s and early 1970s when he was married to actress Jane Fonda, Hayden and Fonda led trips to North Vietnam and other peace campaign rallies across the United States.

Hendrix, Jimi

Considered by many to be the greatest rock guitarist of the 1960s, Jimi Hendrix was born November 27, 1942 in Seattle, Washington. Although he worked as a backing musician in the early 1960s, he first came to the American public's attention as a solo singer-virtuoso guitarist-songwriter in 1967 with his band, the Jimi Hendrix Experience. Hendrix wrote and recorded the psychedelic classic "Purple Haze," considered by some critics one of the most important compositions by an American composer in the twentieth century. He caused considerable controversy among leaders of the Black Power movement, who disliked his attraction to rock, which some considered a "White" musical style. Some of the Black political leaders also objected to Hendrix's sexually charged image, considering it an extension of black-faced minstrelsy. Near the end of his life, Hendrix worked with an all-Black band and made strong anti-war and pro-Black Power statements. He died of drug-related causes in 1970.

Hoffman, Abbie

Born in Worcester, Massachusetts in 1936, Abbie Hoffman became one of the best-known, and certainly most colorful leftist radicals of the counterculture era. While leftists like Angela Davis and Bobby Seale basically took a very businesslike approach to the struggle for equal rights and against the

Vietnam Conflict, Hoffman and his cohort Jerry Rubin undertook a humor–filled street theatre approach. For example, Hoffman organized the attempted exorcism of the Pentagon in which he led 50,000 anti-war protesters on a march surrounding the center of U.S. military power in 1967. While the exorcism and attempted levitation of the Pentagon apparently failed, they captured media attention around the world. Hoffman maintained this ability to be noticed by the media through his audacity throughout the counterculture era. In this respect, Hoffman was closely aligned to the street theatre musicians like the Fugs, who likewise used shock, surprise, and biting satire to mock the establishment. Aside from the attempted levitation of the Pentagon, the most infamous example of Hoffman's anti-establishment modus operandi was his book *Steal This Book*, a work that enumerated ways in which the average citizen could steal from official government entities and big corporations. Along with Jerry Rubin, Hoffman organized the Youth International Party (better known as the yippies). The violence at the 1968 Democratic National Convention, resulted in charges of inciting a riot against Hoffman, Rubin, and several other radicals. After several court cases, however, the defendants were acquitted of all charges. However, charges of involvement with drug activities in 1974 forced Hoffman into hiding until 1980. After serving a short prison sentence he returned to activism for the rest of his life. He committed suicide in 1989.

Hopper, Dennis

Actor Dennis Hopper was born May 17, 1936. Throughout his career Hopper has portrayed societal misfits and insane characters from his appearance in *Rebel Without a Cause* in 1955, through *Apocalypse Now* and *Blue Velvet*, to *Speed*, to his film work in the twenty-first century. Along with Peter Fonda, Hopper co-wrote, co-produced, and co-starred in the counterculture classic *Easy Rider* in 1969. Hopper was largely responsible for compiling the music for the film's soundtrack.

Jesus Christ Superstar

A rock opera written by composer Andrew Lloyd Webber and lyricist Tim Rice. Indeed, some music critics claim that *Jesus Christ Superstar* was the first true rock opera. (Although it predated *Jesus Christ Superstar* by a couple of years, *Hair* is not regarded as a true rock opera by some critics, due both to its more pop, less rock-oriented score and due to its loose structure). The show portrays Jesus of Nazareth as a sort of hippie, counterculture figure and takes the unusual track of looking at Jesus's life story form the viewpoint of Judas Iscariot.

Joplin, Janis

Born in Port Arthur, Texas on January 19, 1943, Joplin was the premiere White, female, blues-based singer of the late 1960s. Joplin's entire persona symbolized the counterculture hippie, sexually active, drug-taking lifestyle. In many respects, these aspects of her life and public persona resembled some of the racier early Black female blues artists of the 1920s. In doing so, Joplin charted new territory for popular White female singers. Due to her lifestyle and music, Janis Joplin helped to blur racial lines and gender role lines during the late 1960s. Joplin never achieved great commercial success and had great difficulty keeping a band together during her brief career. Among devotees of blues-based hard rock, however, she was considered one of the most important musicians of the 1960s. She was one of the premiere musicians to emerge from the San Francisco music scene during the "Summer of Love" (1967). She died of a heroin overdose on October 4, 1970. Bette Midler's movie *The Rose* is based on Joplin's life, a life filled with rejection, few close friendships, drug and alcohol abuse, and incredible musical highs and lows.

Kesey, Ken

Author Ken Kesey (1935–2001), along with his Merry Pranksters, rejected the controls that Dr. Timothy Leary and his associates placed on the use of LSD, looking upon the drug as more of an agent of social change, and one that should be made available to as many people as possible. Royalties that Kesey earned from his best-selling book *One Flew over the Cuckoo's Nest* (1962) financed these "acid tests." Due to Kesey's links with Neal Cassady, Jack Kerouac, and other Beat figures as well as with the younger generation of proto-hippies (like the Grateful Dead, which he hired as a house band when they were known as the Warlocks), he became an important figure bridging 1950s and 1960s counterculture. Although Kesey did not write about his LSD-related exploits with the Pranksters, Tom Wolfe chronicled their exploits in his book *The Electric Kool-Aid Acid Test.*

King, Carole

Born Carole Klein on February 9, 1942 in Brooklyn, New York, King became a leading Brill Building songwriter in the late 1950s. Her collaborations with then-husband Gerry Goffin in the mid-1960s included mildly counterculture songs like "Pleasant Valley Sunday," "Take a Giant Step," and "Wasn't Born to Follow." King emerged as a solo singer-pianist in the early 1970s and recorded the groundbreaking and hugely successful album *Tapestry*. Although *Tapestry* was not a feminist manifesto by any stretch of the imagination, many American women heard King's songs about a very real range of emotions as reflecting their own emotions. As such, it became an important part of the women's movement. In addition, rock critic Robert Christgau, among others, credited King's gospel-inspired piano playing with being the first easily distinguishable instrumental "voice" by a woman in the rock era (Christgau 1972).

Leary, Dr. Timothy

Born October 22, 1920 in Springfield, Massachusetts, Timothy Leary became a Harvard researcher and professor who moved from the study of personality to the study of the effects of mind-altering drugs by the early 1960s. He lost his post at Harvard due to his emergence as a sort of LSD guru, widely promoting use of the drug. Leary's famous statement "Tune in, turn on, drop out" became something of a mantra for those seeking spiritual refuge through psychedelic drugs during the 1960s. Despite his reputation as a radical, Leary believed that LSD should be taken under tightly controlled conditions and for inner exploration; he was dead set against the kind of experimentation endorsed by Ken Kesey and the Merry Pranksters. Leary's influence did not extend much beyond the 1960s as he spent considerable time in the 1970s in prison on various drug-related charges or in a self-imposed exile. Leary eventually lectured and wrote extensively on time and space travel, extrasensory perception, and the cyberculture that emerged near the end of his life. Eventually allegations emerged linking Leary to the CIA and the FBI as an informant. He died in 1996.

Lennon, John

Although perhaps best known as the rhythm guitarist, singer, and songwriting partner of Paul McCartney in the Beatles, John Lennon (1940–1980) enjoyed a solo career after the Beatles disbanded in 1970. "Give Peace a Chance," "Imagine," "Power to the People," and most of the songs on the John Lennon–Yoko Ono album *Sometime in New York City* carried an antiwar, pro-peace, sometimes revolutionary, feminist, and generally antiestablishment message. Interestingly, Lennon put his career on hold in 1975, at the "official" end of the counterculture era. He and his wife and collaborator, singer, songwriter, and artist Yoko Ono, re-emerged in 1980 shortly before Lennon was assassinated by Mark David Chapman, a deranged fan.

LSD

The common name for the drug D-Lysergic acid diethylamide, first used by Albert Hofmann, a chemist with the Swiss firm Sandoz Pharmaceuticals, on August 19, 1943. The drug, also known as "acid," was used by psychiatrists into the early 1960s. The drug came into widespread street usage in the early 1960s and was made illegal in the United States in 1966.

Manson, Charles

The violent escapades of Charles Manson and his "Family" have been well documented. They represented the dark side of the communal, hippie lifestyle when their involvement in the Tate–LaBianca murders came to light. It is significant that one of the ways Manson gained converts was through his music. In fact, Manson's failed attempts to secure a recording contract were said to have played a role in the choice of actress Sharon Tate's residence to stage the murderous act that was designed to ignite a race war.

MC5, The

Although the MC5, a Detroit band whose name is short for the Motor City Five, achieved somewhat limited chart success ("Kick Out the Jams" reached #82 on the *Billboard* pop singles charts, while the album of the same name really did not do much better), the group played a prominent role in espousing manager John Sinclair's radical White Panther Party philosophies of drugs, sex, and revolution in the streets. The MC5 combined a sound that foretold 1970s punk rock, with free improvisation and anti-government rhetoric. The band consisted of Michael Davis, bass; Wayne Kramer, guitar; Fred "Sonic" Smith, guitar; Dennis Thompson, drums; and Rob Tyner, vocals. There first impact in the Detroit area came in 1966, but they became more widely known in 1968 when they released their first album, *Kick Out the Jams*. They were loud, profane, and made a complete mockery of conservative, middle-class sensibilities, and by 1972, they were history.

Merry Pranksters

A loose confederation of young people associated with author Ken Kesey and his infamous LSD "acid tests" of the early to mid-1960s. Kesey and the Merry Pranksters initially listened to avant-garde jazz of musicians like Rahsaan Roland Kirk during their drug trips. The group had a stereo system wired to outdoor speakers all around Kesey's property so that they could listen to music any time they wanted. Eventually, they began hiring the Grateful Dead (then known as the Warlocks) as their house band. Their exploits traveling the country in an old bus, generally acting outrageous, were chronicled by journalist Tom Wolfe in his book *The Electric Kool-Aid Acid Test*.

Mingus, Charles

A highly influential jazz bassist and composer, Charles Mingus (1922–1979) wrote several pieces with strong Black pride–influenced titles in the 1950s and 1960s. Some of Mingus's compositions reached back to early New Orleans–style jazz textures of group improvisation with easily heard references to the blues.

Mitchell, Joni

Born November 7, 1943 in Alberta, Canada, Mitchell gained her greatest notoriety during the counterculture era as the writer of "Woodstock," the song that documented the famous art and music festival of the same name. Mitchell also played a significant role as a female performer who developed an easily identifiable guitar and vocal style.

Monkees, The

Assembled for a popular television show about a rock group, the Monkees consisted of Peter Tork, Michael Nesmith, David Jones, and Micky Dolenz. The group primarily recorded songs by writers under contract to various subsidiaries of their record and television production company. Included among these were a couple of somewhat counterculture songs by Carole King and Gerry Goffin: "Take a Giant Step" and "Pleasant Valley Sunday." More importantly, the television show *The Monkees* brought long-haired musicians and rock music to a wide audience in 1966–1968. The Monkees' 1968 film *Head* included several drug references, psychedelic sequences, and generally exploded the plastic image of the group.

Monterey Pop Festival

The Monterey International Pop Music Festival (June 1967) was significant in that several rock musicians who were not widely known made dazzling appearances. Jimi Hendrix had started his solo career in England, but made his first major impact in the United States at this June 1967 event when he performed scorching electric guitar solos, proclaimed the death of surf music, and ignited his guitar using lighter fluid. Other significant counterculture musicians that appeared at Monterey Pop included Janis Joplin with her band Big Brother and the Holding Company, and Country Joe & the Fish. The Byrds, Eric Burdon and the Animals, and Buffalo Springfield, all of which I have mentioned in this book in conjunction with at least one important counterculture contribution, also appeared.

Morrison, Jim

Singer and principal songwriter of the Doors, Jim Morrison (1943–1971) became a very visible fixture in the period 1967–1970. In his lyrics and stage persona he played the role of a shaman of the dark. Many of his song lyrics and published poems deal with sex and death. Morrison was charged with several crimes near the end of his career, including exposing his penis while performing a concert. Doors keyboardist Ray Manzarek claims in his autobiography that Morrison basically psyched the crowd into thinking that he was exposing himself, but that Morrison never did commit the crime. Manzarek cites this incident as an example of the shaman-like hold Morrison had over his fans (Manzarek 1998). Morrison's death in Paris was also controversial; some claimed that he died of a heroin overdose, while others close to the singer claim that he never used the drug. Some claim that Morrison faked his death and cite evidence in some of his lyrics suggesting that this had been planned for some time.

Motown

The term Motown refers to a record company (and its several subsidiaries, such as Gordy and Tamla) and a style of Black music that the label made popular throughout the counterculture era. Formed by Berry Gordy, Jr., Motown featured a light soul-influenced sound that appealed to largely White audiences as well as to Blacks. Even during most of the turbulent 1960s Motown remained strangely apolitical. All that changed in late 1968 and into 1969 when Motown songwriters and performers issued a series of recordings that dealt with the social problems of the day. These songs included "War," "Stop the War Now," and "Ball of Confusion." Many jaded critics suggested that the reason behind Motown's sudden transformation was that counterculture music was now the popular norm and that to remain apolitical would be to risk record sales.

Musique concrète

A French term describing music that incorporates found, real-life sounds (usually captured on tape). Examples include songs like the Beatles' "Revolution No. 9," in which John Lennon incorporated pieces of electronic tape he found in the studio, the Fugs' "Kill for Peace," which uses the sound of actual machine guns, Eric Burdon and the Animals' "Sky Pilot," which uses the sound of combat, and Chicago's "Prologue, August 29, 1968," with its recording of the actual Black demonstrators at the 1968 Democratic National Convention. This technique was first associated with European avant-garde electronic music composers in the 1950s, but was taken up by pop musicians in the 1960s and 1970s.

Near, Holly

Although most of her pro-feminism, pro-lesbian and gay rights, anti-nuclear, anti-exploitive-multinational-corporation songs came into prominence among activists after the time period covered by this book, Near took part in some of the last major anti-war activities of the Vietnam Conflict, including tours with Jane Fonda, Tom Hayden, and Donald Sutherland. Near's main contribution, however, probably was in her taking the best aspects of the progressive movement and protest music into the 1980s and beyond, thereby extending the influence of the counterculture well beyond 1975. She also happened to be one of the most gifted singers from both a technical and expressive standpoint among her generation of protest musicians. Near, who had appeared as an actor in films and television shows like *Slaughterhouse Five, All in the Family, The Mod Squad,* and *The Partridge Family,* was also active on Broadway, having appeared in the Broadway production of *Hair.* Near then made music, and particularly music for various progressive causes, her focus and formed an independent record company, Redwood Records, in 1972. She was apparently one of the first, if not *the* first, female artist to found an independent recording company. Significantly, she did so just at the ascendancy of the women's movement into the national consciousness.

Newton, Huey

Huey Newton (1942–1989) was one of the leading radical Black activists of the 1960s. He co-founded, along with Bobby Seale, the Black Panther Party for Self Defense in 1966. From their formation, the Black Panthers advocated violent opposition to what they saw as the officially sanctioned racism of the United States. Their violence was specifically directed against the police whom they saw as agents of this repression. In 1967 Newton was convicted of voluntary manslaughter for the killing of a policeman. Newton would eventually be cleared in 1971, but only after three mistrials. In order to avoid drug-related and murder charges, he fled the United States in 1974. When he returned in 1977, he went free after two trials ended with hung juries. Newton would eventually earn a doctorate in social philosophy in 1980. He was shot and killed in 1989.

Ochs, Phil

> One of the leading leftist folk revival singer-songwriters to take up the anti-war cause during the counterculture era, Phil Ochs (1941–1975) never achieved the popular commercial success of Joan Baez, Judy Collins, or Bob Dylan. While he touched relatively few people through his recordings, Ochs performed at countless peace rallies and folk festivals, often rallying the crowds with his best–known anti-war songs, "I Ain't Marching Anymore" and "Draft Dodger Rag." He also wrote influential and effective songs protesting the mistreatment of Blacks ("The Ballad of Medgar Evers" and "Here's to the State of Mississippi") and in support of workers' rights. Apparently convinced that the movement had been all for naught and fighting depression, brought on in part by a mugging in Africa that left his voice permanently damaged, and by an addiction to alcohol, Ochs took his own life. Interestingly, Ochs's recordings from the 1960s and 1970s are virtually all available on compact disc reissues, as well as in elaborate boxed sets. Interest in Phil Ochs as a topical singer-songwriter is perhaps stronger today than it was during his lifetime.

Ono, Yoko

> Born in Japan (1932), Yoko Ono moved to the United States at an early age and became a conceptual artist and composer in the John Cage–influenced avant-garde scene of the 1950s. As a result of one of her art shows in England in the mid-1960s she came to the attention of John Lennon. Lennon and Ono later became musical collaborators and married. Their jointly composed and jointly performed double album *Sometime in New York City* proclaimed a strong pro-feminist, anti-war, pro-radical politics message. It was due in part to Yoko Ono's influence that Lennon produced the avant-garde tape piece "Revolution No. 9" on the Beatles' so-called "White Album."

Paxton, Tom

> Although he would become better known as a composer and performer of children's songs in the 1970s and 1980s, Tom Paxton was a notable protest singer–songwriter in the early and mid-1960s. In songs like "Buy a Gun for Your Son," "The Willing Conscript," "Talking Vietnam Pot Luck Blues," and "What Did You Learn in School Today?" Paxton brought a rare and effective (and sly) sense of humor to the folk revival repertoire. Some of the emotions felt by the protagonists of his songs came out of his own service in the U.S. Army in the early 1960s.

Peel, David

> One of the most famous street musicians in New York City during the 1960s and 1970s, David Peel wrote and performed many humorous pro-marijuana songs. Peel made several recordings including some produced by John Lennon, who acknowledged and championed Peel's unique music. In fact, Lennon mentioned David Peel among the important underground figures in New York in his song "New York City" on the *Sometime in New York City* album.

Peter, Paul & Mary

> This popular acoustic folk revival trio consisted of Peter Yarrow (born 1938), Paul Stookey (born 1937), and Mary Travers (born 1937). They recorded several rhetorically gentle anti-war songs, like "The Cruel War" (sometimes given as "The Cruel War Is Raging") and Bob Dylan's "Blowin' in the Wind" (a #2 pop hit). They deserve credit for bringing this type of material, as well as other folk and folk-revival music, to a wide audience. Some right-wing critics interpreted their 1963 hit song "Puff the Magic Dragon" as a pro-marijuana or pro-opium song, although it seems more likely that it really was meant to be the fanciful children's tale about a dragon that it appears to be on the surface.

Reddy, Helen

> Born October 25, 1941 in Australia, Helen Reddy's first U.S. hit recording was "I Don't Know How to Love Him," from the rock opera *Jesus Christ Superstar*. While songs from that rock opera (in which Reddy did not appear) were of counterculture significance, Reddy's most important link to the movement was her 1972 hit single "I Am Woman." The song became the anthem of the women's movement. Reddy's television performances of "I Am Woman" were fraught with controversy, as she wished to perform bra-less and with unshaven underarms; both were viewed as symbolic of women's rejection of the stereotypes and subservient roles of the past.

Reynolds, Malvina

> Considerably older than most of the folk revival/protest singer–songwriters of the 1960s Malvina Reynolds (1900–1978) had been involved in progressive, socialist politics during the Great Depression and earned her doctorate from the University of California at Berkeley in 1936. She met Pete Seeger and other folk singers in the late 1940s and began to write her own songs at that time. She is probably best known for her songs "Little Boxes," which became Pete Seeger's only pop chart hit single, and for "What Have They

Done to the Rain," which was a top 40 hit for the Searchers. "Little Boxes" mocks late 1940s and 1950s American suburban values and the "cookie-cutter" lifestyle that was common at that time, while "What Have They Done to the Rain" deals metaphorically with environmental degradation. Reynolds also wrote several songs protesting America's role in the Vietnam Conflict. She later wrote songs and performed for Women for Peace and for the boycott of the Nestlé Corporation, as well for other causes.

Rolling Stones, The

Originally consisting of Mick Jagger (vocals), Keith Richards (lead guitar and vocals), Brian Jones (rhythm guitar), Charlie Watts (drums), and Bill Wyman (bass), the Rolling Stones were seen as the darker side of the "British Invasion." Unlike the Beatles, whose earlier covers of American music tended to be Motown and Brill Building songs, the Rolling Stones were more heavily influenced by American rhythm and blues. Controversy arose over songs like "Let's Spend the Night Together" (an invitation to premarital sex) that were written by Jagger and Richards. Their "Something Happened to Me Yesterday" describes a night out on the town while tripping on LSD. In June 1967, Mick Jagger and Keith Richards became the first prominent British rock stars to be arrested on drug charges, making headlines around the world. The Rolling Stones continue to tour and record long after the end of the counterculture era. Many commentators consider them to be the greatest rock and roll band of all time.

Rubin, Jerry

Born July 14, 1938 in Cincinnati, Ohio, Jerry Rubin was exposed to left-leaning philosophies early on: his father was active as a union representative. After the death of Rubin's parents within several months of each other when Rubin was a young man just beginning a career in journalism, he traveled to Israel with his thirteen-year-old brother. There, he became increasingly interested in the plight of the oppressed. Upon his return to the United States and subsequent enrollment as a graduate student at the University of California at Berkeley in 1964, Rubin took part in his first political protest when he participated in a picket of a grocer who refused to hire Blacks. Rubin began organizing protests against the United States' war in Vietnam. His Vietnam Day Committee, an organization with Socialist leanings that supported various youth-oriented, leftist causes, was investigated by the House Un-American Activities Committee. Rubin's appearance before this Justice Department committee created an uproar; he appeared in Revolutionary War garb and handed out copies of the Declaration of Independence to those assembled. The case was thrown out of court in the middle of the proceedings in an apparent attempt to keep Rubin from testifying and garnering even more publicity. After their 1967 march on the Pentagon and attempt at an exorcism and levitation of the center of U.S. military power, Rubin and fellow radical Abbie Hoffman formed the Youth International Party, perhaps better known as the yippies. The yippies were at the center of the catastrophic demonstrations and subsequent police beatings that caught the attention of the entire nation during the 1968 Democratic National Convention in Chicago. In the early 1970s, Rubin became closely associated with John Lennon and Yoko Ono, appearing with them when the couple hosted *The Mike Douglas Show*. He also educated the Lennons about the American radical left, prevailing upon them to perform at benefits to support White Panther Party founder John Sinclair. Rubin later renounced radical politics. He died in 1994 after he jaywalked into the path of an oncoming car in Los Angeles.

Seale, Bobby

Born October 22, 1936, Bobby Seale co-founded the Black Panther Party in 1966 along with Huey Newton. Seale was heavily influenced by Malcolm X and felt that Blacks needed to be armed for self-defense and for a possible future revolutionary struggle. During the riots at the 1968 Democratic National Convention in Chicago, members of the Black Panthers fought with police. Although Seale had been in town for only two days during the convention, he was arrested as one of the primary instigators of the violence. Seale's speech in Chicago's Grant Park was highly inflammatory and caused him to be lumped with organizers who had apparently been much more instrumental in putting the protests together. When it came time for the "Chicago Eight" to be tried, Seale was separated from the others, bound, and gagged. This was seen by many in the movement as a blatantly racist act by the legal system in Chicago and was widely protested. Seale was tried separately and convicted of conspiracy to disrupt the Democratic convention. The conviction was later overturned. In the 1970s Bobby Seale renounced violence and continues to work as an activist for the rights of Blacks into the twenty-first century.

Seeger, Pete

Among the best-known American musicians of the twentieth century, Pete Seeger (born 1919) was performing and recording traditional American folk songs and newly composed folk-like protest songs from the 1940s. He was influenced in part by his father, Charles Seeger, a prominent musicologist who specialized in preservation of American folk music. Pete Seeger was a founding member of two important left-wing protest-folk groups, the Almanac Singers and the Weavers. During the McCarthy era, Seeger was blacklisted by the House Un-American Activities Committee as a Communist. He wrote such well-known songs as "Turn! Turn! Turn! (To Everything There Is a Season)," "Waist Deep in the Big Muddy," "Bring Them Home," and "Where Have All the Flowers Gone?" Seeger performed at numerous political rallies and concerts and returned to television when his blacklisting was lifted in the 1960s. In the 1970s Seeger became increasingly active in the environmental movement, with a focus on water pollution. He has recorded widely and published educational materials related to guitar and banjo performance.

Sgt. Pepper's Lonely Hearts Club Band

Arguably one of the most important record albums of the 1960s, this collection by the Beatles appeared in summer 1967. *Sgt. Pepper*, as it quickly came to be known, featured the Beatles backed up by symphonic strings, electronically manipulated vocal and instrumental parts, instruments recorded with backwards taping techniques—all of these techniques designed to stimulate the senses and enhance the texts of the songs. As a recording production, the album was hailed as one of the major accomplishments in the history of recorded sound. A number of songs, too, reflected the counterculture of 1967, mostly through intentional or unintentional references to drugs like marijuana and LSD. Some people consider *Sgt. Pepper's Lonely Hearts Club Band* to be the first "concept album." The album seemed to be a coherent whole, from its packaging (with many young people of the time noting that the Beatles were pictured on the album's cover standing behind a bed of marijuana plants, surrounded by many of their favorite actors, philosophers, and religious and political figures) through the use of some musical and lyrical themes from song to song. Even though the Beach Boys' *Pet Sounds* or Pink Floyd's *Piper at the Gates of Dawn* precede *Sgt. Pepper* and are more thoroughly integrated as whole works of art in the minds of some critics, *Sgt. Pepper's Lonely Hearts Club Band* made an impact far exceeding that of virtually any other album of the 1960s. *Sgt. Pepper* was not a collection of single records with some filler material; in fact, no singles were issued of any of the songs on the album.

Simon, Paul

Although he and his singing partner Art Garfunkel did not outwardly appear to be part of the counterculture, singer-songwriter-guitarist Paul Simon (born 1941) was responsible for several anti-war compositions during the 1960s. These include "The Side of a Hill" "Scarborough Fair/Canticle," "Seven O'Clock News/Silent Night," and his hilarious anti-war, anti-establishment parody of Bob Dylan, "A Simple Desultory Philippic (Or How I Was Robert McNamara'd into Submission)." Simon became one of the most important male American musical stars of the 1970s and is given some credit for helping to expedite the end of the South African system of apartheid with his groundbreaking *Graceland* album in the 1980s.

Sinclair, John

The manager of the MC5, Sinclair preached radical social change brought upon by drug usage and free love. As historian David Farber writes,

> For Sinclair and the rest of his cohort who would form the White Panther Party in 1968, their acid visions turned them from anomie and isolation to a belief in the possibility of a communal youth consciousness. Acid was a tool, they believed, in achieving a group identity, a new collective social presence that could change society. For Sinclair's group, dropping acid pointed them toward political struggle. (Farber 2002, 27)

Sinclair became a target for the police and was convicted of passing two joints to undercover officers. This was Sinclair's third drug-related conviction so he was sentenced to ten years in prison. Many members of the radical left considered his arrest, conviction, and sentencing to be politically motivated. Sinclair's supporters mounted a Free John Sinclair campaign that included a benefit concert at which Phil Ochs, Stevie Wonder, John Lennon and Yoko Ono, Bobby Seale, and Allen Ginsberg appeared. Within days of this concert the Michigan Supreme Court overturned Sinclair's conviction. During his time in prison Sinclair worked on a book espousing his political views and the sex, drugs, and rock and roll approach to revolution. It was published in 1972 as *Guitar Army*. More recently Sinclair has hosted jazz radio shows, written poetry, worked as an activist for more liberalized marijuana laws, and written articles for a variety of publications.

Sly & the Family Stone

Led by keyboardist and lead singer Sylvester "Sly Stone" Stewart, this multiracial and multigendered band had nineteen singles make the *Billboard* pop charts between 1968 and 1975; all of the songs were written and all of the records were produced by Stone. The band put on a much-heralded show at the Woodstock festival, performing, among other songs, "I Want to Take You Higher." Several of Stone's songs from around 1970 deal with issues of race relations and Black pride, especially "Thank You (Falettinme Be Mice Elf Agin)." Sly Stone was an influence on later funk and disco styles.

Smothers Brothers, The

Tom and Dick Smothers were folksingers and comedians who hosted a comedy-variety television show in 1967–1969. Phil Ochs, Pete Seeger, and other musicians aligned with the counterculture appeared on the program. The anti-war message of Tom and Dick Smothers started out subtly, but by the end of their program's run, it had grown confrontational. Interestingly, this shift took place as the movement grew increasingly violent, making the fate of *The Smothers Brothers Comedy Hour* a reflection of what was happening in U.S. society at large.

Steppenwolf

The performers of counterculture songs such as "The Pusher," "Born to Be Wild," "Draft Resister," and "Magic Carpet Ride," Steppenwolf developed out of the 1964–1967 group Sparrow. Steppenwolf was fronted by the East German–born singer-guitarist John Kay (real name Joachim Krauledat), and also featured guitarist Goldy McJohn, drummer Jerry Edmonton, guitarist Michael Monarch, and bassist Nick St. Nicholas. The group was named after the Herman Hesse novel *Der Steppenwolf*, a favorite of 1960s counterculture youth. Steppenwolf's links to and popularity in biker circles is evidenced by the inclusion of two of their songs in the soundtrack of the classic counterculture film *Easy Rider*.

Summer of Love

The summer of 1967 was called the Summer of Love, due primarily to the happenings in San Francisco. The peaceful hippie lifestyle was glorified in songs, the most prominent of which were the John Phillips composition "San Francisco (Be Sure to Wear Flowers in Your Hair)," a hit for folksinger Scott McKenzie, and Eric Burdon and the Animals' "San Franciscan Nights." At the time, several San Francisco bands that glorified the use of psychedelic drugs and the hippie lifestyle jumped into national prominence, including the Grateful Dead and the Jefferson Airplane. Numerous accounts have been written that challenge the generally held notions about the communal, everyone-loves-everyone-else life at San Francisco's Golden Gate Park (George Harrison's encounter with hippies at the park who angrily chased him after he was unable to perform for them has been detailed in several books about the Beatles), however, the myth of a life free from war with ample psychedelic drugs, free love, and free food, has persisted.

Surrealistic Pillow

This late 1966, early 1967 album by the Jefferson Airplane was an important collection. Although several individual songs, including "White Rabbit" and "She Has Funny Cars" achieved special notoriety because of their psychedelic drug references, the entire album played an important role in introducing America not only to the Airplane, but to the entire musical scene that was developing in San Francisco, California during the year or so leading up to the so-called "Summer of Love."

Tapestry

This 1971 album by Carole King established her as among the elite songwriters of the day. Songs like "I Feel the Earth Move," "You've Got a Friend," "(You Make Me Feel Like) A Natural Woman," and "It's Too Late" covered a range of styles and emotional content that fit in perfectly with the consciousness raising of the women's movement. The album also established King's piano style as "the first widely recognized instrumental signature ever developed by a woman" (Christgau 1972).

Velvet Underground, The

Consisting of guitarist-singer-songwriter Lou Reed, bassist-violist-keyboardist John Cale, guitarist Sterling Morrison, and drummer Maureen Tucker, the Velvet Underground was an influential part of the fringe New York City rock scene in the second half of the 1960s. The band was associated for a period of time with pop artist Andy Warhol, who was responsible for bringing the mysterious singer Nico into the band for a short time. The Velvet Underground's songs, written by Reed, dealt with life on the street, drug abuse and addiction, sexual fantasy, ambiguity and fetishes, and alienation from society. The Velvet Underground achieved little commercial success through the time they disbanded in 1973. Subsequently, however, their albums became increasingly popular, particularly during the punk/new wave musical movement of the late 1970s and early 1980s. The Velvet Underground was an important influence on American punk singer-songwriter Patti Smith and well-known British singer-songwriter David Bowie.

Watson, Doc

Along with "Mother" Maybelle Carter, country-folk musician Doc Watson (born 1923) was a favorite of the Back to the Land movement crowd. Watson was blind since infancy and developed a flat-picking guitar style that influenced numerous younger folk and bluegrass musicians. Watson's style did not keep up with popular trends in country music; rather, he provided a link to earlier traditional folk-country styles.

What's Going On

This 1971 concept album by Motown singer-songwriter Marvin Gaye broke new ground for Motown Records. A commercial success itself, the album also featured three top-10 singles. Motown had been slow to allow its artists to deal with social issues, but this album found Gaye dealing with environmental degredation and society's failure to come to grips with it ("Mercy Mercy Me"), the harshness of ghetto life for Blacks ("Inner City Blues"), and the general breakdown of society ("What's Going On"). It has been suggested that Marvin Gaye's writing, singing, and production on *What's Going On* proved to Motown Records, and to other companies that were hesitant to release material that might be politically controversial, "that it was possible to make a socially conscious statement and still sell records" (Gaye with Basten 2003, 84).

Woodstock

The Woodstock Music and Art Fair, held August 15–18, 1969, on Max Yasgur's farm in Bethel, New York. Woodstock was organized by an executive staff consisting of Michael Lang, John Roberts, Joel Rosenman, and Artie Kornfeld. The festival attracted some 400,000, and featured performances by Richie Havens, Jimi Hendrix, Crosby, Stills, Nash & Young, the Who, Country Joe & the Fish, Creedence Clearwater Revival, John Sebastian, the Incredible String Band, Sweetwater, Ravi Shankar, Melanie, Arlo Guthrie, Joan Baez, Santana, Canned Heat, Mountain, Sly & the Family Stone, the Jefferson Airplane, Joe Cocker, Ten Years After, Sha Na Na, Blood, Sweat & Tears, the Paul Butterfield Blues Band, Janis Joplin, and the Grateful Dead. The demographics of the festival's attendees are detailed in Weiner and Stillman (1979). Woodstock is considered by many historians to represent the high point of the counterculture movement, at least the high point of how the philosophy of "peace, love, and understanding" could effectively work in a real-life situation. Due to the size of the crowd, inadequate sanitation and food, audience members had to live a communal life of sharing and cooperation for three days; by and large they succeeded. The film synopsis of the festival, entitled *Woodstock: Three Days of Peace & Music*, brought this sociological phenomenon to the entire world.

Yasgur, Max

Yasgur owned the farm in Bethel, New York on which the famed Woodstock Music and Art Fair took place. As documented in the film of the music festival, Yasgur and festival attendees seemed to develop a mutual respect, if not admiration, despite their generational differences. In fact, part of Yasgur's motivation in leasing his property to the festival's organizers was that he felt that the promoters had been wronged by citizens of Wallkill, New York who had driven the music festival from their town. Max Yasgur was immortalized in several songs about Woodstock, including Mountain's "For Yasgur's Farm" (which was performed at the 1969 festival) and Joni Mitchell's composition "Woodstock" (which became a hit for Crosby, Stills, Nash & Young in early 1970).

Zappa, Frank

A musician better known for his albums (many of which featured songs with sophomoric, scatological lyrics) and extended improvisations than for chart singles, Frank Zappa (1940–1993) became a figure of major importance in the musical counterculture. For one thing, the extended group improvisations performed by his band (the Mothers of Invention), which he called "freak-outs," were said to simulate the sensory overload of the LSD experience; this despite the fact that Zappa totally abstained from drugs and alcohol. By 1968, Zappa was seen as a figure of sufficient "hip-ness" that his recognition of *The Monkees* as a television program that brought an at-least-mildly counterculture lifestyle to the American public in a positive light caused at least some sociologists to view the "counterculture" in broader terms than they previously had. Interestingly, Zappa openly mocked the hippies who listened to his music for its drug-like stimulation. He also openly mocked musicians who he considered to be overly commercial. For example, the Mothers of Invention album *We're Only in It for the Money* is a biting indictment of the Beatles (the title and cover photo mock *Sgt. Pepper's Lonely Hearts Club Band*). During the late 1980s, Zappa became an outspoken proponent of freedom of speech and an outspoken critic of the Parents Music Resource Center, which sought to place warning labels on recordings in order to steer young people away from listening to music dealing with sex, drugs, and violence.

Bibliography

Aarons, Leroy F. 1965. FBI Checks Folk Songs—Then Mum's the Word. *Washington Post*, November 6, 6.

Aarons, Leroy F. 1969. Sgt. Pepper Makes a Pitch for Peace. *Los Angeles Times*, June 15, 14 (Calendar).

Adams, Rebecca G. and Robert Sardiello, eds. 2000. *Deadhead Social Science: You Ain't Gonna Learn What You Don't Want to Know*. Walnut Creek, CA: AltaMira Press.

Agnew, Spiro T. 1972. Talking Brainwashing Blues. Reprinted in *The Sounds of Social Change*, ed. R. Serge Denisoff and Richard A. Peterson, 307–10. Chicago: Rand McNally.

All Music Guide: Stand! 2002. *All Music Guide*. http://www.allmusic.com. Accessed December 17.

All Music Guide: There's a Riot Goin' On. 2002. *All Music Guide*. http://www.allmusic.com. Accessed December 17.

Allen, Gary. 1969. That Music: There's More to It Than Meets the Ear. *American Opinion* 12 (February): 49–62. (See also: Allen 1972.)

Allen, Gary. 1972. More Subversive Than Meets the Ear. In *The Sounds of Social Change*, ed. R. Serge Denisoff and Richard A. Peterson, 151–66. Chicago: Rand McNally. (Note: The present article is a reprint of Allen 1969.)

Anderson, Omer. 1966. Army Drops Bomb on "Protests." *Billboard* (January 15): 3.

Anderson, Terry H. 1995. *The Movement and the Sixties*. New York: Oxford University Press.

Ankeny, Jason. 2000. Review of *The Great American Eagle Tragedy* by Earth Opera. *All Music Guide*. http://www.allmusic.com. Accessed October 11.

Ankeny, Jason. 2002. MC5. *All Music Guide*. http://www.allmusic.com. Accessed June 12.

Antlfinger, Carrie. 2002. Panel Denies License for Dead Reunion. Associated Press Wire Report (June 12).

Armstrong, Dan. 1963. "Commercial" Folksongs—Product of "Instant Culture." *Sing Out!* 13 (February–March): 20–22. (Note: The present article is a response to Fiott 1962–1963.)

Arnold, Ben. 1993. *Music and War: A Research and Information Guide.* New York: Garland Publishing.

Artists Support U.S. Servicemen in Vietnam. 1966. *Billboard* (January 8): 35.

Baez, Joan. 1969. *Daybreak.* New York: Avon Books.

Baez, Joan. 1987. *And a Voice to Sing With.* New York: New American Library.

Banners, Buttons, and Songs. 1968. *Variety* (September 11): 88.

Battle of Ideologies Set to Music Meets Deejay Resistance Movement. 1965. *Variety* (October 13): 63.

Beard, Rick and Leslie Cohen Berlowitz, eds. 1993. *Greenwich Village: Culture and Counterculture.* New Brunswick, NJ: Published for the Museum of the City of New York by Rutgers University Press.

Begler, Lewis. 1970. *Rock Theology: Interpreting the Music of the Youth Culture.* New York: Bengizio Press.

Belasco, Warren James. 1989. *Appetite for Change: How the Counterculture Took on the Food Industry, 1966–1988.* New York: Pantheon Books.

Belz, Carl. 1967. Popular Music and the Folk Tradition. *Journal of American Folklore* 80 (April–June): 130–42.

Belz, Carl. 1972. *The Story of Rock,* 2nd ed. New York: Oxford University Press.

Berger, Bennett M. 1981. *The Survival of a Counterculture: Ideological Work and Everyday Life among Rural Communards.* Berkeley: University of California Press.

Bewley, John M. 2000. Personal library reference e-mail to the author, August 29.

Bindas, Kenneth J. and Craig Houston. 1989. "Takin' Care of Business": Rock Music, Vietnam and the Protest Myth. *Historian* 52 (November): 1–23.

Birchall, Ian. 1969. The Decline and Fall of British Rhythm and Blues. In *The Age of Rock,* vol. 1, ed. Jonathan Eisen, 94–102. New York: Vintage Books, Random House.

Biskind, Peter. 1998. *Easy Riders, Raging Bulls: How the Sex-Drugs-and-Rock'n'Roll Generation Saved Hollywood.* New York: Simon & Schuster.

Bloom, Alexander and Wini Breines, eds. 1995. *Takin' It to the Streets: A Sixties Reader.* New York: Oxford University Press.

Bodroghkozy, Aniko. 2001. *Groove Tube: Sixties Television and the Youth Rebellion.* Durham, NC: Duke University Press.

The Boston Women's Health Book Collective. 1971. *Our Bodies, Ourselves: A Book by and for Women.* New York: Simon & Schuster.

Botkin, B. A. 1967. The Folksong Revival: Cult or Culture? In *The American Folk Scene: Dimensions of the Folksong Revival,* ed. David A. DeTurk and A. Poulin, Jr., 95–102. New York: Dell Publishing, Laurel Editions.

Boy, 10, Leads Viets to Father's Hideout. 1964. Associated Press Wire Report (December 18).

Braunstein, Peter. 1999. Disco. *American Heritage* 50(7) (November): 43–57.

Braunstein, Peter and Michael William Doyle. 2002a. Historicizing the American Counterculture of the 1960s and '70s. In *Imagine Nation: The American Coun-*

terculture of the 1960s and '70s, ed. Peter Braunstein and Michael William Doyle, 5–14. New York: Routledge.

Braunstein, Peter and Michael William Doyle, eds. 2002b. *Imagine Nation: The American Counterculture of the 1960s and '70s*. New York: Routledge.

Brownmiller, Susan. 1975. *Against Our Will: Men, Women, and Rape*. New York: Simon and Schuster.

Budds, Michael J. and Marian M. Ohman, eds. 1993. *Rock Recall: Annotated Readings in American Popular Music from the Emergence of Rock and Roll to the Demise of the Woodstock Nation*. Needham Heights, MA: Ginn Press.

Cahn, Edgar S. 1969. *Our Brother's Keeper: The Indian in White America*. Washington, DC: New Community Press.

Carr, Roy and Tony Tyler. 1978. *The Beatles: An Illustrated Record*, revised and updated ed. New York: Harmony Books.

Cash, Johnny. 1964. A Letter from Johnny Cash. *Broadside* 41 (March 10): 10.

Cavan, Sherri. 1972. *Hippies of the Haight*. St. Louis: New Critics Press.

Chalmers, David. 1996. *And the Crooked Places Made Straight: The Struggle for Social Change in the 1960s*. Baltimore: Johns Hopkins University Press.

Chepesiuk, Ronald. 1995. *Sixties Radicals, Then and Now: Candid Conversations with Those Who Shaped the Era*. Jefferson, NC: McFarland.

Chilcoat, George W. 1992. Popular Music Goes to War: Songs about Vietnam. *International Journal of Instructional Media* 19(2): 171–82.

Chomsky, Noam. 1967. The Responsibility of Intellectuals. *New York Review of Books* (February 23): 16.

Christgau, Robert. 1972. Carole King: Five Million Friends. *Newsday* (November). (Reprinted in Christgau 1973.)

Christgau, Robert. 1973. *Any Old Way You Choose It*. Baltimore: Penguin Books.

Clark, Charlie. 1986. The Tracks of Our Tears—When Rock Went to War: Looking Back on Vietnam and Its Music. *Veteran* (February): 10–23.

Cleaver, Eldridge. 1968. *Soul on Ice*. New York: McGraw-Hill. Reprint, New York: Dell, 1992.

Clymer, Kenton J., ed. 1998. *The Vietnam War: Its History, Literature and Music*. El Paso: Texas Western Press.

Cohn, Nik. 1969. *Rock from the Beginning*. New York: Stein and Day.

Coker, Wilson. 1972. *Music and Meaning*. New York: Free Press.

Cook, Bruce. 1971. *The Beat Generation*. New York: Scribner.

Cooper, B. Lee and Wayne S. Haney. 1997. *Rock Music in American Popular Culture II: More Rock 'n' Roll Resources*. New York: Harrington Park Press.

Corliss, R. 1967. Pop Music: What's Been Happening. *National Review* 19 (April 4): 371–74.

Cott, Jonathan and Christine Doudha, eds. 1982. *The Ballad of John and Yoko*. Garden City, NY: Rolling Stone Press.

Cunningham, Sis and Gordon Friesen. 1965. An Interview with Phil Ochs. *Broadside* 63 (October 15).

Cuscuna, Michael. 1969. A New Music of Political Protest. *Saturday Review* 52 (December 13): 55–56.

Dachs, David. 1964. *Anything Goes: The World of Popular Music*. Indianapolis: Bobbs-Merrill.

Dachs, David. 1969. *American Pop*. New York: Scholastic Book Services.

Dalton, David. 1971. *Janis*. New York: Simon & Schuster—A Fireside & Stone Hill Book.

Dane, Barbara. 1969–1970. If This Be Treason. *Sing Out!* 19 (Winter): 2–7.

Dane, Barbara and Irwin Silber, comps. and eds. 1969. *The Vietnam Songbook*. New York: The Guardian.

Daniels, Robert V. 1989. *Year of the Heroic Guerrilla: World Revolution and Counter-revolution in 1968*. New York: Basic Books.

Darlington, Sandy. 1969. Country Joe & The Fish: 1965–1968. In *Rock and Roll Will Stand*, ed. Greil Marcus, 150–69. Boston: Beacon Press.

Darnovsky, Marcy, Barbara Epstein, and Richard Flacks, eds. 1995. *Cultural Politics and Social Movements*. Philadelphia: Temple University Press.

Dawbarn, B. 1968. Don't Laugh, But the Next Step Could Be Pop as a Political Power. *Melody Maker* 43 (October 6): 13.

Dean, Maury. 1966. *The Rock Revolution*. Detroit: Edmore Books.

DeBenedetti, Charles with Charles Chatfield, assisting author. 1990. *An American Ordeal: The Antiwar Movement of the Vietnam Era*. Syracuse, NY: Syracuse University Press.

Deloria, Vine, Jr. 1969. *Custer Died For Your Sins: An Indian Manifesto*. New York: Macmillan.

Denisoff, R. Serge. 1969. Folk Rock: Folk Music, Protest, or Commercialism? *Journal of Popular Culture* 3 (Fall): 214–30.

Denisoff, R. Serge. 1970a. Kent State, Muskogee and the White House. *Broadside* 108 (July–August): 2–3.

Denisoff, R. Serge. 1970b. Protest Songs: Those on the Top Forty and Those on the Street. *American Quarterly* 22 (Winter 1970): 807–23.

Denisoff, R. Serge. 1971. *Great Day Coming: Folk Music and the American Left*. Urbana: University of Illinois Press.

Denisoff, R. Serge. 1972a. The Evolution of the American Protest Song. In *The Sounds of Social Change*, ed. R. Serge Denisoff and Richard A. Peterson, 15–25. Chicago: Rand McNally.

Denisoff, R. Serge. 1972b. Folk Music and the American Left. In *The Sounds of Social Change*, ed. R. Serge Denisoff and Richard A. Peterson, 105–20. Chicago: Rand McNally.

Denisoff, R. Serge. 1972c. *Sing a Song of Social Significance*. Bowling Green, OH: Bowling Green State University Popular Press.

Denisoff, R. Serge. 1973. *Songs of Protest, War & Peace*. Santa Barbara, CA: American Bibliographical Center–Clio Press. (Note: There are a number of factual errors in the various discographies in the present volume. Due to the date of the publication, use of the discographies is dependent upon access to the original issues of the listed recordings on vinyl. For an updated and corrected discography of Vietnam Conflict–related recordings, see Perone 2001.)

Denisoff, R. Serge. 1990. Fighting Prophecy with Napalm: "The Ballad of the Green Berets." *Journal of American Culture* 13 (Spring): 81–94.

Denisoff, R. Serge and Mark H. Levine. 1971. The Popular Protest Song: The Case of the "Eve of Destruction." *Public Opinion Quarterly* 35 (Spring): 119–24. (See also Denisoff and Levine 1972.)

Denisoff, R. Serge and Mark H. Levine. 1972. Brainwashing or Background Noise: The Popular Protest Song. In *The Sounds of Social Change*, ed. R. Serge Denisoff and Richard A. Peterson, 213–21. Chicago: Rand McNally. (Note: The present article is an expanded version of Denisoff and Levine 1971.)

Denisoff, R. Serge and Richard A. Peterson, eds. 1972. *The Sounds of Social Change: Studies in Popular Culture.* Chicago: Rand McNally.

DeTurk, David A. and A. Poulin Jr., eds. 1967. *The American Folk Scene: Dimensions of the Folksong Revival.* New York: Dell Publishing, Laurel Editions.

Deutsch, Didier C. 1988. Liner notes to *Hair.* Compact disc reissue. RCA 1150-2-RC.

Diggins, John P. 1992. *The Rise and Fall of the American Left.* New York: W. W. Norton.

Dotter, Daniel. 1987. Growing Up Is Hard to Do: Rock and Roll Performers as Cultural Heroes. *Sociological Spectrum* 7: 25–44.

Downey, Pat, George Albert, and Frank Hoffman. 1994. *"Cash Box" Pop Singles Charts, 1950–1993.* Englewood, CO: Libraries Unlimited.

Dunson, Josh. 1965. *Freedom in the Air.* New York: International Publishers.

Dunson, Josh. 1966. Thunder without Rain. *Sing Out!* 15 (January): 12–17.

E. D. 1964. Letters. *Broadside* 47 (June 30).

Echols, Alice. 1999. *Scars of Sweet Paradise: The Life and Times of Janis Joplin.* New York: Metropolitan Books.

Echols, Alice. 2002. *Shaky Ground: The Sixties and Its Aftershocks.* New York: Columbia University Press.

Eder, Bruce. 2002a. Paul Revere & The Raiders. *All Music Guide.* http://www.allmusic.com. Accessed June 28.

Eder, Bruce. 2002b. Review of *The Life and Times of Country Joe & the Fish* by Country Joe & the Fish. *All Music Guide.* http://www.allmusic.com. Accessed October 10.

Eder, Bruce. 2002c. Review of *Steppenwolf* by Steppenwolf. *All Music Guide.* http://www.allmusic.com. Accessed November 11.

Eder, Bruce. 2002d. Review of *Steppenwolf the Second* by Steppenwolf. *All Music Guide.* http://www.allmusic.com. Accessed November 11.

Eddy, Chuck. 1998. *Stairway to Hell: The 500 Best Heavy Metal Albums in the Universe.* New York: Da Capo Press.

Edmonds, Ben. 1997. Track by Track. In liner notes for *Farewells & Fantasies* (Phil Ochs): 63–89. Three compact discs. Elektra R2-73518.

Edwards, Emily and Michael Singletary. 1984. Mass Media Images. *Popular Music and Society* 9(4): 17–26.

Eliot, Marc. 1979. *Death of a Rebel: A Biography of Phil Ochs.* New York: Anchor Books.

Epstein, Jonathan S., ed. 1994. *Adolescents and Their Music: If It's Too Loud, You're Too Old.* New York: Garland Publishing.

Erlewine, Stephen Thomas. 2002a. Review of *Stand!* by Sly & the Family Stone. *All Music Guide.* http://www.allmusic.com. Accessed December 17.

Erlewine, Stephen Thomas. 2002b. Review of *There's a Riot Goin' On* by Sly & the Family Stone. *All Music Guide.* http://www.allmusic.com. Accessed December 17.

Erlewine, Stephen Thomas. 2003. Led Zeppelin. *All Music Guide.* http://www.allmusic.com. Accessed August 20.

Escot, Colin. 1988. Liner notes to *Hi Records: The Blues Sessions.* Two 33⅓-rpm phonodiscs. Hi Records D-HIUKLP 427.

Etzkorn, K. Peter. 1977. Popular Music: The Sounds of the Many. In *Music in Amer-*

ican Society 1776–1976, ed. George McCue, 119–32. New Brunswick, NJ: Transaction Books.

Evans, Paul. 1992. *Rolling Stone Album Guide*, 3rd ed. Ed. Anthony DeCurtis, James Henke, and Holly George-Warren. *S.v.* "Creedence Clearwater Revival." New York: Random House.

Fager, C. E. 1970. Chilling Outrage: "Ohio" by Crosby, Stills, Nash and Young. *Christian Century* 87 (August 19).

Farber, David. 1994. *The Age of Great Dreams: America in the 1960s*. New York: Hill and Wang.

Farber, David. 2002. The Intoxicated State/Illegal Nation: Drugs in the Sixties Counterculture. In *Imagine Nation: The American Counterculture of the 1960s and '70s*, ed. Peter Braunstein and Michael William Doyle, 17–40. New York: Routledge.

Fariña, Richard. 1969. Baez and Dylan: A Generation Singing Out. In *The Age of Rock*, vol. 1, ed. Jonathan Eisen, 200–207. New York: Vintage Books, Random House.

Fields, Carletta. 1969. Persecution of the Young Lords. *Black Panther Newspaper*, May 19. Reprinted as Hispanic Revolutionaries in *Sixties Counterculture*, ed. Stuart A. Kallen, 206–208. San Diego: Greenhaven Press, 2001.

Fiott, Stephen. 1962–1963. In Defense of Commercial Folksingers. *Sing Out!* 12 (December–January): 43–45. (See also Armstrong 1963.)

Firestone, Shulamith. 1970. *The Dialectic of Sex: The Case For Feminist Revolution*. New York: Morrow.

Folk Music in Vietnam. 1968. *New York Times*, February 13. Reprinted in *Sing Out!* 18 (June–July): 1.

Folk Songs and the Top 40—A Symposium. 1966. *Sing Out!* 16 (March): 12–21.

Fonda, Peter. 1998. *Don't Tell Dad: A Memoir*. New York: Hyperion.

Forbes, C. A. 1971. New Folk Musical: Do the Answers Ring True? New Vibrations. *Christian Century* 15 (March 26): 38.

Fort Hood Three Defense Committee. 1966. *The Fort Hood Three: The Case of the Three G.I.'s Who Said "No" to the War in Vietnam*. New York: Fort Hood Three Defense Committee.

Foster, Alice. 1970. Merle Haggard: "I Take a Lot of Pride in What I Am." *Sing Out!* 19 (March–April).

Friedan, Betty. 1963. *The Feminine Mystique*. New York: Norton.

Friesen, Agnes. 1962. Singing on the Peace Walk. *Sing Out!* 12 (Summer): 35+.

Frith, Simon. 1981. *Sound Effects: Youth, Leisure, and the Politics of Rock 'n' Roll*. New York: Pantheon Books.

Gabree, John. 1969. Rock: Art, Revolution or Sell-Out? *High Fidelity* 19 (August): 10–11.

Garlock, Frank. 1971. *The Big Beat: A Rock Blast*. Greenville, SC: Bob Jones University Press.

Gaye, Frankie with Fred E. Basten. 2003. *Marvin Gaye, My Brother*. San Francisco: Backbeat Books.

Geltman, M. 1966. Hot Hundred: A Surprise! Patriotic Songs. *National Review* 18 (September): 894–96.

George, Nelson. 1988. *The Death of Rhythm and Blues*. New York: Pantheon Books.

Gilroy, Paul. 1993. *The Black Atlantic: Modernity and Double Consciousness*. Cambridge, MA: Harvard University Press.

Ginsberg, Allen. 1966. Liner notes to *The Fugs* (The Fugs). 33⅓-rpm phonodisc. ESP-Disk 1028.

Gitlin, Todd. 1987. *The Sixties: Years of Hope, Days of Rage*. New York: Bantam Books.

Glazer, Tom, ed. and collector. 1970. *Songs of Peace, Freedom, and Protest*. New York: David McKay Company.

Gleason, Ralph J. 1965a. Surrounded by "Subversive" Music. *San Francisco Chronicle*, November 14, 23.

Gleason, Ralph J. 1965b. "The Times They Are a Changin'": The Changing Message of America's Young Folksingers. *Ramparts* (April): 36–48.

Gleason, Ralph J. 1966. Liner notes for *Parsley, Sage, Rosemary and Thyme* (Simon and Garfunkel). 33⅓-rpm phonodisc. Columbia 9363. Reissued on compact disc, Columbia CK-9363.

Gleason, Ralph J. 1972. A Cultural Revolution. In *The Sounds of Social Change*, ed. R. Serge Denisoff and Richard A. Peterson, 137–46. Chicago: Rand McNally.

Goines, David Lance. 1993. *The Free Speech Movement: Coming of Age in the 1960s*. Berkeley, CA: Ten Speed Press.

Goines, David Lance. 2001. The Free Speech Movement in Berkeley. In *Sixties Counterculture*, ed. Stuart A. Kallen, 33–43. San Diego: Greenhaven Press.

Goldman, Albert Harry. 1971. *Freakshow: The Rocksoulbluesjazzsickjewblackhumor-sexpoppsych Gig and Other Scenes from the Counter-Culture*. New York: Atheneum. Republished as *Freakshow: Misadventures in the Counterculture, 1959–1971*. New York: Cooper Square Press, 2001.

Goldstein, Richard. 1968. The New Rock: Wiggy Words that Feed Your Mind. *Life* (June 28): 67+.

Goldstein, Richard. 1989. *Reporting the Counterculture*. Boston: Unwin Hyman.

Graubard, Mark. 1974. *Campustown in the Throes of the Counterculture (1968–1972)*. Minneapolis: Campus Scope Press.

Gravel, Senator Mike, ed. 1972. *The Pentagon Papers: The Defense Department History of the United States Decisionmaking on Vietnam*. Boston: Beacon Press.

Greenfield, Robert. 1996. *Dark Star: An Oral Biography of Jerry Garcia*. New York: William Morrow.

Greenwald, Matthew. 2002a. Review of "Mama Told Me (Not to Come)." *All Music Guide*. http://www.allmusic.com. Accessed October 10.

Greenwald, Matthew. 2002b. Review of "Something Happened to Me Yesterday." *All Music Guide*. http://www.allmusic.com. Accessed October 10.

Greenwald, Matthew. 2003. Review of "Jesus Is Just Alright." *All Music Guide*. http://www.allmusic.com. Accessed January 21.

Guterman, Jimmy. 2000. Liner notes to *The Big Bang! The Best of the MC5*. Compact disc. Rhino R2 79783.

Hale, Jeff A. 2002. The White Panthers' "Total Assault on the Culture." In *Imagine Nation: The American Counterculture of the 1960s and '70s*, ed. Peter Braunstein and Michael William Doyle, 125–55. New York: Routledge.

Hall, Mildred. 1968. Congress Faces R 'n' R Revolution and Rights. *Billboard* (December 28).

Hamilton, Neil A. 1997. *The ABC-CLIO Companion to the 1960s Counterculture in America*. Santa Barbara, CA: ABC-CLIO.

Harrington, Joe S. 2002. *Sonic Cool: The Life and Death of Rock 'n' Roll*. New York: Hal Leonard Corporation.

Harris, Bruce. 1972. Liner notes to *Weird Scenes Inside the Gold Mine* (The Doors). Two 33⅓-rpm phonodiscs. Elektra 8E-6001.

Harrison, Hank. 1973. *The Dead Book*. New York: Links Books.

Hayden, Tom. 1988. *Reunion: A Memoir*. New York: Random House.

Hedgepeth, William. 1970. *The Alternative: Communal Life in New America*. New York: Macmillan.

Heineman, Kenneth J. 2001. *Put Your Bodies Upon the Wheels: Student Revolt in the 1960s*. Chicago: Ivan R. Dee.

Helander, Brock. 1996. *The Rock Who's Who*, 2nd ed. New York: Schirmer Books.

Helen's Hymn. 1972. *Newsweek* (December 18): 68–69.

Henderson, David. 1978. *Jimi Hendrix: Voodoo Child of the Aquarian Age*. Garden City, NY: Doubleday.

Henderson, David. 1983. *'Scuse Me While I Kiss the Sky: The Life of Jimi Hendrix*. New York: Bantam Books. Republished 1996. (Note: This book is condensed and revised from Henderson 1978.)

Hentoff, Nat. 1967. The Future of the Folk Renascence. *Sing Out!* 17 (February–March): 10–13.

Hero-Hitting Tune Stirring Rhubarb. 1970. *Billboard* 82 (October 10): 72.

Herr, Michael. 1978. *Dispatches*. New York: Avon.

Hersch, Charles B. 1987. Liberating Forms: Politics and the Arts from the New York Intellectuals to the Counterculture. Master's thesis, University of California at Berkeley.

Hersch, Charles B. 1998. *Democratic Artworks: Politics and the Arts from Trilling to Dylan*. Albany NY: State University of New York Press.

Hesse, Hermann. 1927. *Der Steppenwolf*. Berlin: S. Fischer.

Hey Brother! Let the People Sing. 1970. *Broadside* 110 (November–December): 3.

Hirsch, Paul. 1969. *The Structure of the Popular Music Industry: The Filtering Process by Which Records Are Preselected for Public Consumption*. Ann Arbor: Survey Research Center, Institute for Social Research, The University of Michigan.

Hirsch, Paul. 1971. *A Progress Report on an Exploratory Study of Youth Culture and the Popular Music Industry*. Ann Arbor: Survey Research Center, Institute for Social Research, The University of Michigan.

Hodenfield, Chris. 1970. *Rock '70*. New York: Pyramid Books.

Hoffman, Abbie. 1969. *Woodstock Nation*. New York: Vintage Books, Random House.

Hoffman, Abbie. 1971. *Steal This Book*. New York: Pirate Editions. (Note: Author credits also include the following: "Co-conspirator: Izack Haber. Accessories after the fact: Tom Forcade [and] Bert Cohen.") Republished with a new introduction, New York: Four Walls Eight Windows, 1996.

Hoffman, Abbie. 1980. *Soon to Be a Major Motion Picture*. New York: Perigee Books.

Hoffman, Frank. 1983. *The Cash Box Singles Charts, 1950–1981*. Metuchen, NJ: The Scarecrow Press.

Hoffman, Frank and George Albert. 1994. *The Cash Box Charts for the Post-Modern Age, 1978–1988*. Metuchen, NJ: The Scarecrow Press.

Holdship, Bill. 1991. Liner notes to *Songs of Protest*. Compact disc. Rhino 70734.

Hopkins, Jerry. 1970. *The Rock Story*. New York: New American Library.

Hopkins, Jerry and Daniel Sugerman. 1980. *No One Here Gets Out Alive*. New York: Warner Books.

Horowitz, David, Michael Lerner, and Craig Pies, eds. 1972. *Counterculture and Revolution*. New York: Random House.

Hoskyns, Barney. 1997. *Beneath the Diamond Sky: Haight-Ashbury, 1965–1970*. New York: Simon & Schuster.

Hoskyns, Barney. 2001. The Birth of Hippie Culture. In *Sixties Counterculture*, ed. Stuart A. Kallen, 107+. San Diego: Greenhaven Press. (Note: This article is excerpted from Hoskyns 1997.)

Hunt, Richard A. 1988. A Battle for the People's Hearts and Minds. In *The Vietnam War*, ed. Ray Bonds, 106–13. New York: Military Press.

India: Merseysiders at the Ganges. 1968. *Time* 91 (March 1): 25. Reprinted in *Rock Recall: Annotated Readings in American Popular Music from the Emergence of Rock and Roll to the Demise of the Woodstock Nation*, ed. Michael J. Budds and Marian M. Ohman, 252. Needham Heights, MA: Ginn Press, 1993.

Interview with Phil Ochs, Part 1. 1968. *Broadside* 89 (February–March): 11–14.

Jancik, Wayne and Tad Lathrop. 1995. *Cult Rockers*. New York: Fireside.

Jasper, Tony. 1972. *Understanding Pop*. London: SCM Press.

Jay, Karla and Allen Young. 1972. *Out of the Closets: Voices of Gay Liberation*. New York: New York University Press. Reprint, New York: New York University Press, 1992.

Jezer, Marty. 2001. From City Protesters to Country Communes. In *Sixties Counterculture*, ed. Stuart A. Kallen, 132–37. San Diego: Greenhaven Press.

Jones, LeRoi. 1963. Liner notes for *Coltrane Live at Birdland*. 33⅓-rpm phonodisc. Impulse A-50.

Jones, LeRoi. 1968. *Black Music*. New York: William Morrow.

Jonnes, Jill. 1996. *Hep-Cats, Narcs, and Pipe Dreams: A History of America's Romance with Illegal Drugs*. New York: Scribner.

Joseph, Peter. 1973. *Good Times: An Oral History of America in the Nineteen Sixties*. New York: Charterhouse.

Judah, J. Stillson. 1974. *Hare Krishna and the Counterculture*. New York: Wiley.

Kaiser, Charles. 1988. *1968 in America*. New York: Weidenfeld & Nicolson.

Kallen, Stuart A., ed. 2001. *Sixties Counterculture*. San Diego: Greenhaven Press.

Kelly, Linda. 1995. *Deadheads: Stories from Fellow Artists, Friends, and Followers of the Grateful Dead*. Secaucus, NJ: Carol.

Keltz, Iris. 2000. *Scrapbook of a Taos Hippie: Tribal Tails from the Heart of a Cultural Revolution*. El Paso, TX: Cinco Puntos Press.

Kemp, Mark. 1997. Song of a Soldier: The Life and Times of Phil Ochs. In liner notes for *Farewells & Fantasies* (Phil Ochs): 13–62. Three compact discs. Elektra R2-73518.

Kent, Stephen A. 2001. *From Slogans to Mantras: Social Protest and Religious Conversion in the Late Vietnam War Era*. Syracuse, NY: Syracuse University Press.

Kesey, Ken. 1962. *One Flew Over the Cuckoo's Nest*. New York: New American Library.

Khan, Chaka with Tonya Bolden. 2003. *Chaka! Through the Fire*. New York: Rodale.

Kingman, Daniel. 1998. *American Music: A Panorama*, concise ed. New York: Schirmer Books.

Korall, Burt. 1968. The Music of Protest. *Saturday Review* (November 16): 36+.

Kostelanetz, Richard, ed. 1997. *The Frank Zappa Companion: Four Decades of Commentary*. New York: Schirmer Books.

Kurutz, Steve. 2002. Review of *Have a Marijuana* by David Peel. *All Music Guide.* http://www.allmusic.com. Accessed October 10.

Laing, David. 1970. *The Sounds of Our Time.* Chicago: Quadrangle Books.

Lamm, Robert et al. 1970. Liner notes to *Chicago II.* Two 33⅓-rpm phonodiscs. Columbia PG24.

Landau, Jon. 1969. John Wesley Harding. In *The Age of Rock,* vol. 1, ed. Jonathan Eisen, 214–29. New York: Vintage Books, Random House.

Landau, Jon. 1972. *It's Too Late to Stop Now.* San Francisco: Straight Arrow Books.

Larkin, Rochelle. 1970. *Soul Music.* New York: Lander Books.

Leary, Timothy. 1968. *The Politics of Ecstasy.* New York: G. P. Putnam's Sons. Reprint, Berkeley, CA: Ronin, 1998.

Leary, Timothy. 1983. *Flashbacks: A Personal and Cultural History of the Era.* Los Angeles: Jeremy P. Tarcher.

Lees, Gene. 1970. Rock, Violence, and Spiro T. Agnew. *High Fidelity* 20 (February): 108.

Leitch, Donavan. 1999. Liner notes to *Donovan's Greatest Hits* (Donovan). Compact disc. Epic EK-65730.

Lelyveld, Joseph. 1966. Ravi Shankar Gives West a New Sound That's Old in East. *New York Times,* June 20, 22. Reprinted in *Rock Recall: Annotated Readings in American Popular Music from the Emergence of Rock and Roll to the Demise of the Woodstock Nation,* ed. Michael J. Budds and Marian M. Ohman, 252. Needham Heights, MA: Ginn Press, 1993.

Lembcke, Jerry. 1998. *The Spitting Image: Myth, Memory, and the Legacy of Vietnam.* New York: New York University.

Lennon, John and Yoko Ono. 1972. Liner notes and lyrics to *Sometime in New York City* (John & Yoko/Plastic Ono Band). Two 33⅓-rpm phonodiscs. Apple PCSP 716. Reissued on compact disc, Capitol CDP 0777 7 93850 2 7.

Liner notes to *J. B. Lenoir* (J. B. Lenoir). 1970. 33⅓-rpm phonodisc. Crusade/Polydor 24-4011.

London, Jack. 1913. *Valley of the Moon.* New York: Macmillan Company.

Long Time Gone: Sixties America Then and Now, ed. Alexander Bloom. 2001. Oxford: Oxford University Press.

Lorber, Alan. 1996. Boston Sound 1968—The Music & The Time. Liner notes to *Bosstown Sound—1968: The Music and the Time.* Two compact discs. Big Beat Records CDWIK2 167.

Lund, Jens and Denisoff, R. Serge. 1971. The Folk Music Revival and the Counter Culture: Contributions and Contradictions. *Journal of American Folklore* 84 (October–December): 394–405.

Macan, Edward. 1996. *Rocking the Classics: English Progressive Rock and the Counterculture.* New York: Oxford University Press.

Makower, Joel. 1989. *Woodstock: The Oral History.* New York: Doubleday—A Tilden Press Book.

Manzarek, Ray. 1998. *Light My Fire: My Life with The Doors.* New York: G. P. Putnam.

Marcus, Greil, ed. 1969a. *Rock and Roll Will Stand.* Boston: Beacon Press.

Marcus, Greil. 1969b. A Singer and a Rock and Roll Band. In *Rock and Roll Will Stand,* ed. Greil Marcus, 90–105. Boston: Beacon Press. (See also Marcus 1972.)

Marcus, Greil. 1972. A New Awakening. In *The Sounds of Social Change,* ed. R. Serge

Denisoff and Richard A. Peterson, 127–36. Chicago: Rand McNally. (Note: The present article is basically a reprint of Marcus 1969b.)

Marcus, Greil. 1984. In Your Heart You Know He's Right. *Artforum* (November): 95.

Martin, Bradford. 2001. Politics as Art, Art as Politics: The Freedom Singers, the Living Theatre, and Public Performance. In *Long Time Gone: Sixties America Then and Now*, ed. Alexander Bloom, 159–87. New York: Oxford University Press.

Martin, Harris. 1966. *Music City News* Goes to Vietnam. *Music City News* (January): 11.

McCombs, Larry. 1967. Broadside of Boston. *Sing Out!* 17 (April–May): 49.

McLuhan, Marshall and Quentin Fiore. 1967. *The Medium Is the Massage*. New York: Touchstone.

McLuhan, Marshall and Quentin Fiore. 1968. *War and Peace in the Global Village*. New York: Bantam.

McNamara, Robert S. with Brian VanDeMark. 1995. *In Retrospect*. New York: Times Books.

McRuer, Robert. 2002. Gay Gatherings: Reimagining the Counterculture. In *Imagine Nation: The American Counterculture of the 1960s and '70s*, ed. Peter Braunstein and Michael William Doyle, 215–40. New York: Routledge.

Means, Russell. 1995. *Where White Men Fear to Tread: The Autobiography of Russell Means*. New York: St. Martin's Press.

Mele, Christopher. 2000. *Selling the Lower East Side: Culture, Real Estate, and Resistance in New York City*. Minneapolis: University of Minnesota Press.

Mellers, Wildrid. 1969. New Music in a New World. In *The Age of Rock*, vol. 1, ed. Jonathan Eisen, 180–88. New York: Vintage Books, Random House.

Melton, Barry. 2001. Everything Seemed Beautiful: A Life in the Counterculture. In *Long Time Gone: Sixties America Then and Now*, ed. Alexander Bloom, 145–57. New York: Oxford University Press.

The Message of History's Biggest Happening. 1969. *Time* 94 (August 29): 32–33. Reprinted without song lyrics in *Rock Recall: Annotated Readings in American Popular Music from the Emergence of Rock and Roll to the Demise of the Woodstock Nation*, ed. Michael J. Budds and Marian M. Ohman, 295. Needham Heights, MA: Ginn Press, 1993.

Michals, Debra. 2002. From "Consciousness Expansion" to "Consciousness Raising": Feminism and the Countercultural Politics of the Self. In *Imagine Nation: The American Counterculture of the 1960s and '70s*, ed. Peter Braunstein and Michael William Doyle, 41–68. New York: Routledge.

Miles, Barry. 1997. *Paul McCartney: Many Years from Now*. New York: Henry Holt.

Miller, James. 2001. The Antiwar Movement Is Born. In *Sixties Counterculture*, ed. Stuart A. Kallen, 57–66. San Diego: Greenhaven Press.

Miller, Lloyd. 1967. The Sound of Protest. *Case Western Reserve Journal of Sociology* 1 (June): 41–52.

Minstrel with a Mission. 1964. *Life* (October 9): 61–68.

Morrison, Joan and Robert K. Morrison. 1987. *From Camelot to Kent State: The Sixties Experience in the Words of Those Who Lived It*. New York: Times Books. Updated, New York: Oxford University Press, 2001.

MTV.com. 2003. Bob Dylan. *MTV.com*. http://www.mtv.com. Accessed May 4.

Murray the K. 1967. The New Music—Telling It Like It Is. *Wall Street Journal*, July 5, 12.

Music. 1965. *Time* 86 (September 17): 102.

My Generation. 1995. VHS-format videocassette. Gary Busey, narrator; Obie Benz, writer, producer director; Andrew Solt, Quincy Jones, Bob Metrowitz, David Salzman, executive producers; Jeffrey Peisch, series producer. Chicago: Time-Life Video & Television. Warner Home Video 13865.

Nakai, R. Carlos and James DeMars. 1996. *The Art of the Native American Flute.* Phoenix: Canyon Records Productions.

National Public Radio. 2004. "The 100 Most Important American Musical Compositions of the 20th Century." *NPR.* http://www.npr.org/programs/specials/vote/100list.html#P. Accessed January 7.

Naughton, Francis Patrick. 1978. Making the Greenwich Village Counterculture: An Analysis of the Construction of an Urban Intellectual Community. Ph.D. dissertation, New School for Social Research.

Near, Holly. 1974. What Are My Songs? *Sing Out!* 22(6): 14.

Neihardt, John G. 1972. *Black Elk Speaks.* Lincoln: University of Nebraska Press.

Neufeld, Jacob. 1988. Disengagement Abroad—Disenchantment at Home. In *The Vietnam War,* ed. Ray Bonds, 210–17. New York: Military Press.

Newsom, Jim. 2000. Review of *Mixed Bag* (Richie Havens). *All Music Guide.* http://www.allmusic.com. Accessed September 26.

Newsom, Jim. 2002. Review of *It Ain't Easy* (Three Dog Night). *All Music Guide.* http://www.allmusic.com. Accessed October 10.

Newsweek. 1965. (September 20): 90.

Newton, Huey. 1967. Killuminati. *Black Panther Newspaper,* July 20. Reprinted as How to Run a Revolution, in *Sixties Counterculture,* ed. Stuart A. Kallen, 200–205. San Diego: Greenhaven Press, 2001.

Noebel, David A. 1966. *Rhythm, Riots, and Revolution.* Tulsa, OK: Christian Crusade Publications.

O. S. 1965. Letter to *Broadside. Broadside* 55 (February 12): 12.

Obst, L. Rosen, ed. 1977. *The Sixties: The Decade Remembered Now, by the People Who Lived It Then.* New York: Rolling Stone Press.

Ochs, Phil. 1963. The Need for Topical Music. *Broadside* 22 (March): 6–7.

Ochs, Phil. 1965. Topical Songs and Folksinging, 1965: A Symposium. *Sing Out!* Reprinted in *The American Folk Scene,* ed. David A. DeTurk and A. Poulin, Jr. New York: Dell Publishing, 1967.

Ochs, Phil. 1967. Have You Heard? The War Is Over! *Village Voice* (November 23): 16+. Reprint of an article that originally appeared in the *Los Angeles Free Press* (June 1967).

Onkey, Lauren. 2002. Voodoo Child: Jimi Hendrix and the Politics of Race in the Sixties. In *Imagine Nation: The American Counterculture of the 1960s and '70s,* ed. Peter Braunstein and Michael William Doyle: 189–214. New York: Routledge.

Orloff, Katherine. 1974. Interview with Grace Slick. In *Rock 'n' Roll Woman.* Los Angeles: Nash. Excerpted in *Rock Recall: Annotated Readings in American Popular Music from the Emergence of Rock and Roll to the Demise of the Woodstock Nation,* ed. Michael J. Budds and Marian M. Ohman, 264. Needham Heights, MA: Ginn Press, 1993.

Orth, Michael. 1966. The Crack in the Consensus: Political Propaganda in American Popular Music. *New Mexico Quarterly* 36 (Spring): 62–79.

Parsons, Talcott. 1951. *The Social System.* New York: Free Press.

Paul's Dream. 1966. *National Guardian* (February 19).

Peel, David. 1984. *The David Peel Interview.* Interview conducted by Albert Goldman. 1⅞ ips audio cassette. Orange Records Q&A 48421.

Perone, James E. 2001. *Songs of the Vietnam Conflict.* Westport, CT: Greenwood Press.

Perry, Paul. 1996. *On the Bus: The Complete Guide to the Legendary Trip of Ken Kesey and the Merry Pranksters and the Birth of the Counterculture.* New York: Thunder's Mouth Press.

Pielke, Robert G. 1986. *You Say You Want a Revolution: Rock Music in American Culture.* Chicago: Nelson-Hall.

Planer, Lindsay. 2003. Review of "Almost Cut My Hair." *All Music Guide.* http://www.allmusic.com. Accessed April 19.

Prato, Greg. 2002a. Gloria Gaynor. *All Music Guide.* http://www.allmusic.com. Accessed June 28.

Prato, Greg. 2002b. Grace Jones. *All Music Guide.* http://www.allmusic.com. Accessed June 28.

Pratt, Ray. 1994. *Rhythm and Resistance: Political Uses of American Popular Music,* 2nd ed. Washington, DC: Smithsonian Institution Press.

Pratt, Ray. 1998. "There Must Be Some Way Outta Here!": The Vietnam War in American Popular Music. In *The Vietnam War: Its History, Literature and Music,* ed. Kenton J. Clymer, 168–89. El Paso: Texas Western Press.

Protest Disker Hits Draft Vandals. 1965. *Variety* (October 27): 60.

Protest Songs with a Rock Beat. 1965. *Life* 59 (November 5): 44.

Puterbaugh, Parke. 1993. Liner notes to *The Very Best of Tommy James and The Shondells* (Tommy James and The Shondells). Compact disc. Rhino R2-71214.

Pyes, Craig. 1970. *Rolling Stone* Gathers No Politix. *Sundance* 2 (October): 34–35.

Rabbi Chides Folkniks on "Destruction" Fears. 1965. *Variety* (October 13): 63.

Ragogna, Mike. 2000. Liner notes to *Easy Rider: Music from the Soundtrack.* Compact disc reissue. MCA 088-119-153-2.

Randal, Jonathan. 1967. Rock 'n' Roll Song Becoming Vietnam's "Tipperary." *New York Times,* June 14.

Reagon, Bernice Johnson. 1975a. In Our Hands: Thoughts on Black Music. *Sing Out!* (November): 1–2.

Reagon, Bernice Johnson. 1975b. Songs of the Civil Rights Movement, 1955–1965: A Study in Culture History. Ph.D. Dissertation, Howard University.

Reeve, Andru J. 1994. *Turn Me On, Dead Man: The Complete Story of the Paul McCartney Death Hoax.* Ann Arbor, Michigan: Popular Culture, Ink.

Reich, Steve. 1987. Liner notes to *Steve Reich: Early Works.* Compact disc. Elektra Nonesuch 9 79169-2.

Reynolds, Malvina. 1968. Letters to *Broadside. Broadside* 90 (April): 9.

Ribakove, Sy and Barbara Ribakove. 1966. *The Bob Dylan Story.* New York: Dell Publishing Company.

Rinzler, Alan. 1971. A Conversation with Charles Reich: Blowing in the Wind. *Rolling Stone* 75 (February 4): 30–34.

Robinson, John P. and Hirsch, Paul M. 1972. Teenage Responses to Rock and Roll Protest Songs. In *The Sounds of Social Change: Studies in Popular Culture,* ed. R. Serge Denisoff and Richard A. Peterson, 222–32. Chicago: Rand McNally.

Rodnitzky, Jerome L. 1971a. The Decline of Contemporary Protest Music. *Popular Music and Society* 1 (Fall): 44–50.

Rodnitzky, Jerome L. 1971b. The New Revivalism: American Protest Songs, 1945–1968. *The South Atlantic Quarterly* 70 (Winter): 13–21.

Rodnitzky, Jerome L. 1999. *Feminist Phoenix: The Rise and Fall of a Feminist Counterculture.* Westport, CT: Praeger.

Rosenstone, Robert A. 1969. "The Times They Are A-Changin": The Music of Protest. *Annals of the American Academy of Political and Social Science* 382 (March): 131–44.

Rossinow, Doug. 2002. Revolution Is about Our Lives. In *Imagine Nation: The American Counterculture of the 1960s and '70s,* ed. Peter Braunstein and Michael William Doyle: 99–124. New York: Routledge.

Rothstein, Jeffrey. 1999. The Apotheosis of Discontent: Representations of the Counterculture in 1960's Film and Television. Master's thesis, Youngstown State University.

Rubin, Jerry. 1970. *Do It!* New York: Ballantine.

Ruhlmann, William. 2000a. Holly Near. *All Music Guide.* http://www.allmusic.com. Accessed October 11.

Ruhlmann, William. 2000b. Review of *Hang in There* (Holly Near). *All Music Guide.* http://www.allmusic.com. Accessed October 11.

Ruhlmann, William. 2002. Review of *Jesus Christ Superstar* (MCA Original Cast Recording). *All Music Guide.* http://www.allmusic.com. Accessed July 2.

Sardiello, Robert. 1994. Secular Rituals in Popular Culture: A Case for Grateful Dead Concerts and Deadhead Identity. In *Adolescents and Their Music: If It's Too Loud, You're Too Old,* ed. Jonathon S. Epstein, 115–39. New York: Garland Publishing.

Sardiello, Robert. 1998. Identity and Status Stratification in Deadhead Subculture. In *Youth Culture: Identity in a Postmodern World,* ed. Jonathon S. Epstein, 118–47. Malden, MA: Blackwell.

Sardiello, Robert. 2000. Studying Deadhead Subculture. In *Deadhead Social Science: You Ain't Gonna Learn What You Don't Want to Know,* ed. Rebecca G. Adams and Robert Sardiello. Walnut Creek, CA: AltaMira Press.

Sasfy, Joe. 1988. Liner notes to *Classic Rock: 1968.* Compact disc. Time-Life 2CLR-04.

Scaduto, Anthony. 1971. *Dylan: An Intimate Biography.* New York: Grosset and Dunlap.

Schieber, Curtis. 2000a. New Boxed Set Salutes Incubator of Modern Folk. *The Columbus Dispatch,* October 1, F1.

Schieber, Curtis. 2000b. Ochs's Brilliance Helped Define Protest Genre. *The Columbus Dispatch,* October 1, F1.

Schoenfeld, Herm. 1965. Fresh Talent Lifts Disk. B.O. *Variety* (October 13): 63.

Seale, Bobby. 1978. *A Lonely Rage.* New York: Times Books.

Shaw, Arnold. 1971. *The Rock Revolution.* New York: Macmillan.

Sheehan, Neil. 1988. *A Bright Shining Lie: John Paul Vann and America in Vietnam.* New York: Random House.

Shelton, Robert. 1963. New Folk Singers. *New York Times,* June 13.

Silber, Irwin. 1967a. Fan the Flames. *Sing Out!* 17 (April–May): 33+.

Silber, Irwin. 1967b. Songs to Fight a War By: A Study in Illusion and Reality. *Sing Out!* 17 (August–September): 20–25.

Silber, Irwin. 1968. Country Joe Unstrung. *Sing Out!* 18 (June–July): 19+.

Sinclair, John. 1969. A Letter from Prison, Another Side of the MC5 Story, and (Incidentally) the End of an Era. *Creem* 2 (November): 9–14+.

Sinclair, John. 1970. Liberation Music. *Creem* 2 (November): 18–22.

Sinclair, John. 1972. *Guitar Army: Street Writings/Prison Writings*. New York: Douglas Books.

Sinclair, John and Robert Levin. 1971. *Music and Politics*. New York: World Publishing.

Singleton, Carl, 1999. *The Sixties in America*, Pasadena, CA: Salem Press.

Skolnick, Jerome H. 1969. *The Politics of Protest*. New York: Ballantine Books.

Smith, Paul Chaat and Robert Allen Warrior. 1996. *Like a Hurricane: The Indian Movement from Alcatraz to Wounded Knee*. New York: W. W. Norton.

Smucker, Tom. 1970. The Politics of Rock: Movement vs. Groovement. In *Age of Rock*, vol. 2, ed. Jonathan Eisen, 83–91. New York: Vintage Books, Random House.

Solomon, Maynard. 1964. Liner notes for *It's My Way!* (Buffy Sainte-Marie). 33⅓-rpm phonodisc. Vanguard VRS-9142.

Songs and Vietnamese Clientele Are Sad at Nightclub in Saigon. 1969. *New York Times*, December 14, 7.

Sternfield, Aaron. 1965. *Billboard* (August 21): 12.

Sternfield, Aaron. 1966. The Vietnam Conflict Spawning Heavy Barrage of Disk Tunes. *Billboard* (June 4): 1+.

Stevens, Jay. 1988. *Storming Heaven: LSD and the American Dream*. New York: Harper & Row.

Stine, Peter, ed. 1995. *The Sixties*. Detroit: Wayne State University Press.

Strunk, Oliver, ed. 1965. *Source Readings in Music History: Antiquity and the Middle Ages*. New York: W.W. Norton.

Stuessy, Joe. 1990. *Rock and Roll: Its History and Stylistic Development*. Englewood Cliffs, NJ: Prentice-Hall.

Szatmary, David. 1996. *A Time to Rock: A Social History of Rock 'n' Roll*. New York: Schirmer Books.

Tate, Greg. 2003. *Midnight Lightning: Jimi Hendrix and the Black Experience*. Chicago: Lawrence Hill Books.

Thomas, Stephen. 2002. The New York Dolls. *All Music Guide*. http://www.allmusic.com. Accessed June 7.

Thompson, Hunter S. 1967. *Hell's Angels: A Strange and Terrible Saga*. New York: Random House.

Thompson, Hunter S. 1971. *Fear and Loathing in Las Vegas: A Savage Journey to the Heart of the American Dream*. New York: Warner Books.

Tin Soldiers and Nixon's Coming. 1970. *Rolling Stone* 61 (June 25): 9.

Townshend, Pete. 1970. In Love with Meher Baba. *Rolling Stone* 71 (November 26): 25–26. Excerpted in *Rock Recall: Annotated Readings in American Popular Music from the Emergence of Rock and Roll to the Demise of the Woodstock Nation*, ed. Michael J. Budds and Marian M. Ohman, 253. Needham Heights, MA: Ginn Press, 1993.

Traum, Artie. 1968. Richie Havens. *Sing Out!* 18 (September–October): 3+.

Unger, Irwin and Debi Unger eds. 1998. *The Times Were a Changin': The Sixties Reader*. New York: Three Rivers.

Universal Song. 1966. *Broadside* 71 (June): 13.

Unterberger, Richie. 2000. Review of *Death, Glory and Retribution. All Music Guide.* http://www.allmusic.com. Accessed October 4.

Unterberger, Richie. 2003a. Review of *Are You Experienced?* by The Jimi Hendrix Experience. *All Music Guide.* http://www.allmusic.com. Accessed June 19.

Unterberger, Richie. 2003b. Review of "Hurdy Gurdy Man" by Donovan. *All Music Guide.* http://www.allmusic.com. Accessed June 11.

The Vietnam War: Its History, Literature, and Music, ed. Kenton J. Clymer. 1998. El Paso: Texas Western Press.

Van Ronk, Dave. 1966. Quoted in *Sing Out!* 16 (February–March): 21.

Viglione, Joe. 2003. Review of "I Am Woman." *All Music Guide.* http://www.allmusic.com. Accessed January 21.

Von Hoffman, Nicholas. 1968. *We Are the People Our Parents Warned Us Against.* Chicago: Quadrangle Books.

Waddell, Ray. 2002 "Dead Members Find 'Other' Touring Opportunities." *Billboard* 114 (August 24).

Warmbrand, Ted. 1971. Singing Against the War in Washington. *Broadside* 113 (May–June): 2.

Waksman, Steve. 1998. Kick Out the Jams! The MC5 and the Politics of Noise. In *Mapping the Beat: Popular Music and Contemporary Theory,* ed. Thomas Swiss, John Sloop, and Andrew Herman, 47–75. Malden, MA: Blackwell Publishers.

Walley, David and Patricia Kennely. 1968. Country Joe & The Fish. *Jazz & Pop* 7 (November): 36–39. Excerpted in *Rock Recall: Annotated Readings in American Popular Music from the Emergence of Rock and Roll to the Demise of the Woodstock Nation,* ed. Michael J. Budds and Marian M. Ohman, 269. Needham Heights, MA: Ginn Press, 1993.

Weberman, Alan. 1968. Interpretations of John Lennon's "Fool on the Hill" and Jim Morrison's "Love Street." *Broadside* 95 (November–December): 1+.

Weiner, Rex and Deanne Stillman. 1979. *Woodstock Census: The Nationwide Survey of the Sixties Generation.* New York: Viking.

Weinraub, Bernard. 1969. A Vietnamese Guitarist Sings of Sadness of War. *Broadside* 99 (June): 4.

Werbin, Stuart. 1972. *Sometime in New York City:* John & Jerry & David & John & Leni & Yoko. *Rolling Stone* (February 17). Reprinted in *The Ballad of John and Yoko,* ed. Jonathan Cott and Christine Doudna, 126–34. Garden City, NY: Rolling Stone Press, 1982.

Westergaard, Sean. 2000. Review of *Band of Gypsys* (Jimi Hendrix). *All Music Guide.* http://www.allmusic.com. Accessed November 15.

Whitburn, Joel. 1997. *Top Pop Singles 1955–1996,* 8th ed. Menomonee Falls, WI: Record Research Inc.

White, Timothy. 1983. A Man out of Time Beats the Clock. *Musician* 60 (October 1983).

Whitmer, Peter O. with Bruce Van Wyngarden. 1987. *Aquarius Revisited: Seven Who Created the Sixties Counterculture and Changed America.* New York: Macmillan.

Wiener, Jon. 1984. *Come Together: John Lennon in His Own Time.* New York: Random House.

Williams, Roger Neville. 1971. *The New Exiles: American War Resisters in Canada.* New York: Liveright Publishers.

Wilson, Brian with Todd Gold. 1991. *Wouldn't It Be Nice*. New York: HarperCollins Publishers.

Wolfe, Paul. 1964. Report on the Newport Folk Festival of 1964. *Broadside* 53 (December 20): 11.

Wolfe, Paul. 1972. Dylan's Sellout of the Left. In *The Sounds of Social Change*, ed. R. Serge Denisoff and Richard A. Peterson, 147–50. Chicago: Rand McNally.

Wolfe, Tom. 1968. *The Electric Kool-Aid Acid Test*. New York: Farrar, Straus and Giroux. Reprint, New York: Bantam Books, 1969.

Woody's Boy. 1966. *Newsweek* (May 23): 110.

Yinger, J. Milton. 1960. Contraculture and Subculture. *American Sociological Review* 25(4) (October): 625–35.

Yorke, Ritchie. 1970. John, Yoko and Year One. *Rolling Stone* 62 (June 28). Reprinted in *The Ballad of John and Yoko*, ed. Jonathan Cott and Christine Doudna, 58–73. Garden City, NY: Rolling Stone Press, 1982.

Young, Hugo. 1967. The Stones: A Case of Social Revenge. *The Sunday Times* [London] July 2, 10. Reprinted in *Rock Recall: Annotated Readings in American Popular Music from the Emergence of Rock and Roll to the Demise of the Woodstock Nation*, ed. Michael J. Budds and Marian M. Ohman, 254. Needham Heights, MA: Ginn Press, 1993.

Young, Israel G. 1967. Frets and Frails. *Sing Out!* 17 (April–May): 35.

Zwonitzer, Mark with Charles Hirshberg. 2002. *Will You Miss Me When I'm Gone? The Carter Family & Their Legacy in American Music*. New York: Simon & Schuster.

Song Title Index

General Index

About the Author

JAMES E. PERONE is the author of ten books, including *Paul Simon: A Bio-Bibliography*, *Songs of the Vietnam Conflict*, and *Louis Moreau Gottschalk: A Bio-Bibliography*. He is Associate Professor of Music at Mount Union College, where he teaches Music in America, Vernacular Music and the Vietnam Conflict, Music Theory, and Clarinet.